GOING COMPREHENSIVE IN ENGLAND AND WALES

THE WOBURN EDUCATION SERIES

General Series Editor: Professor Peter Gordon

GOING COMPREHENSIVE IN ENGLAND AND WALES:

A Study of Uneven Change

ALAN KERCKHOFF, *Duke University*

KEN FOGELMAN, *University of Leicester*

DAVID CROOK, *University of London*

DAVID REEDER, *University of Leicester*

THE WOBURN PRESS

LONDON • PORTLAND, OR.

First published in 1996 in Great Britain by
THE WOBURN PRESS
Newbury House, 900 Eastern Avenue, London IG2 7HH, England

and in the United States of America by
THE WOBURN PRESS
c/o ISBS, 5804 N.E. Hassalo Street, Portland, Oregon 97213-3644

British Library Cataloguing in Publication Data

Going comprehensive in England and Wales : a study of
uneven change. – (Woburn education series)
1. Comprehensive high schools – Great Britain – History –
20th century 2. Public schools – Great Britain – History –
20th century 3. Education, Secondary – Great Britain –
History – 20th century
I. Kerckhoff, Alan C.
373.2′5′0941

Library of Congress Cataloging in Publication Data

Going comprehensive in England and Wales : a study of uneven change /
Alan Kerckhoff ... [et al.].
    p.   cm. — (The Woburn education series)
Includes bibliographical references and index.
ISBN 0-7130-0199-2. – ISBN 0-7130-4026-2 (pbk.)
1. Education, Secondary—Great Britain. 2. Comprehensive high
schools—Great Britain. 3. Educational change—Great Britain.
I. Kerckhoff, Alan C. II. Series
LA635065 1996
373.41—dc20   96-11875
                                                           CIP

ISBN 0 7130 0199 2 (cloth)
ISBN 0 7130 4026 2 (paper)

Typeset by Vitaset, Paddock Wood, Kent
Printed in Great Britain by
Bookcraft (Bath) Ltd, Midsomer Norton, Avon

Contents

Acknowledgements

This book arises out of a research project, entitled 'When a Society Changes its School System: The Introduction of Comprehensive Schools in Great Britain', prosecuted jointly by the Department of Sociology, Duke University, North Carolina and the School of Education, University of Leicester, during the period 1991–93. We are grateful to the Spencer Foundation, Chicago, for generously sponsoring the project.

Jennifer Manlove, a doctoral candidate at Duke University, was an active participant in the analysis of the data from the National Child Development Study. We are indebted to her for her many contributions.

Thanks are also due to the many archivists and librarians who facilitated the process of locating sources. Some of the research involved examining records which are still held by local education authorities or which are restricted in terms of access. Keith Wood-Allum, former Director of Education for Leicestershire, and Christopher Tipple, Director of Education for Northumberland (and their colleagues), were especially helpful in this respect, allowing us access to still-current LEA files. In Manchester, Lady Pariser kindly allowed us to look at the papers of her late husband, Sir Maurice Pariser, which constitute an important source.

Many other individuals have also assisted our research, by agreeing to be interviewed, by lending private papers or by commenting on interim case study reports. Particular thanks are owed to Caroline Benn, Ernest Butcher, Bob Cant, Clyde Chitty, John Dunn, Reg Eyles, Keith Fenwick, Maurice Galton, Peter Gosden, Andy Green, Ruth Jennings, Don Jones, Sir Peter Newsam, Ted Owens, Frank Pedley, Lesley Pedley, E.R. Perraudin, David Reynolds and Eric Woodward. Brian Simon read and perceptively commented on each of the ten interim case studies which we produced. His support and encouragement throughout the project was unstinting and we owe him a special debt of gratitude.

Abbreviations

AAM	Association of Assistant Mistresses (papers housed at Warwick University Modern Records Centre)
AASE	Association for the Advancement of State Education (local associations were affiliated to CASE; papers housed at Warwick University Modern Records Centre)
AEC	Association of Education Committees (papers housed at the Brotherton Library, University of Leeds)
BBC	British Broadcasting Corporation
BP	Boyle Papers (housed at the Brotherton Library, University of Leeds)
BRO	Bristol Records Office
CASE	Campaign for the Advancement of State Education (papers housed at Warwick University Modern Records Centre)
CEO	Chief Education Officer
CES	Collège Enseignement Secondaire
CHL	County Hall, Leicester
CHM	County Hall, Morpeth
CSC	Comprehensive Schools Committee
CTC	City Technology College
DES	Department of Education and Science
DFE	Department for Education
GCE	General Certificate of Education
GLRO	Greater London Record Office
GM	Grant Maintained
HMI	Her Majesty's Inspectorate (of schools)
IAHM	Incorporated Association of Head Masters
ILEA	Inner London Education Authority
IQ	Intelligence quotient
LCA	Leeds City Archives
LCC	London County Council
LEA	Local Education Authority
MCL	Manchester Central Library
NCDS	National Child Development Study
NEA	National Education Association

NRO	Northumberland Record Office (Morpeth)
PRO	Public Records Office
SP	Spicer Papers (housed at County Hall, Morpeth)
TES	Times Educational Supplement
ULBL	University of Leeds Brotherton Library
WL	Wakefield Library
WPL	Worthing Public Library
WSRO	West Sussex Record Office (Chichester)
WUMRC	Warwick University Modern Records Centre
WYAS	West Yorkshire Archives Service (Wakefield)

The European Context of British Educational Reform

In the post-Second World War years in western Europe a new cycle of educational reform was initiated. An ideology of hope and belief in the importance of educational expansion was complemented by growing dissatisfaction with the stratified systems of schooling that most countries had inherited. Social, economic and demographic pressures combined to put structural reform on the agenda not only of popular movements and political groups but also of governments and educational policy-makers in several countries. Norway led the way in the 1950s, by extending an existing common school tradition. In the 1960s, several countries in Europe began to initiate programmes of secondary reorganisation to replace older parallel systems of schooling with comprehensive schools. A move to comprehensive reorganisation was made in countries such as Sweden, France, Scotland and England and Wales. In the 1970s, other European countries, including the West German states, followed suit, while France, which had restricted comprehensive reorganisation to five-year middle schools, began to reorganise higher secondary education.

Ideas about common schooling in Europe can be traced back to the nineteenth century as represented by the emergence of the concept of the Scandinavian basic school and the early ideas in France and Germany of *Écoles Uniques* and *Gesamtschule*. In most countries, however, including these and Britain too, a generally similar system of elementary schools plus selective secondary schooling eventually emerged. Recent studies of the rise of modern educational systems in Europe have emphasised the underlying structural similarities among these systems. Ringer argues, for example, that in the late nineteenth and early twentieth centuries, European educational systems were characterised by an attempt to retain the exclusivity of higher status schooling while expanding the provision of lower status *modern* or post-elementary schooling (Ringer, 1979; Müller, Ringer and Simon, 1987).

In the post-Second World War period, however, the concept of the *multilateral* or *comprehensive* school, as an aspect of reformist educational policy, challenged, at least in theory if not necessarily in practice, the principles of selection and differentiation embodied in the way that most western European educational systems had evolved. This meant that when the idea of comprehensive education began to gain support as a viable policy, it represented a challenge to prevailing assumptions about the functions of secondary schools, and threatened the status and future of schools that participated to some degree in élite recruitment or shared the values of such schools. There were, nevertheless, important differences between countries in the degree of ideological support which comprehensive reorganisation received and the extent and effectiveness of the opposition to the comprehensive movement. There were also differences among countries in the rapidity and thoroughness with which the change to a comprehensive system was achieved.

CENTRALISED AND PLURALIST SYSTEMS

In the literature on educational reform, Norway and Sweden are frequently cited as examples of countries that pushed through a comprehensive system in a relatively short time and in a thorough-going way, based on a clearly defined model of what a comprehensive school should be, not only in terms of recruitment but internal organisation, curricula and ethos. In both countries there was a tradition of support for the principles of common schooling associated with popular movements, and that support became widespread in the period of economic expansion of the 1950s and 1960s. Change was led by government but rested on a broad consensus about the need for educational reform to help bring about the good society in social democratic terms. Thus, in Sweden, after a short period of experimentation in the 1950s, and in line with the principle of continuous educational reform, the government legislated a change to nine-year comprehensive schools (ages 7 to 16) in 1962, imposing the same pattern of organisation and curricula on all schools at the same time. A similar process characterised the integration of higher secondary education in the early 1970s (Boucher, 1982; Thompson, 1975).

Commentators on educational change in Nordic countries have drawn attention to the role of their political systems, which can be regarded as characterised by centralist and corporatist features. In the political sphere, it is argued, the pluralist paradigm associated with such countries as the United States and England and Wales is not appropriate in considering the political systems in many European countries – not only Scandinavian countries but also the Netherlands, Belgium and France to an extent. Norway and Sweden have been seen as the 'purist' examples of social corporatism, with public policy an outcome of deliberate proceedings between government and bureaucratised interest groups and, in regard to educational policy, incorporating educational professions in the decision-making process of the state (Paulston, 1968, pp. 142–6; Rust, 1990). The way in which comprehensive schooling was carried through in Norway, Rust has argued, shows how a political system with corporate features has provided viable mechanisms for dramatic and ultimately revolutionary policy formation. This throws a different light on a political system that has been previously represented as a powerful tool of social control (Rust, 1990, pp. 25–6).

Similarly, it has been argued that the centralist political system of Fifth Republic France was a key factor in explaining how a nearly uniform scheme of comprehensive reorganisation was achieved in the 1960s (Gaziell, 1989). In France there was no national consensus in favour of structural reform, and earlier projects failed to secure the consent of all the interest groups involved. In the early 1960s, comprehensive reorganisation was regarded still as a controversial issue and was subject to widespread public debate, as it was in England and Wales. But a new project was initiated from the centre, more for economic and demographic than social reasons. Outsiders brought into the Ministry of Education in 1961–62 guided a reform project based on the *Collège Enseignement Secondaire* (CES), a five-year middle school. The changeover to the CES was carried through by ministerial decree and involved a process described as interest group 'co-optation'. While the central government was able to take advantage of the extra powers in the Fifth Republic constitution to initiate and promote the project, the consent and participation of interest groups such as business and the Catholic church was necessary to ensure the adoption of the reform in practice. This support meant that comprehensive reorganisation in France pushed ahead, despite continuing opposition from teachers' unions and some parental groups.

Such corporatist and centralised political systems seem to be able to bring about institutional change more rapidly and more fully than pluralist political systems such as those found in England and Wales. One commentator has contrasted the rapidity and thoroughness of the reform process in France with that in England and Wales, where a move to comprehensive education based on a wider range of models

3

was also under way in the 1960s (Neave, 1975b). By 1971, 60 per cent of 11–15-year-olds in state secondary education in France were in the reformed sector, compared with six per cent in 1964. The comparable figures for England and Wales were 36 per cent (38 per cent using a wider definition) in 1971, compared with seven per cent (nine per cent using a wider definition) in 1964. Put another way, in the period 1963–72, the average incremental turnover in terms of pupils moving into the reorganised schools was 7.7 per cent in France compared with 4.25 per cent in England and Wales. In addition, the French centralised system ensured a much greater uniformity not only of institutions, but of school size and definitions of catchment areas.

On the other hand, as in some other European countries, a second phase of reform was needed in France to deal with higher secondary education (age 15+), whereas the British comprehensive school movement involved the entire age range from 11 to 18. Moreover, in the late 1960s and through the 1970s in Britain, there was an accelerating shift from the selective system of grammar and secondary modern schools to the widespread introduction of comprehensive schools. Although reform began more slowly, it ultimately developed considerable momentum.

Given the strength of vested interests and ideological opposition to comprehensive reorganisation in Britain, the extent of comprehensivisation by the end of the 1970s, with 82 per cent of the secondary school population enrolled in comprehensive schools of some kind, must count as a considerable achievement. A comparison with the experience of West Germany, a decentralised federalist system is apposite. In the West German states, the pace and extent of comprehensive reorganisation closely followed party political lines, but overall progress was relatively slow. The first comprehensive schools appeared in West Berlin in 1968, but in the period to 1980 there were only 178 comprehensive schools in existence, to which might be added another 175 schools which would rather be called 'multilateral'. Together, they accounted for less than 16 per cent of the secondary school population in West Germany in the late 1970s. In West Berlin and the state of Hessen, the most comprehensivised areas, the proportion reached 25 per cent and 40 per cent respectively, the latter state providing the one and only fully comprehensivised area, in a rural district (Geddes, 1980; Korner, 1981).

From a European perspective, then, the importance of England and Wales is that structural reform was carried through in the context of a political system generally recognised as having strong pluralist features. Most important were the open competition of pressure groups and the strong role of decentralised forms of government, as represented by the large number of local authorities.

The changeover from selective to comprehensive schooling has been a proving ground for theories of educational policy-making in Britain, with the leading authorities finding in comprehensive reorganisation in Britain a pluralist and indeterminate interplay between policy and practice, centre and periphery (Kogan, 1975, pp. 231–3; Archer, 1979, pp. 589–99; McPherson and Raab, 1988, p. 347). However, the significance of these pluralist features in shaping the nature and impact of comprehensive reform has not been given the same degree of attention. Hence, this book which focuses on the process of change and which can be described as a study of policy in action in a pluralist society.

REORGANISATION IN ENGLAND AND WALES

Great Britain, like most western European countries, has had a highly stratified educational system throughout most of the twentieth century. The 1944 Education Act organised British education in what was then viewed as a more liberal form than before the Second World War because it provided universal secondary schooling, and it offered at least an opportunity for students to follow advanced secondary school academic courses. At the secondary school level, the system clearly separated the more and less accomplished students into grammar and secondary modern schools, however. That separation was made at age 11 (10½ for many), dependent in large part on the so-called 11+ examination. Transfers between the two types of secondary schools were seldom possible.

Although it did provide better schooling than in the past to less accomplished or less privileged students, such a selective system was not viewed with favour by all, and there were outspoken critics from the beginning, especially within the Labour Party. That dissatisfaction fuelled the reform movement calling for the establishment of comprehensive schools.

The creation of comprehensive schools in England and Wales can be traced from at least the immediate post-war period. Only a handful of local education authorities (LEAs) established comprehensives that early, however. Before the mid-1960s, which we designate a period of experimentation, a few pioneering and progressive LEAs introduced comprehensives. Although such experimentation is an indication of the pluralist nature of educational decision-making, those LEAs were still dependent on having their plans accepted by the centre, represented by the Ministry of Education, and there were undoubtedly fewer comprehensive schools established because of that central government involvement.

It was not until the mid-1960s that a national political initiative was taken by the central Labour administration to 'go comprehensive'. This took the form of 'Circular 10/65', a call by the central government for LEAs to submit plans for the establishment of comprehensive schools. Despite an overt ideological commitment on the part of Anthony Crosland, the minister concerned, to promote greater social equality through school reform, the circular only *requested* the local authorities to submit plans. Although the circular undoubtedly provided a major impetus, the pace of change was still dependent on the nature and timing of LEA responses.

Moreover, despite Crosland's preference for an 11–18 'all-through' model of reorganisation, the circular endorsed five other ways in which secondary schools might be organised on a non-selective basis. This flexibility of approach to comprehensive reorganisation was condoned and encouraged by the DES whose policy, Benn and Simon (1972, pp. 86–7) have argued, was 'to get as much agreement as possible by pursuing a consensus line – [and] a strategy of an accelerated rate of growth for comprehensives within a bipartite structure'. Again, we see the results of a pluralist approach to reform.

By way of contrast, even within Great Britain, the implementation of comprehensive education in Scotland was more uniform than in England and Wales. This was partly because Circular 600, the Scottish equivalent to Circular 10/65, prescribed a single form of reorganisation, and the Scottish Education Department took a stronger line in securing its implementation. Although the pace of reform was dependent in Scotland, as in England and Wales, on the policies and attitudes of local education authorities, there was a different relationship between centre and periphery (McPherson and Raab 1988, pp. 396–7). For these reasons, the present study has been confined to England and Wales.

One element in the movement to comprehensive education in the 1960s was the growing dissatisfaction with the so-called 11+ examination, a mechanism used to separate students into the levels of the selective system. Discarding the 11+ examination made it possible to loosen the definition of the appropriate age at which secondary school begins. We will see that one of the features of the comprehensive movement in England and Wales was the introduction of different age ranges of students in secondary schools. In addition to the 'all-through' pattern, various 'tiered' systems were introduced, which sometimes involved some kind of middle school.

One reason to establish tiered systems was the frequent need to fit newly established comprehensive schools into buildings that had originally been used in the selective system of grammar and secondary modern schools. A large proportion of English and Welsh secondary school students left school at the age of 16, while others entered the sixth form, where study was focused on preparation for advanced (A-Level) examinations. Under the selective system, the great majority of secondary modern school students left at 15 (16 from 1974) or shortly thereafter, and the great majority of grammar school students stayed on for the sixth form. Secondary modern schools could thus have relatively large age 11 intakes but function without sixth forms, and grammar schools could have relatively small age 11 intakes and assume most students would stay into the sixth form. Most 'all-through' comprehensives were quite large because, to have an adequately sized sixth-form student body, it was necessary to have a relatively large pool of younger students from which the sixth formers would emerge. Many of the existing buildings were too small to accommodate enough of the full range of 11–18-year-old students and still have a viable sixth form. So, one solution to the problem was to establish middle schools and take students into the comprehensives at older ages (Jones, 1989).

Another way in which some LEAs coped with this problem of school size was to use secondary schools that enrolled students only until the age of 16. In such cases, some other source of sixth-form instruction was provided. One way was to establish a 'sixth-form college', a separate location at which only sixth-form courses were offered (Bright, 1972). In other cases, only some comprehensives had sixth forms, and students enrolled in schools without sixth forms had to transfer if they were to stay on for post-compulsory education.

Thus, the 1960s and 1970s not only saw rapid change in the overall *form* of secondary education (from selective to comprehensive), but also *diversity* in the institutional arrangements used to provide that education. The diversity of changes in secondary schools did not stop there, however. Account has to be taken also of the manner in which different local authorities implemented reorganisation, whether as a uniform scheme or with a more *ad hoc* approach, and whether in terms of dealing with the local area as a whole or on a school-by-school basis. And, of course, the LEAs varied in the rapidity and the degree of comprehensivisation. Some LEAs changed completely to comprehensive schools. Others resisted the comprehensive movement entirely and had still not implemented reorganisation schemes by the mid-1970s.

These kinds of variation among LEAs provide the basis for the analysis in this book. What differentiated the LEAs that took one form of action rather than another? Can we explain why some LEAs were at the forefront of the movement and others resisted it throughout? What led to the decisions about the ways the comprehensives were organised? In a pluralist society, can we make any general statements, or is every case a unique mixture of multiple forces? We will not claim to have answered those questions, but they have guided the work that is reported here.

STUDYING DIVERSITY AND UNEVEN EDUCATIONAL CHANGE

The diversity of patterns of implementation and the variety of organisational features are then key features of the process of structural reform in England and Wales. The introduction of comprehensive schools was not a uniform process in the 1960s and 1970s. There was diversity, both in the ways LEAs changed their educational systems and the organisation of individual schools within many LEAs. To understand the nature of this diversity and the reasons for it necessitates pursuing the story of comprehensive reorganisation at both the national and the local level, so as to identify the nature and sources of variation and to assess the influences at work. Two factors that have received attention in previous discussions of educational reform are political party positions and social class.

Since the majority of local authorities that had started to reorganise by 1970 were Labour-controlled (Litt and Parkinson, 1979), the first question to arise concerns the role of political influence. Although comprehensive education appeared on the agenda of the Labour Party conferences in the 1950s, a number of writers have commented on the divided attitudes of the Labour Party towards selection and comprehensive reorganisation (Banks, 1955; Parkinson, 1970; Barker, 1972; Benn and Simon, 1972; Fenwick, 1976). These divisions were reflected in the range of opinions to be found among members of local Labour parties. In some authorities, such as, for example, Sheffield and Leicester, an 'old guard' among the controlling Labour group was only reluctantly converted to comprehensive education (Reeder, 1993). Conversely, as other studies have shown, some Conservative and Independent-controlled authorities, especially in rural areas, more readily accepted comprehensive reorganisation schemes (Jones, 1989; Fenwick, 1976).

We are not only concerned to study the origins of the demand for comprehensive reorganisation at the local level and the differences in the responses of LEAs to Circular 10/65, but also to examine the implementation process. There are a number of studies, mostly unpublished, which provide information about the sources of demand and forms of response in particular cases. In a review of some of these, Ribbins and Brown found that 'in the great majority of cases the demand for reorganisation entered the system through the agency of the local political party' (Ribbins and Brown, 1979, p. 190, quoted in McPherson and Raab, 1988, p. 396). But, they warn, 'the argument that the pace of reorganisation has depended on the political colour of the controlling party locally needs to be used with some care' (p. 191).

The review by Ribbins and Brown and subsequent reviews by other commentators have identified a variety of influences on the implementation process. They highlight the role of Chief Education Officers (CEOs) and consider how far local pressure groups and parental associations influenced the process of change (Ribbins and Brown, 1979; James, 1980; Fearn, 1980, 1983, and 1989). In what follows, we seek to extend this earlier work by engaging in a more systematic comparative investigation of the variations in the experiences of local authorities based on qualitative studies, combined with the analysis of statistical data. The aim is to illuminate further the nature and implications of a process of uneven educational change in a pluralist system.

THE EFFECTS OF REORGANISATION

School reforms in many countries during the twentieth century have been, at least in part, motivated by a desire to weaken the influence of social class on educational attainment. Although the research results relevant to that association have not always been consistent, they are not especially reassuring. A recent attempt to assess the impact of twentieth-century educational expansion, using a carefully controlled common method of analysis in 13 countries, has confirmed the general weakness of educational reform as a mechanism of weakening the social class influence on educational attainment (Shavit and Blossfeld,

9

1993). The study included western and non-western industrial countries, as well as western socialist countries, all of which had experienced educational reforms. With the exception of Sweden and the Netherlands, where the class–attainment association declined, there was virtual stability across cohorts in the other 11 countries. Even in Sweden and the Netherlands, the decline is not clearly attributable to the educational reforms, but seems to have been due to more general equalisation processes in those countries.

The analysis of England and Wales included in the 13-country study (Kerckhoff and Trott, 1993) focused on the post-war reform outlined in the 1944 Education Act, and that analysis showed the same degree of continuity of class–attainment patterns as were found elsewhere. All of those analyses, however, were directed more towards assessing the *amount* of educational attainment and social mobility rather than towards an examination of the factors that serve to maintain the observed level of continuity. The movement to comprehensive schools in England and Wales involved a change from a selective system that has been consistently viewed as perpetuating class differences. It is too early to assess the overall impact of that change on social mobility patterns, and we do not have adequate data to make that assessment, but the present investigation can help us understand the *process* of change.

In Britain some of the early studies of the changeover to comprehensive schools took an optimistic view of what the comprehensive school was achieving. In particular, Scottish studies reported an improvement in the educational attainments of working-class children (McPherson and Willms, 1987). The two major studies of the effects of comprehensivisation in England and Wales have reached contradictory conclusions, however. Although Marks, Cox and Pomian-Srzednicki (1983) claimed superior results for selective LEAs, these results have been severely criticised (Fogelman, 1984; Lacey, 1984) and contrast with those of Steedman (1983), who concluded that the differences between the two sectors were very small.

An important question with respect to the English and Welsh experience is whether the manner in which comprehensive reorganisation was implemented served to perpetuate the selective system's class–attainment association. Did the process reflect social class considerations? Was the varied rate of reorganisation the result of social class considerations? Were the new comprehensive schools wholly different from the selective schools or did their varied characteristics continue some of the features of the selective system? Did the new schools function in ways that served to perpetuate some of the class-linked patterns? These are some of the questions that guide our analysis in later chapters.

ORGANISATION OF THE PRESENTATION

The book provides several different views of the period of changeover from a largely selective to a largely comprehensive secondary school system. First, Chapter 2 provides an overall description of the process of comprehensivisation in England and Wales, concentrating largely on the national scene and the major national social and political forces that shaped the pattern of change. Chapters 3 to 9 then offer historical reconstructions of the process of comprehensive reorganisation in ten local authority areas. These chapters take into account variations in socioeconomic characteristics, political control and a number of highly varied local conditions in seeking to understand the quite different actions taken in these ten local areas. The analyses are presented in case studies, as illustrations of different types of reorganisation processes and outcomes.

Chapters 10 to 12 return to a broad, national perspective, but they still maintain a focus on variations within the overall changeover process. The analyses in these three chapters are based on data from the National Child Development Study (NCDS), a longitudinal study of a birth cohort of British children who were in secondary school during the period of rapid reorganisation. The analyses take into account variations among the local authorities, among the schools these young people attended, and among the students' own backgrounds, experiences and achievements. Finally, Chapter 13 provides an overview of the investigation and suggests some tentative conclusions and recommendations.

Throughout, our interests are twofold. First, we seek to understand the dynamics of change, to identify and assess the importance of the factors that influenced the introduction of comprehensive schools and led to the varied nature of those schools. Second, we attempt to chart the actual change process at the level of the schools and the students involved, to see how much change actually occurred and what difference it made in the way schools functioned and in the academic achievements of the students.

2

Comprehensive Reorganisation in England and Wales: An Overview

This chapter provides an overview of the evolution of policy and its impact on the process of comprehensive reorganisation. It is a narrative account, based mainly on secondary sources, which illustrates the interplay between national politics and local developments. It introduces several themes to be pursued later, in particular the role of local education authorities in the process of educational change. But it is primarily concerned with tracing the shifts in governmental policies towards comprehensive reorganisation. It also seeks to develop a perspective on the key phase of reorganisation in the period 1965–74, by dealing with a longer time span. Thus, the main account of the politics of reorganisation is prefaced with a brief commentary on the evolution of a tripartite orthodoxy to show how the principle of differentiation, as embodied in that orthodoxy, was challenged by the demand for comprehensive schools. The chapter also contains a postscript – a review of the ways in which changes in policy since 1974 have affected the pace of change and the future of the comprehensive school. Implicit in our discussion, therefore, is the view that comprehensive reorganisation in the 1960s and 1970s was but one phase in a continuing process of educational reconstruction in Britain that began in the nineteenth century and carries on today.

THE EMERGENCE OF A TRIPARTITE ORTHODOXY

The idea of providing parallel schools for secondary-age children emerged in the late 1930s, as a consequence of inter-war thinking and developments in secondary education. To understand these it is necessary to bear in mind that the transformation of British education during the nineteenth century had resulted in an hierarchical system of schooling whereby the division between elementary and secondary education was based primarily on social class, rather than chronological progression. The idea of state secondary education derived from the reform of middle-class education in this period. With the Education

Act of 1902, middle-class education was formally constituted as grammar school education, incorporating both the old endowed grammar schools and the new municipal grammar schools. The provision of secondary grammar schooling remained patchy, however, and a case can be made for saying that the decision to subsidise the grammar schools via the rates actually *reinforced* class divisions in education despite the availability of scholarships. The latter did little to extend access to secondary schooling, and the opportunity ration remained very low during the inter-war period though rising slightly to 14.34 per cent of the secondary school-age population in 1938 (Simon, 1992, p. 29).

It must be borne in mind that local authority schools other than grammar schools were managed under the *elementary* and not the *secondary code*, even when they contained pupils of secondary age. At the same time, the local authority-maintained grammar schools were having to establish their place within a status hierarchy of secondary education at the local level in which the most prestigious schools lay outside local authority control. At the top of the hierarchy were the independent schools – the so-called public schools which, by 1938, were educating about seven per cent of the nation's children. They were followed closely by those old endowed grammar schools which obtained direct grants from the central government office (the Board of Education) in return for offering a certain proportion of their places free to local children. These schools tended to be more prestigious than local authority grammar schools on account of their historical traditions, as well as their independence from local authority control. But there were also distinctions between the municipal grammar schools according to their level of fees and the proportion of scholarship children they took in. All these distinctions persisted into the post-1944 period, modified only by the abolition of fee-paying for municipal grammar schools and the ending of direct grant status in 1976.

The local authority (municipal) grammar schools had succeeded in securing a position within the local status hierarchy during the inter-war years. They grew in numbers and confidence during this period, and adopted some of the values of the upper-class public schools, thereby forming an association with traditional and prestigious elements in British society. They also developed an ethos of meritocracy and academic endeavour appropriate to schools whose social composition had been enlarged in varying degrees by the inclusion of children from lower middle and upper working-class backgrounds.

As early as 1913, about 21 per cent of boys and 20 per cent of girls attending these schools had fathers in lower middle-class occupations (minor officials, clerks, travellers, agents), while 18.2 per cent of the boys and 19 per cent of the girls came from a skilled manual background. Only 2.4 per cent of the boys and 2.6 per cent of the girls had parents in unskilled occupations (Board of Education Return, quoted in Reeder 1987, p. 149).

The problem for educational reformers during the inter-war years was how to extend the concept of secondary education to cover elementary school children older than age 11 once the school-leaving age had been raised to 14. Earlier attempts to develop an alternative secondary sector based on higher-grade elementary schools had been suppressed or diverted after 1902, but there was a renewed demand in the 1920s for improving the education of elementary school children after the age of 11.

It is possible to trace the emergence of the concept of comprehensive education to the demand for multilateral schools that began to emerge in this period. Among the organisations giving support to multilateralism at various times from the 1920s were the Independent Labour Party, the National Union of Teachers (NUT) and a few local authorities, notably the West Riding Authority. This small but growing support for the multilateral school can be seen as foreshadowing a demand for comprehensive education in the post-Second World War period.

However, the dominant view of educational policy-makers in the inter-war years was that no reorganisation should affect the status or integrity of the grammar school but should be carried through by the creation of *separate* secondary schools. Thus, the authors of the most influential of the inter-war reports on education, the Hadow Report of 1926, concluded that children's secondary education should be determined on the grounds of ability, and the authors apparently had no doubts that it was possible to distinguish between academic children, who would benefit from a traditional examination-orientated education in a grammar school, and the less able, who would benefit from courses of practical instruction in a modern school.

The Hadow enquiry had been set up by a Labour government, and the committee membership included the radical historian, R.H. Tawney, whose influential pamphlet, 'Secondary Education for All: A Policy for Labour', had argued that 'all normal children, irrespective of their income, class, or occupation of their parents, may be transferred at the age of 11+ from the primary or preparatory school to one type or another of secondary school, and remain in the latter till sixteen'. The notion of separate schools, reflecting children's differing levels of intelligence, was a pervasive one. The work of researchers, including Cyril Burt, psychologist to the London County Council (LCC) from 1913,[1] fostered a widespread acceptance of psychometric tests as a measure of IQ. 'Such tests were as attractive to Labour educationalists as to others since they appeared to offer a neutral means of assessing the aptitudes of children from deprived backgrounds and of allocating them to appropriate schools' (Thane, 1982, p. 204).

At the local level, the more progressive authorities, such as the City of Leicester, pressed forward with building new senior schools on the Hadow model, although these schools continued to be categorised as in the public elementary sector. There was also a new attempt on the part of some LEAs to develop commercial and technical courses for working-class pupils in central schools and junior technical schools. These schools too had an inferior status to the state secondary (grammar) schools. In any case, the pace of change was uneven. State education was low on the political agenda and vulnerable to financial stringency. The serious economic situation of the early 1930s, combined with the perpetuation of the so-called dual system of voluntary and LEA-maintained schools and the existence of large numbers of rural, all-age schools, all conspired to limit incidences of Hadow-style reorganisation in the years before the Second World War.

One historian has argued that the slow rate of reorganisation in the 1930s, in particular the patchy and incomplete adoption of mental testing, is the key to the survival of a group of secondary schools that favoured élite groups (Sutherland, 1984, Chapters 9 and 10). A more common view is that the ideology of mental testing *reinforced* the idea of differentiated schooling, as eventually set out by the Consultative Committee on Secondary Education, chaired by Sir Will Spens, at the conclusion of its five-year deliberations in 1938. This report expressed satisfaction that, 'in a high proportion of cases', a selective examination at the age of 11+ was capable of selecting '(a) those pupils who quite certainly have so much intelligence, and intelligence of such character, that without doubt they ought to receive a secondary education of a grammar school type; and (b) those pupils who quite certainly would not benefit from such an education' (Board of Education, 1938, p. 379).

The main concern of the Spens Committee was to reflect growing demands for a diversification of the academic secondary curriculum, particularly on the part of those educationists and local authorities supportive of technical education. The solution which Spens arrived at was the secondary technical school. The committee rejected the idea of incorporating the technical into secondary education by means of a single secondary school organised on bilateral or multilateral lines. Thus they dismissed evidence in favour of such a school from teachers' organisations, representatives of the Labour movement and from local government organisations. The report as finally published noted 'with some reluctance' that it could not advocate the adoption of multilateralism as a general policy, while conceding – and this represented an important pointer to future developments – that multilateral schools might be the right solution in sparsely populated rural areas and new housing estates. This concession apart, the report came down firmly for a tripartite organisation, to accommodate the technical school in accordance with its brief. Hence Brian Simon's judgement that 'generally speaking the historical importance of the Spens Report lies in its powerful support for the tripartite system' (Simon, 1992, p. 182).

However, this version of the origins of tripartite thinking in Britain has been criticised for giving the impression that a consensus view was already in place before the Second World War. As McCulloch points out, both Spens and the subsequent Norwood Report on examinations (1943) endorsed tripartism but for different reasons and with very different stances towards the nature and scope of secondary education which reflected important policy differences. The general argument is that ideological debate leading up to and following on from Spens was more open and contested than has previously been implied. The Spens proposal for a tripartite system embodying secondary technical schools, for example, was initially resisted by Board of Education officials (McCulloch, 1993, pp. 163–80; 1989, pp. 35–42).

What is not disputed is the existence of a consensus among members of the policy-making community in favour of doing nothing to undermine the position of the grammar schools. This conviction, along with the belief in the possibilities of selecting children according to different abilities as reiterated in the Norwood Committee's report, underpinned wartime planning to expand opportunities for secondary education to all children over the age of 11. Tripartism or a system of three parallel schools was the preferred solution to wartime pressures for reform, and the Board of Education's secret, but much leaked 1941 'Green Book', entitled 'Education after the War' came down firmly in favour of three parallel schools.[2] It is worth noting, however, that the Board of Education officials responsible for drafting the

Green Book were divided as to whether 13, rather than 11, might be a more suitable age for children to sit a selection examination (Gosden, 1976, pp. 256–8).

THE EVOLUTION OF A NATIONAL POLICY

Despite the absorption of tripartism into the mainstream thinking of policy-makers, the 1944 Education Act certainly did not close the door on multilateral – or comprehensive – education, and, in requiring LEAs to submit detailed development plans for scrutiny, the new ministry did not specify that non-selective secondary schools would be unacceptable. This at least left the way open for local initiative, and what limited progress was made in the immediate post-1944 years towards bringing in comprehensive schools was the result of local LEA actions. For the most part, these actions reflected the special circumstances of and some progressive thinking by particular LEAs, rather than any concerted national political effort. Most LEAs were more concerned about coping with the aftermath of the war and with the new requirements of the 1944 Act than educational innovations.

Comprehensives Overlooked: 1945–51

Faced with the task of creating a new order for education, LEAs had different starting points. The case studies in the following chapters of this report indicate, for example, that London and Bristol were, because of severe wartime bomb damage, in a unique position to contemplate the development of housing and educational provision simultaneously, and they judged that the comprehensive school was especially suitable to serve new urban communities (see Chapters 4 and 5). The example of these two LEAs suggests that support for comprehensives in the immediate post-war period was an urban phenomenon, led by Socialist ideologues. But that hypothesis is challenged by the fact that the West Riding, which also expressed a preference for comprehensive schools, was a predominantly rural county and, at that time, Conservative-controlled (Clegg, 1965, p. 75). The relationship between socioeconomic conditions, political activity and the timing and nature of reorganisation plans is a theme which will be studied in detail subsequently. The role of central government in this early period was to respond to applications rather than to give a lead. Paradoxically, the Labour government, up to 1951, provided a less coherent positive response to proposals for comprehensive

17

schools than did the Conservative government which followed. This is surprising, given the record of the post-war Labour government in implementing progressive welfare policies and taking account of the tradition of support for the multilateral school within the Labour movement. Indeed, in discussions following the Spens Report, the Labour Party's wartime Education Advisory Committee had recommended that: 'local education authorities should be required to plan a systematic development of multilateral schools as an immediate practical policy'. This was followed by a resolution at the Labour Party conference of 1942 calling on the Board of Education 'to encourage, as a general policy, the development of a new type of multilateral school' (Simon, 1991, p. 47).

It would be misleading to suggest, therefore, that the failure to develop a national policy for comprehensive education in the post-war years was due simply to the dominance of tripartite thinking within the policy-making establishment in British education. It also reflected a failure of political will. Labour's general election victory of 1945 apparently did not alter the course of national education policy very much. Indeed, in some ways, the policies of Clement Attlee's two Ministers of Education, Ellen Wilkinson (1945–47) and George Tomlinson (1947–51) can be seen as more conservative than those of both the wartime coalition government and the long period of Conservative government between 1951 and 1964. As far as the comprehensive school issue is concerned, there has been a hotly contested academic debate about whether these ministers set back the incipient movement to end selective schooling.

Shortly after Labour's 1945 victory, while LEAs were grappling with the problems of enforcing the new Education Act, the Ministry of Education issued a pamphlet entitled *The Nation's Schools* (Ministry of Education, 1945), which addressed organisational questions associated with tripartism, but had little to say about multilateral schools, except that they might be most appropriate in sparsely populated areas or as 'judicious experiments' elsewhere. Ellen Wilkinson is widely regarded as a radical figure in the Labour movement, but her views on the subject of comprehensive schools appear to have been ambiguous. However, in his 'defence' of Ellen Wilkinson, her former Parliamentary Private Secretary recalls a 1946 speech in the House of Commons in which she said of multilateral schools:

> I welcome experiments of this kind and on these lines. They have some great attractions. They mix all the children together in the

corporate life of one community ... they avoid snobbish distinctions between schools of different grades ... they make it easier for children to switch from one course to another (Hansard, H of C, Vol. 424, 1 July 1946, quoted in Hughes, 1979, p. 158).

There is, nevertheless, an inconsistency in Wilkinson's expressed fear that comprehensive schools should not become 'unreasonably large' (Hughes 1979, p. 158) and that of her former Parliamentary Secretary, John Redcliffe-Maud. The latter's autobiography recalls that 'the Inspectorate thought that such a school would have to be large enough to take some two thousand pupils if it was to meet the needs of children of both the highest and the lowest intellectual ability without an unjustifiably high ratio of staff to pupils' (Redcliffe-Maud, 1981, p. 55)

Another ministerial pamphlet, issued after Wilkinson's sudden death in 1947, entitled *The New Secondary Education* (Ministry of Education, 1947) also reflected the assumption that LEAs would opt for a selective secondary system. Despite his background as a former LEA chairman and chairman of the Labour Party Education Advisory Committee, the new minister, George Tomlinson, 'preferred a policy of cautious experimentation to the adoption of what was as yet an untried system' (Hughes, 1979, p. 159), and warned in 1950 that 'the (Labour) Party are kidding themselves if they think that the comprehensive idea has any popular appeal' (Parkinson, 1970, p. 47). Rubinstein finds both Wilkinson and Tomlinson guilty of setting back the movement for comprehensive education, 'the most important development in English secondary education since 1945' by 'the better part of 20 years' (Rubinstein, 1979 p. 161), but, in fairness, it should be pointed out that both ministers appear to have been representative of the party position. There are, in fact, just six examples of Labour MPs expressing support for comprehensive schools during the 1945–51 ministry (Fenwick, 1976, p. 58). This had much to do with the educational background and outlook of Labour members at this time.

The climate of indifference did not prevent a number of local authorities from pressing ahead with plans to establish comprehensive schools. Without apparent enthusiasm, the ministry sanctioned a limited number of experimental comprehensive schools during the late 1940s, with Anglesey, a rural Welsh authority, together with Coventry and London (see Chapter 4) taking the lead. Educational arguments for the common school were at least as influential as political ones, and educational innovation depended upon the willingness of both administrators and local politicians to look to the future, as well as the present. Rarely were both camps equally progressively minded and enthusiastic, and in Bristol, for example, the radical plan for comprehensive schools drawn up by a young and highly able Chief Education Officer (CEO) was unattractive to Labour councillors who typified the old, rather than new, order (see Chapter 5). In other authorities as well, such as the City of Leicester, older Labour councillors were reluctant to contemplate drastic change to a selective system which they had helped to bring into being, and they concentrated their efforts on making the system more flexible (Reeder, 1993). At the ministerial level, the two formidable hurdles which blocked a number of LEA proposals were, first, a concern about whether the size of proposed comprehensives would be adequate to sustain a viable sixth form and, second, a reluctance to permit LEAs to close or amalgamate existing grammar schools which were popular with parents.

Cautious Experimentation: 1951–64

During the early years of the Conservative ministry, there seemed little for comprehensive enthusiasts to be positive about. The last-minute intervention of the Minister of Education, Florence Horsbrugh, to prevent the London County Council (LCC) from closing the Eltham Hill Girls' Grammar School in 1954 ensured that London's first purpose-built comprehensive was not, in fact, comprehensive. The decision prompted widespread – and in some cases, unlikely – rebukes from those who feared that Horsbrugh was intent on destroying the principle of LEA autonomy to organise its school pattern as it saw fit (see Chapter 4), but during the next four years the LCC led the way by establishing a total of 26 trail-blazing comprehensives. Among Horsbrugh's successors, Sir David Eccles and Edward Boyle stand out as more progressive, and Brian Simon has recently argued that the successful Soviet launch of Sputnik in 1957 reinforced Prime Minister Anthony Eden's message that educational advance was essential if Britain was to play a part in the scientific revolution (Simon, 1991, pp. 198–9). This required an overhaul of both the higher and secondary education sectors. By this time, several developments had begun to undermine the tripartite orthodoxy, and these, along with the growing body of criticism of the selection process, were helping to change the climate of thinking.

First, it had become clear that tripartism was a misleading concept, because only a very few LEAs – Manchester, for example, among our case-study examples (see Chapter 5) – had taken seriously the provision of distinct technical schools. In 1958 there were 279 secondary technical schools in England and Wales, with a total of 95,239 pupils, around only four per cent of the total number of secondary school pupils. More than 40 per cent of LEAs still did not provide any secondary technical schools at all. In part this situation was due to insufficient funds being available to provide specialist facilities, but it also reflected a lack of confidence among LEAs in the idea of the technical school and the possibility of discerning technical aptitudes at 10–11 years. Historical analysis has shown that the failure of the secondary technical schools was in large part due to the resistance of parents and industry, and that Sir David Eccles helped to prevent further development of the schools in the 1950s (McCulloch, 1989, p. 7 and Chapters 4 and 8). Despite some notable individual successes, and the enthusiastic proselytising of a group of educationists committed to the idea of an alternative route in secondary and higher education to that of the conventional academic, the secondary technical schools failed to generate much popular support.

As Boyle later privately confided, 'we really had a bipartite system of selective and non-selective schools – and the idea of "parity of esteem" between them was a sham', also citing the growth of grammar school sixth forms and the way that Her Majesty's Inspectorate (HMI) 'foolishly' opposed the development of GCE courses in the secondary moderns, as important in reinforcing life-long notions of 11+ 'success' or 'failure'.[3] He also suggested that, during the 1950s, the ministry had become interested in the ideas of Robin Pedley, a Leicester University academic, whose research indicated that abandoning the 11+ examination in favour of a comprehensive system did not necessitate huge comprehensives with 1,500 or more on the roll.

Pedley himself recalled in 1980:

> during the early and mid-fifties there was growing interest in the possibility of beating, at one stroke, both of the bogeys which had hitherto seemed to create an 'either/or' situation: selection at 11 and giant comprehensives. The solution was essentially simple: that of putting secondary modern and grammar schools end-on in a two-tier comprehensive system. A far-sighted Minister of Education, Sir David Eccles, took a personal interest; and at a meeting with him and senior officials in 1956 I was left in no doubt of their readiness to encourage experiment which went along these lines (*Education*, 30 May 1980, p. 458).

Undoubtedly influenced – despite his denial (Jones, 1988, p. 57) – by

Pedley's thinking, Stewart Mason, Director of Education for Leicestershire, unveiled, in April 1957, an 'experiment' in non-selective education to the age of 14 in two parts of the county. This was the beginning of a 12-year piecemeal process which scrapped the 11+ and led to the development of a two-tier comprehensive school system (see Chapter 7).

The White Paper issued by Minister of Education Geoffrey Lloyd at the end of 1958, entitled *Secondary Education for All: A New Drive*, welcomed the Leicestershire experiment. The document tentatively suggested, for the first time, that such schools might be particularly suitable in country districts with sparse populations and areas of new housing (where they would not force the closures of well-established grammar, technical or modern schools). However, the proviso was added that:

> ... it is quite another matter when a local authority proposes to bring to an end an existing grammar school ... simply in order that a new comprehensive school may enjoy a monopoly of the abler children within its area. It cannot be right that good existing schools should be forcibly brought to an end, or that parents' freedom of choice should be so completely abolished (Ministry of Education 1958, pp. 5–6).

Simon describes this as a 'highly aggressive and totally unsympathetic formulation' (Simon, 1991, p. 204), and it is certainly true that Lloyd's refusal to sanction a number of LEA proposals for comprehensive schools which involved the merger or disestablishment of grammar schools confirmed the government's prevailing scepticism about comprehensives (ibid., p. 211). Despite the fact that this did not amount to a glowing testimonial, the 1958 White Paper did represent the comprehensive school in a more positive light than any previous ministerial document, and it may be seen as the first stage in an evolutionary Conservative secondary education policy which became less attached to 11+ selection during the following decade.

These years also saw an LEA-led 'break-out in secondary education' (ibid., Chapter 6; see also Simon, 1985, pp. 283–97), and they were crucial to the development of comprehensive education in England and Wales. What lay behind this change was growing parental dissatisfaction with the 11+, despite the efforts of several authorities to develop academic work in the secondary modern schools. By the late 1950s and early 1960s, Simon argues, 'pressures were building up from all parts of the country, but perhaps particularly from the great conurbations in the north', and:

> it was becoming clear by now that a social movement of some significance was under way – reflecting increased aspirations and mounting frustration on the part of parents (including new social strata emerging from technological change) and the local politicians representing them (Simon, 1991, p. 271).

The new Education Minister from July 1962, Edward Boyle, was aware that dissatisfaction with the 11+ was increasing, and that, in the light of evaluations of comprehensive school experiments, such as that published by the LCC in 1961, 'support for the development of secondary education along comprehensive lines was gaining considerable momentum' (Boyle, 1972, p. 31). According to one writer, tensions within the Conservative Party which were to become manifest later in the decade were already present, as defenders of the grammar schools 'were alarmed not only by the egalitarian impulse to change the social pattern of schooling but by, what appeared to them to be, the possibility of an ill-considered, headlong rush towards a monolithic system of comprehensive schools' (Knight, 1990, p. 17).

However, Boyle was always more in tune with grass-roots feelings about the 11+ than were his detractors in the party (Crook, 1993). Encouraged by Boyle's assurance in a party television broadcast in May 1963 that LEA schemes for the reorganisation of secondary education would be judged strictly on their educational merits, regardless of the authority's political complexion,[4] the Labour-controlled Education Committees of Liverpool, Manchester and London all announced proposals to discontinue the 11+ and establish city-wide comprehensive school systems over the following months. While Labour-dominated big city authorities such as these took the lead, the ambition to reorganise was developing into a more widespread phenomenon, affecting authorities with a variety of different socio-economic circumstances and political complexions. Ministry officials estimated that a majority of LEAs had completed or were working on reorganisation proposals by 1963 (Boyle, 1972, pp. 32–3), with a number of Conservative LEAs among the most determined to end selection. Boyle reported to Prime Minister Macmillan that the tendency to move away from formal selection examinations had been 'quietly encouraged' by his ministry and that the time was right to go beyond the doctrine of the 1958 White Paper by ending 'the strict neutrality which my department has maintained in public towards local selection methods'.[5] This cleared the path for Bradford to become the first English city to completely abolish 11 + selection from September 1964 (Chitty, 1989, p. 37).

Although its long-term significance could not be predicted at the time, Boyle's 1964 Education Act removed the outdated obstacle of compulsory school transfer at 11, which the 1944 Education Act had imposed. This was a direct response to pressure exerted by Alec Clegg, CEO of the West Riding LEA, who, because of demographic pressures and building constraints in parts of his diverse county, sought a three-tier comprehensive school system, incorporating middle schools for 9–13-year-olds (see Chapter 7). The three-tier option was later widely favoured – especially by Conservative-controlled LEAs – as authorities wishing to go comprehensive saw it as the cheapest and least contentious means of doing so. Opting for lower, middle and upper schools, it should be remembered, allowed reorganisation to occur with minimal extra building work, necessitated few (if any) enforced school closures, and allowed the former grammar schools to maintain their examination courses and sixth forms. These were sensitive issues for politicians, parents and ratepayers alike.

The question of the age of school transfer was part of the brief given to a committee of enquiry, headed by Lady Plowden in 1963, and, at the time of Labour's narrow general election victory in October 1964, there was some talk of 'waiting for Plowden' before attempting to put into effect the manifesto promise that 'secondary education will be reorganised on comprehensive lines' (Short, 1989, p. 104). However, the tide of reform which the LEAs were leading was becoming irresistible.

The Background to Circular 10/65

The middle years of the 1960s were a crucial phase in the development of comprehensive reorganisation, during which central government came more into the picture. Progress was now dependent on the relationships between national and local policies. In one sense, it might be argued that activity at the local level was forcing the hand of central government. On the other hand, this activity also put a brake on the kind of powers that central government adopted once the political will to have a comprehensive system was in place.

A week-by-week survey of the *Times Educational Supplement* (TES) from 1963 indicates the interest which LEAs, acting entirely of their own volition, were showing towards comprehensive education.

That same year, at its autumn conference, the Labour Party belatedly adopted a policy to establish universal comprehensive education and to end 11+ selection everywhere, but no time limits for the completion of reorganisation were indicated. At the highest levels of the party, it was widely felt that coercion would be both unnecessary and unwise. Indeed, reports from the localities were most encouraging. Practices of parental and teacher consultation, previously unheard of in education – or indeed in any other area of British local government – were developing, in addition to the established democratic checks and balances imposed by council, committee and sub-committee votes. The public meeting became an increasingly important forum for the exchange of information and opinions, particularly after 1964 when the Bristol (see Chapter 5) and Liverpool city-wide comprehensive proposals were criticised more for their secrecy than for their substance. The ideas and experiences of various LEAs were exchanged both formally, by means of fact-finding visits, and informally, through correspondence and friendships, and alternative reorganisation models were widely discussed.

Although the simplest and most common reorganisation pattern involved the adoption of 'all-through' 11–18 comprehensive schools, a number of authorities were attracted by the widely publicised Leicestershire two-tier plan. But by the early 1960s, doubts were being raised about 14+ transfer, in view of the much anticipated, but slow to arrive, raising of the school leaving age to 16. Moreover, committed comprehensive supporters were suspicious of the way that some of Leicestershire's upper schools continued to style themselves 'grammar' schools. Alternatives to the 'all-through' and 'Leicestershire' patterns were beginning to proliferate by the early 1960s. The 'Croydon' scheme, featuring a sixth-form college, based on the American 'junior college' principle (see Chapter 6), aroused a great deal of curiosity, although it was not widely popular among teachers. Other LEAs, while evidently uncomfortable with the 11+, preferred to opt for the 'Doncaster' semi-comprehensive scheme (which retained just a small number of grammar schools), or sought to investigate alternative, fairer procedures for selection, such as the West Riding's 'Thorne' scheme (see Chapter 7). Also, the 1964 legislation permitting the establishment on a trial basis of three-tier schemes aroused interest in areas other than the West Riding.

This local activity, and the variety of schemes already under discussion, were important in shaping the way that central government sought to accelerate change under a new Labour administration ostensibly committed to the principle of comprehensive reorganisation. In addition, account has to be taken of the attitudes and sensibilities of the chief political players, and, in particular, the two responsible ministers, in the period immediately preceding the issue of Circular 10/65.

Labour's first Secretary of State for Education in the 1964 Wilson Cabinet was Michael Stewart. His credentials, as Tony Benn, a fellow minister, noted in his diary, were impressive: 'He is a passionate believer in comprehensive education and sees the danger of allowing the direct grant schools to obstruct the development of fully comprehensive education' (Benn, 1987, p. 179). In his first Cabinet paper, Stewart introduced the idea of issuing a circular 'requiring local authorities to submit appropriate plans', but with the proviso that there be 'legislation in the next session, both to deal with the particular difficulties and, if necessary, to deal with uncooperative local authorities' (Stewart, 1980, p. 132).

Although the idea of a circular was well-received, the Cabinet preferred that it should 'request', rather than 'require' LEAs to co-operate. This decision represented a third manifesto retreat in as many weeks, according to Ted Short, Wilson's Chief Whip (and a future Education Secretary himself), who has described his apprehension at the time (Short, 1989, pp. 104–5). Stewart, however, decided to be content with 'three-quarters of the loaf' (Stewart, 1980, p. 132) and in the subsequent Commons debate announced his intention not to seek legislation 'unless it proved essential for the continuation of the comprehensive policy' (Hansard, H of C, 21 January 1965).

Stewart subsequently pointed out that he was helped by the divisions within Conservative ranks over the comprehensive school issue (Stewart, 1980, p. 132). But Labour policy was not without its own contradictions, exemplified by the amendment finally approved in the Commons debate, which welcomed 'the efforts of local authorities to reorganise secondary education on comprehensive lines which will preserve all that is valuable in grammar-school education for those children who now receive it and make it available to more children' (Hansard, H of C, 21 January 1965, quoted in Chitty, 1989, p. 40).

This illogical reasoning exactly reflected that of Prime Minister Wilson, who saw the comprehensive school as a 'grammar school for all', and was on record as having said that grammars would be abolished 'over my dead body'.[6] Later, in 1969, Tony Benn's diary notes Wilson's apparent inability to see a contradiction between comprehensives and continuing selective practices (Benn, 1988, p. 218).

Chitty has, however, suggested that the way in which comprehensive education was constantly misrepresented by Wilson and others was not wholly counter-productive:

> the slogan of 'grammar schools for all', in fact, served a number of useful functions: it silenced the opponents of reorganisation within the party itself; it appealed to growing demands for a more meritocratic system of secondary education; and it dispelled the fears of parents who placed their trust in the traditional grammar school curriculum (Chitty, 1989, p. 36).

Stewart's successor, Tony Crosland, arrived at the DES just as much-publicised difficulties at two London comprehensives, Risinghill and Kidbrooke (see Chapter 4) had placed the whole issue of comprehensive education under press and public scrutiny. But he showed no signs of wavering from the course set by his predecessor, and believed, according to his wife, that the forthcoming departmental circular on comprehensives would be more effective if it sought the voluntary co-operation of LEAs:

> the department couldn't cope with the pace already set. He didn't want the new system threatened by botching it – throwing together buildings that lacked the physical requirements for a sixth form; or amalgamating a grammar school and a secondary modern school so quickly that instead of creating a genuinely new school the grammar school ethos prevailed (Crosland, 1982, p. 144).

DES figures show how, between 1960 and 1965, the total number of comprehensive schools in England and Wales more than doubled (from 130 to 262). During these years, the number of pupils in comprehensives also rose from 128,835 (representing 4.7 per cent of the total maintained secondary school population) to 239,619 (8.5 per cent) (Simon, 1991, p. 586, Table 6a). If proof is needed that it was developments at the LEA level which shaped a national comprehensive schools policy, this surely fits the bill. It was not difficult for Crosland to play down any suggestions made in the press of conflict between his department and LEAs, and he reminded an audience at the end of May 1965 that almost two-thirds of the secondary school population already lived in areas where the LEA was implementing or planning a comprehensive schools policy:

the fact is that there has been a growing movement against the 11+ examination and all that it implies. This movement has not been politically inspired or imposed from the centre. It has been a spontaneous growth at the grass roots of education, leading to a widespread conviction that separatism is an offence against the child as well as a brake on social and economic progress ... The whole notion of a selection test at this age belongs to the era when secondary education was a privilege of the few.[7]

Crosland recognised the LEA's unique local knowledge and respected the fact that there was undoubtedly more expertise to oversee re-organisation in the localities than there was within his own ministry. Pragmatism determined that any insistence upon a single model would thwart – or be used as an excuse to delay indefinitely – comprehensive reorganisation in areas with small but serviceable schools. For this reason, Crosland indicated that the forthcoming circular would high-light alternative patterns, based on the diverse experiences of the pioneering authorities (Simon, 1991, p. 281). But he also, ominously, avoided mentioning the availability of additional funding to enable LEAs to effect change.

Circular 10/65: Labour's Modest Proposal

Circular 10/65 was eventually published on 14 July 1965, and it received a predictably mixed reception from the press. Despite the *Daily Telegraph*'s protestations to the contrary (15 July 1965), there was nothing dictatorial about it. Above all else, the circular was a planning document for LEAs, indicating six alternative methods of 'going comprehensive'. LEAs were free to decide, on the basis of educational preference and existing building stock, whether an all-through solution – which the circular noted was still the favoured option at the DES – was appropriate, or whether they wished to introduce a tiered system. Of the two-tier alternatives, each contemplated secondary education beginning at 11, with a transfer to another school (or sixth form college) at 13, 14 or 16. The newly permissible three-tier solution, with middle schools catering for the 8–12 or 9–13 age group, was also outlined, indicating the willingness of the DES to see this scheme applied – though experimentally at first – beyond the West Riding.

It seems unlikely that any of the six models would have been unfamiliar to CEOs or Education Committee chairmen. Over the previous ten years, the journal *Education*, as well as the *TES* (and, indeed, the national daily press from time to time) had charted the progress – though rarely uncritically – of comprehensives. Moreover, since 1958 a radical education journal, *Forum*, initially co-edited by Robin Pedley and Brian Simon of Leicester University, had concentrated on the comprehensive school issue, carrying regular regional – and comparative – surveys and articles on new trends, written by academics, politicians, administrators and teachers (Simon, 1991, pp. 204–7).

Two months after the publication of the circular, the Comprehensive Schools Committee (CSC) was formed, composed of 'a formidable group of educationalists' (Benn, 1987, p. 322), headed by Tony Benn's wife, Caroline, and Brian Simon. The group were by no means impressed by Crosland's progress to date, and took him to task for approving Doncaster's semi-comprehensive plan, while rejecting the – to their mind sounder – proposals of Liverpool, Stoke-on-Trent and Luton (Simon, 1991, pp. 281–2). The influence which the CSC exerted upon DES documents during this period was marked, and represented 'an interesting lesson in the operation of pressure politics' (Benn, 1987, p. 482). For the remainder of the decade, and the first part of the next, the CSC produced an annually updated comprehensive schools survey, indicating the progress – or otherwise – of every English, Welsh and Scottish LEA.

The formulation of local responses to Circular 10/65 usually involved the transmission of ideas through a hierarchy of working parties, sub-committees, the Education Committee and full Council. As the pages of the *TES* from this era show, draft proposals were constantly being rejected or withdrawn, revised and re-submitted, but the CSC, operating from the basement of the Benns' house in Holland Park, managed to keep track of the local scene rather better than the DES officials who often requested updates (conversation with Caroline Benn, 30 March 1992).

Conservatives and Comprehensives: A Vexing Issue

In subsequent years, the *raison d'être* for Circular 10/65 was to become the focus of heated controversy between the pro- and anti-comprehensive lobbies, but the question of comprehensive education has never been a simple party political matter. For Conservatives, at both the national and local levels, it was a particularly vexing issue. At the beginning of 1966, *The Economist* commented that comprehensive education was attracting bipartisan support, re-christening Sir Edward Boyle, the Shadow Education Minister, 'Sir Edthony Crossboyle' (15 January 1966, p. 172). Boyle had declined to support isolated campaigns to defy Crosland's request, reminding a fellow Tory MP that 'it is worth remembering that as long ago as 1963, more than half the local authorities were contemplating reorganisation of either the whole or part of their area, and that this was true of a number of non-Socialist authorities as well as the Socialist-administered big cities.' A drive back to bipartism would, he argued, 'lead into headlong collision with a great many Local Authorities – not only those administered by the left'.[8] In response to another enquiry, he advised:

> ... no Conservative government could reverse this trend without having to take far more dictatorial powers over Local Authorities than any socialist government has ever proposed.[9]

Both before and after the more decisive Conservative general election defeat of March 1966, Boyle refused to appease critics who called for an unequivocal statement, promising that he would withdraw Circular 10/65 if he became Secretary of State. Knight (1990) portrays Boyle as 'not a traditional Tory politician', but rather a 'radical social democrat' (p. 34), thus explaining the ever-increasing attacks – for example in the first two *Black Papers* – to which he was subjected by the emerging 'new right' of the party between 1965 and his resignation in 1970 (ibid., pp. 35–53).

In view of the fact that a significant number of Conservative-controlled LEAs responded enthusiastically to the challenge of Circular 10/65, it can be argued that Boyle was more closely in touch with local feelings than his detractors. Moreover, while his party leader, Ted Heath, shared Boyle's objections to 'the bogus hotch-potch of so-called comprehensive schemes', he welcomed, in 1967, 'the variety of patterns of secondary education which avoid selection at 11+', and particularly seemed to favour tiered reorganisation schemes. By 'continuing to adapt themselves', Heath added, 'grammar schools have a vital part to play'.[10] The Party Chairman, Anthony Barber, also acknowledged, in a private letter to Boyle dated 11 March 1968, that 'you have had a difficult time with the question of comprehensive education, but I am sure that our approach – although not always popular with the Party activists – is right and is now being seen to be right'.[11] It is difficult to argue, however, that Boyle and Barber reflected the dominant position in the parliamentary party, which was precisely the problem. The Conservative Party was divided on the matter, and thus the pressure from the local authorities was more successful than it might otherwise have been.

TOWARDS A COMPREHENSIVE EDUCATION SYSTEM

The combination of the fact that Labour's Circular 10/65 provided six acceptable forms of reorganisation and the lack of a clear position by the Conservatives encouraged LEAs to consider alternatives. Thus, rather than representing a major move towards a national education policy, the initial effect of Circular 10/65 was to encourage consideration of a wide range of reorganisation alternatives, including the alternative of refusing to reorganise.

LEA Responses 1965–68: New Flexibility

Among the scores of LEA plans which arrived at the DES in the months following the publication of Circular 10/65, each of the reorganisation models outlined in the circular's appendix featured to a greater or lesser degree. Some authorities determined that no single scheme was appropriate for the entirety of their administrative area, and they submitted hybrid or partial reorganisation proposals. By no means would it be true to say that the Labour government which had sought to accelerate the pace of change accepted these plans uncritically. Many were sent back for further revision, or accepted as interim solutions only, though DES officials were sometimes aware of 'pressure from above to push through schemes despite any shortcomings they might have' (Chitty, 1989, p. 39). A small number – around 20 – of LEAs had indicated, by the autumn of 1965, that they were unwilling to reorganise. When the near certainty of a full five-year term ahead was achieved by Labour the following March, there was a moment when 'the government could have introduced legislation to speed the transition, having wide popular support and a powerful Parliamentary majority' (Simon, 1991, pp. 283–4). The temptation was resisted, however, and the moment passed.

The municipal elections held in the spring of 1967 posed some difficulties for the central government strategy of *requesting*, rather than requiring co-operation. A number of former Labour city strongholds, including Bristol, Manchester, Liverpool, Birmingham and London, were won by the Conservatives, and some LEAs immediately withdrew comprehensive school proposals already submitted to the DES. At this stage, legislation to force the hand of recalcitrant authorities was again contemplated by the Secretary of State (Crosland, 1982, p. 144), but again, no action was taken.

It was the country's economic difficulties, rather than secondary education policy, however, that largely determined the poll results.

There was no backlash against the tendency to do away with the 11+ examination, and local Conservative politicians assuming the chairs of Education Committees were quick to recognise this. Among our case-study authorities, London made a token gesture towards the preservation of its county grammar schools between 1967 and 1970, but it did not seek to prevent secondary moderns from either closing or amalgamating to form new comprehensive schools. The changeover to comprehensive education barely slowed, in fact, during the years of Conservative rule in the capital (see Chapter 4). It was a similar story in Bristol and Manchester (see Chapter 5).

The middle school reorganisation model received a boost in 1967, when the Plowden Report was issued, although the bulk of LEAs opting for a three-tier approach during the late 1960s and early 1970s still tended to favour the 9–13 school, rather than the 8–12 one advocated by a narrow majority of Plowden Committee members. Middle schools offered welcome flexibility for cash-starved LEAs which wished to abandon selection without creating huge comprehensives or attracting school closure or merger protests. In Leeds, it is interesting to note that the arrival of a Conservative Chairman of Education keen on middle schools *accelerated* the move towards a comprehensive city-wide pattern, which had been dogged by political wranglings during the years of Labour control (see Chapter 5; Fenwick and Woodthorpe, 1980, pp. 18–28). This is another indication of the lack of consistent association between forms of reorganisation and political party control.

Demands for Legislation: 1968–70

The widespread acceptance of the comprehensive principle, together with greater flexibility in devising patterns of schooling were both critical in explaining the significant growth in the total number of English and Welsh comprehensives. In 1965 there were 262 comprehensive schools, rising dramatically to 748 in 1968, by which time more than a fifth of the secondary school population attended such a school. But despite this success, a small number of LEAs had still not submitted proposals to the DES, three years after the publication of Circular 10/65, angering some Labour MPs. One revised plan submitted by Birmingham City Council – and promptly rejected by Secretary of State, Edward Short – envisaged retaining 20 of the 25 remaining grammar schools. At the 1968 Labour Party conference, to the apparent approval of most of the audience, one enraged city MP called for legislation to force change. Another backbencher saw legislation as the surest guarantee of securing genuine comprehensive proposals rather than 'half-baked' schemes (*TES*, 4 October 1968).

However, the *TES*, in an editorial in the same issue, sprang to the defence of the laggard LEAs, blaming the 'ridiculous comprehensive schemes now staining the educational scene' on the government's refusal to provide additional money for reorganisation. Ted Short, Secretary of State for Education since April 1968, privately acknowledged this point, admitting in his autobiography that 'the government's refusal to legislate and the Chancellor's refusal to make funds available meant that comprehensive reorganisation was often a botched-up job from the start' (Short, 1989, p. 108).

Short had privately discussed with Tony Benn the possibility of an Education Bill immediately after his appointment (Benn, 1988, p. 62), and after the party conference there was open speculation that legislation was imminent, although at first the government sought to play the rumours down (*TES*, 11 and 18 October 1968). However, the government's patience finally ran out, and it was revealed towards the end of 1969 that the next Queen's Speech would announce the introduction of a Bill giving the Secretary of State powers to legislate for comprehensive education.

This marks, in many ways, a watershed in the history of comprehensive reorganisation, because the proposed legislation sought to destroy the central–local government balance on educational affairs which had prevailed since 1944. Already this relationship was showing signs of strain. In March 1969, the CEO for Southport, a Tory-controlled LEA which had only submitted an interim plan to the DES, complained to the AEC Secretary, Sir William Alexander, that DES tactics amounted to little short of 'blackmail', and warned that some of his elected members would 'want to fight':

> it seems clear from informal discussions with the Department of Education and Science that they are now taking the line that they require the Authority to commit itself to a specific fully comprehensive scheme before any secondary school building projects can be considered. I accept the need to show that a building project should not be incompatible with comprehensive reorganisation, but this is not the same thing as requiring compatibility with a specific scheme to which an Authority is committed as policy.[12]

The prospect of legislation prompted a similar gesture of defiance from the Bournemouth Education Committee,[13] but Alexander was content to wait and see the exact wording of Short's Bill, having been assured by the Secretary of State that LEAs 'will not think it unreasonable'.[14]

In October 1969, Prime Minister Wilson called for 'an objective approach' to the forthcoming Bill,[15] which was introduced in the wake of a further *Black Paper* controversy and the replacement of Boyle on the opposition front bench by the more right-wing Margaret Thatcher. Ironically, Short's Bill helped to unite the opposition behind their new Shadow Minister, since even those who welcomed comprehensives tended to reject the notion of compulsion. The 'rigidly authoritarian' Bill was also unacceptable to the AEC, which judged it to be inconsistent with the government's declared statements about 'freeing local government from meticulous central supervision and direction'.[16] Short's impatience, Alexander argued, was unnecessary and likely to be counter-productive in view of the grass-roots nature of the drive towards comprehensivisation:

> tremendous strides have been taken towards forms of organisation which meet local needs and broadly meet the criteria suggested in Circular 10/65. There is nothing to suggest that acceptance of the principle of comprehensive education will not in time operate in all areas, including the small number who for a variety of reasons have not yet made formal proposals. My Committee feel most deeply that all that has so far happened points the way to continued development by local consent ... the advantage to be gained from forcing the present Bill through the House will be more than countered by the resulting suspicion and bitterness which would inevitably attend the introduction of new major legislation.[17]

Short retorted that he valued LEA freedoms, but that these 'can scarcely include the possibility of frustrating national policy'. 'If it is wrong to select and segregate children it must be wrong everywhere', he replied.[18] Though he regretted education becoming a 'political football',[19] the Secretary of State's view was that the government had a duty to ensure that the minority of LEAs which had not yet begun to plan for comprehensive education were regulated.

Margaret Thatcher and Circular 10/70

In the event, plans to legislate were aborted by political changes consequent on the general election. Not only was the Education Bill sacrificed, the new Conservative Secretary of State for Education,

Margaret Thatcher, published Circular 10/70 on 30 June 1970, effectively withdrawing Labour's circular of five years earlier. LEAs would be, it was claimed, 'freer' to determine secondary school patterns in their areas. This represented, according to Thatcher's critics, 'a specific threat to the further development of comprehensive education' (Simon, 1991, p. 408), but the circular came 'none too soon' for Conservatives on the right of the party 'who readily associated comprehensive schooling with "progressive" styles of teaching and learning' (Knight, 1990, p. 64). At the local level, a number of Conservative strongholds decided to abandon their plans to end selection over the following months. A Lancashire CASE branch correspondent reported to the national Secretary in October 1970 that 'we now have a local battle on to try and prevent the Tories from reversing the plans for comprehensive secondary education here (the Tories are proposing to make the Sixth Form college, which is slowly rising at the bottom of the road, into a super Grammar School!)'.[20] A despondent resolution, passed by the CASE Executive in the autumn of 1970, illustrates the confusion which Circular 10/70 wreaked upon areas where the battle for comprehensives seemed to have been won. However, there was still a belief that pressure group activity could make a real difference:

> CASE deplores the publication of Circular 10/70, and the encouragement this has given to some Local Education Authorities to go back on their intention to abandon selection for secondary education; CASE ... urges local authorities to continue without slackening the movement towards fully comprehensive secondary education; CASE welcomes the appearance of associations of all those working together to achieve comprehensive education, and urges local associations to give their full support to such groups.[21]

Divisions in the Conservative ranks were no less apparent during Margaret Thatcher's stewardship at the DES than they had been in the Boyle era, however. In many Conservative-controlled areas, reorganisation attracted bipartisan support, and Circular 10/70 merely served to provoke embarrassing quarrels about party loyalties. In Bedfordshire and Surrey, for example, County Councillors found themselves at odds with Tory Education Committee members, as well as teachers and parents (Simon, 1991, pp. 409–13), while in Leeds, one of our case-study LEAs (see Chapter 5), the Conservative Chairman of Education was farcically reduced to telephoning the Secretary of State, urging her not to reject the LEA's carefully constructed comprehensive schools plan (Fenwick and Woodthorpe, 1980).

Curiously, the outer London Tory borough of Richmond-upon-Thames, which had fiercely resisted all pressures to abandon selection during the late 1960s, underwent 'a very sudden change of heart'[22] by opting to go comprehensive shortly after the 1970 General Election. Joan Sallis, a local CASE branch member, and later a respected *TES* columnist, attributed this surprising decision to an alliance of local heads, teachers and parents opposed to selection procedures, combined with national pressures for comprehensives and the influence of a small group of pro-comprehensive local Conservatives who succeeded in persuading the centre group of the case for reform.

The Slowly Shifting Tide, 1970–74

Although, as Knight has illustrated, the years 1970 to 1974 witnessed 'a proliferation of educational right-thinking' and the 'absorption of "the *Black Paper* spirit"' into national Conservative Party thinking (Knight, 1990, pp. 65 and 68), LEA comprehensive school proposals continued to arrive at the DES at a steady rate. Chitty reminds us that, despite her personal intervention to 'save' grammar schools from amalgamation or closure, Mrs Thatcher presided over the creation of more comprehensives than any of her predecessors or successors, and that these were crucial years, during which, for the first time, a majority of English and Welsh secondary school children attended a comprehensive school (Chitty, 1989, pp. 54–5).

Sixty-two per cent of English and Welsh maintained secondary school children attended 2,677 comprehensives by 1974, according to DES figures, compared with figures of 32 per cent and 1,250 four years previously (Simon, 1991, p. 586, Table 6a). In Mrs Thatcher's own words, the 'universal comprehensive thing' could not be resisted:

> ... this great roller coaster of an idea was moving, and I found it difficult, if not impossible to stop [it].
>
> (interview in the *Daily Mail*, 13 May 1987, quoted in Chitty, 1989, pp. 54–5).

Nevertheless, comprehensive education did suffer severe setbacks during these years. The Secretary of State's decision to examine LEA proposals to amalgamate or close individual schools by the terms of section 13 of the 1944 Act – rather than continuing the long-established practice of considering plans for the whole of the administrative unit – had the effect of slowing down the comprehensive trend. The tactic undoubtedly reflected Mrs Thatcher's early legal training, and, according to one critic, resulted in 'a series of arbitrary, indeed capricious decisions concerning school policy', building to a climax of public dissatisfaction during the late summer and autumn of 1973 (Simon, 1991, p. 418).

More controversial still was the use (or abuse) of section 13 powers to veto an LEA's proposal to redesignate a school. A total of 94 grammar schools, nominated by various LEAs for amalgamation or closure were 'saved' by Mrs Thatcher between 1970 and 1974. These interventions raised fundamental questions about the rights of central government to interfere in local affairs which seemed to have been laid aside when the 1970 Education Bill was lost. But the policy of supporting grammar schools delighted preservationist groups, some of which were associated with the right wing of the Tory Party. Maynard Potts, chairman of the ultra-right National Education Association, reported in January 1973 that the NEA had helped 287 groups mount opposition to school closures (*TES*, 26 January 1973, letter). On the other hand, critics alleged that Mrs Thatcher's decisions were sometimes inconsistent with her declared intention to speak on behalf of local government electors. Labour supporters claimed that she had overlooked pro-comprehensive petitions and did not consider the wishes of the electors as a whole (*Guardian*, 4 September 1973). Alarm was expressed at the fact that, although DES figures now indicated that 41 per cent of the secondary school population attended a comprehensive, only around 12 per cent were in LEAs with a fully comprehensive system. The simultaneous existence of grammar schools and comprehensives was clearly at odds with the comprehensive philosophy, and parents' overwhelming dissatisfaction with the situation was evident from the results of opinion polls.

THE DECLINE OF COMPREHENSIVE EDUCATION

Although the period 1969–70 represents a watershed in the comprehensive schools movement, it does not necessarily represent a clear 'victory' for either the supporters of comprehensive education or their opponents. The number of comprehensive schools subsequently continued to grow at a rapid rate. At the same time, the balance between the influence of local and central government began to tip away from local dominance. Strangely, the watershed year was marked by defeats for both Labour and the Conservatives, Labour at the polls, the Conservatives in their efforts to stop the comprehensive schools movement. But although both parties were somewhat in disarray, the effect was to weaken the drive towards comprehensive education. The future belonged to the forces of resistance to the movement and, even when Labour were again in power, the setbacks continued.

Comprehensive Education Betrayed, 1974–79

Recent assessments of the education policies of Labour during the premierships of Harold Wilson (to March 1976) and James Callaghan (to May 1979) have portrayed this period as crucial in the battle for the comprehensive school. In part, this was due to the deteriorating economic environment and the industrial and political problems of the government. But there was also evidence of uncertainty and confusion in Labour's attitude to the future of the comprehensive school.

Labour's first move, upon returning to power in 1974, was to replace Circular 10/70 by Circular 4/74, and the co-operation of LEAs was again sought to extend comprehensive education. The new Secretary of State, Reginald Prentice, approved proposals from seven LEAs during his first month of office, and more thereafter, although the subject of legislation was not initially discussed (Simon, 1991, p. 436). However, the anti-comprehensive alliance formed between Mrs Thatcher, the new Conservative Party leader from February 1975, Norman St John Stevas, the Shadow Education Minister, and political and academic representatives of the so-called 'new right' – including Brian Cox, Rhodes Boyson, Keith Joseph and Christopher Patten – urged LEAs which had not yet submitted comprehensive proposals to use stalling tactics and wait for the return of the Conservatives (Knight, 1990, pp. 94–9).

A survey in February 1975 indicated that only 20 of the English and Welsh LEAs were 'truly comprehensive', and a quarter of all pupils still sat the 11+ examination (Simon, 1991, p. 439). Labour's confidence in its policy of seeking co-operation collapsed in the face of the more 'abrasive, aggressive, assertive outlook of the radical right within the Tory party' (ibid., 1991, pp. 438–9), and Secretary of State Fred Mulley indicated that a Parliamentary Bill requiring authorities to go comprehensive would be introduced.

The more sympathetic response of Lord Alexander, Secretary of the AEC, to this move, compared with five years earlier, showed how much the political climate had changed. Alexander particularly regretted the 'party political polarisation' which had worsened since St John Stevas' elevation to the shadow education portfolio. Having in mind the difficulties which Birmingham's CEO had faced in meeting the wishes of his alternating political masters over many years, Alexander suggested that legislation might liberate the issue of reorganisation from politics.[23] However, as in 1970, he thought the actual wording of the Bill, as published in December 1975, was inadvisably confrontational towards LEAs. The passage of the Bill through Parliament took almost a year, during which time Alexander, citing the views of his Executive, urged Mulley to think again:

> they fear that the power now being taken by the Secretary of State creates a very dangerous situation. It could, for example, allow a future Secretary of State to require local education authorities to organise secondary education on a selective basis; and changes of this kind would be utterly destructive of progress in the education service, and harmful to the children.[24]

Alexander's executive believed that 'if the present provisions of the Education Act were maintained without amendment, in due course, a fully comprehensive system throughout the country would be evolved as a natural process in the carrying into effect of consensus opinion, which has been the basis of educational development over the years'.[25] In any case, Alexander continued, since the serious economic condition of the country ruled out the possibility of providing further resources to effect reorganisation, compulsion might lead to the submission of inferior 'makeshift schemes'. He also represented the feeling of his committee that in view of mounting concern about the organisation of education for 16–19 year-olds, the time had perhaps now come for the DES to indicate their preferences for a particular model of reorganisation. To rush new schemes through in the present circumstances was not, he concluded, 'to the advantage of those who firmly believe in the comprehensive principle, and indeed could cause a reaction which could endanger the principle itself'.[26] But Mulley was adamant that legislation had become a necessary evil. His views contrast markedly with Tony Crosland's confidence in the 'grass roots' evolution of comprehensive education, 11 years earlier:

> one would obviously wish that all government policy might be achieved by agreement rather than legislation, but this is rarely feasible. If comprehensive education had been left to evolve by a natural process, in pace with public opinion and without a lead from central government, we would certainly not have seen such great advance in the past ten years. Only by bringing

reorganisation to as speedy a conclusion as possible in the present economic climate – and you will realise that no date has been set for the completion of the reorganisation nationally, precisely in part because we want to guard against the possibility of makeshift schemes through lack of resources – can there be an opportunity for the development of a fully, and hence truly, comprehensive system of secondary education.[27]

By the time the Bill received the Royal assent on 22 November 1976, Shirley Williams had succeeded Mulley in Callaghan's government, and the so-called 'Great Debate' about the future of education, launched in part to raise the profile of the new Prime Minister (Chitty, 1989, p. 71), was under way. In October, a copy of a confidential document written by Mulley (before his departure) and DES officials, known as the 'Yellow Book' had been leaked to the press. It contained, in the *Guardian*'s words, 'a severe indictment of the failure of secondary schools to produce enough scientists and engineers' (13 October 1976, quoted in Chitty, 1989, p. 82). The paper, whose themes were echoed by a much-hyped speech by the Prime Minister at Ruskin College, foreshadowed the education reforms of the Conservative government in the following decade, by proposing the introduction of a national curriculum to particularly emphasise mathematics and science.

The notion that there was a 'crisis' in education had been further accentuated by a series of stories carried by newspapers and television documentaries around this time, which conspired to paint a picture of schools – and comprehensives, in particular – as out of control, walled off from parental concerns and subject to the influence of Marxist ideology (Morris and Griggs, 1988, pp. 5–6; Chitty, 1989, pp. 63–6). This was all symptomatic of the retreat from optimism that character-ised the rhetoric of educational debate at that time (Bernbaum, 1979). Callaghan, who had 'decided to make educational reform a key theme of his new administration' (Chitty, 1989, p. 70), was significantly swayed by the gloomy conclusions of the 'Yellow Book', which 'cast doubt in the most biased way on the work of the comprehensives' (Morris and Griggs, 1988, pp. 6–7), and allowed the political right to seize control of the educational agenda three years before the Conservative Party returned to power in 1979.

In the month following the enactment of the 1976 Bill, Shirley Williams continued publicly to push the comprehensive principle, and had written to 38 LEAs, requiring them to submit plans by April 1978 (Simon, 1991, p. 454). However, as Tony Benn has revealed, doubts at

the highest level ensured that the 'Great Debate' ended any possibilities of comprehensivisation proceeding further (Chitty, 1989,
p. 69). Though he had stolen the Tories' clothing by concentrating
upon the undefined concepts of 'quality' and 'standards' in education,
Callaghan's government was crippled by debt and – notably during the
1978–79 'winter of discontent' – industrial unrest. Education policy
was unclear and budgets for schools, colleges, polytechnics and
universities were all slashed (Morris and Griggs, 1988, p. 12). Significantly, a 1978 DES report, entitled 'Comprehensive Education' (DES,
1978) was more retrospective than forward-looking. The report also
confirmed the Labour government's unwillingness to differentiate
between genuinely comprehensive and quasi-comprehensive solutions,
adopted by various LEAs. 'Whatever the geographical area of the
pattern of organisation', wrote Margaret Jackson, Under-Secretary of
State, 'all have their merits' (ibid., pp.13–14).

The Assault on Comprehensive Education, 1979–95

Margaret Thatcher's general election victory in May 1979 gave the
Conservatives a comfortable parliamentary majority, and within six
months of its taking office, two Education Acts had been passed. The
first of these effectively repealed Labour's 1976 Act, which had, it was
suggested, infringed LEA autonomy. Ironically, LEA autonomy was,
in due course, to become perhaps the principal target of four successive
Conservative governments which have dramatically increased central
control of the curriculum, governance and funding of schools. Nevertheless, freedom was the watchword of the 1979 Act, an emphasis
which Brian Simon interprets as a declaration 'that comprehensive
education was no longer "national policy", so giving the green light to
authorities that wished not only not to reorganise their schools as
comprehensive systems but to go further and split up existing schools
to bring back the grammar school/secondary modern division' (Simon,
1991, p. 474). Yet despite the legislation, the 1980s brought more
examples of LEAs belatedly going comprehensive, including Bolton,
Tamesside, Cornwall and Cumbria, and more grammar schools were
merged or redesignated to become comprehensives (Simon, 1991,
pp. 482–3). There were, it might be argued, several years of lag time
between the strong shift in the central government and the parallel
reaction at the local level.

Instances of LEAs attempting to reverse the process of reorganisation during the past 13 years have been exceptional, but there was an
interesting episode from the West Midlands, dubbed by Simon 'The

Solihull Adventure', which warns against the misjudgement of local councillors regarding community attachment to local schools. In that case, large-scale protests by parents and teachers during 1983 and 1984 forced the abandonment of an attempt to introduce a selective scheme. Similar situations prevailed in Berkshire, Wiltshire and the outer London borough of Redbridge (which had sought to extend its partially selective system). These defeats undoubtedly disappointed the Prime Minister and her free-marketeer Secretary of State for Education and Science from 1981 to 1986, Sir Keith Joseph (Simon, 1991, pp. 498–500). They also undoubtedly encouraged the intro-duction of rather more subtle policy initiatives aimed at establishing specialised ('differentiated') secondary schools and providing for parental choice. These ideas were to find expression in the 1988 Education Reform Act.

Comprehensive Education: A Bleak Future

The notion of 'differentiation' underpins the 'magnet' school model seemingly favoured by John Major, Thatcher's successor as Prime Minister. In July 1992, Secretary of State John Patten suggested that comprehensives in future 'can indeed do a little bit of "picking and choosing" on the side, without coming to me for permission to change their character', adding:

> ... selection is not, and should not be, a great issue of the 1990s as it was in the 1960s. The S-word for socialists to come to terms with is, rather, 'specialisation'. The fact is that children excel at different things; it is foolish to ignore it, and some schools may wish specifically to cater for these differences
>
> (*New Statesman and Society*, 16 July 1992).

In the event, comprehensive schools and selection were far from being dead issues in 1992. Just a day after the above-mentioned article appeared, the press reported that, for the third time in five years, the Conservative-controlled Buckinghamshire County Council had rejected the recommendation of their Education Committee to found a gram-mar school in Milton Keynes and bring the town into line with the southern area of the county, where LEA-maintained grammar schools had never been discarded (*The Times*, 18 July 1992). Two Milton Keynes comprehensives had already used the newly introduced mechanism of opting out of LEA control in order to protect their comprehensive status, thus exploiting the landmark 1988 Education Reform Act in a way that had not been envisaged.

Comprehensive education was, in fact, more of an issue in the 1992 general election, which resulted in another Conservative victory, than it had been at any time since 1974. In February 1992 the issue was rarely out of the newspapers. A statement by Kenneth Clarke, then Secretary of State for Education, in which he claimed to have no objection to grammar schools re-emerging through the process of opting out (*The Times*, 3 February 1992) attracted particular attention. Labour, on the other hand, vowed to 'upgrade' the remaining 170 secondary moderns (in 19 LEAs, accommodating around 95,000 children) and 159 maintained grammar schools (in 28 LEAs) into comprehensives (*Independent*, 26 February 1992).

The contents of a letter, written by Prime Minister John Major to a former General Secretary of the NUT were also widely reported, including his view that 'the problem of low standards stems in large part from the nature of the comprehensive system which the Labour Party ushered in in the 1960s' (*Guardian*, 28 February 1992). Although he later modified that view to concede that parents should have a choice of good schools, the press tended to magnify his criticisms of mis-management of comprehensive schools by left-wing LEAs and suggested that these schools would benefit from opting out (*The Times*, 29 June 1992). This overlooked the many Conservative LEAs which had established comprehensives and still wanted to back them. Although the government has not yet specifically sought to link the issue of segregating children – whether by ability or 'specialisation' – and Grant Maintained (GM) Schools, research is already showing that they are allied. Basing their findings on questionnaire responses from 83 out of 219 English and Welsh opted-out schools, Leicester University researchers disclosed that almost a third of GM schools were using interviews or school reports to select pupils for over-subscribed places (*TES*, 10 April 1992). Of the new GM schools, only one (in West Yorkshire) had by this time officially applied to the DES for a status change to become a selective grammar school, but there were strong indications that others were set to follow. While some Conservative LEAs began to seek mass opt-outs to facilitate the creation of 'magnet' schools, a number of Labour LEAs have contemplated following the Milton Keynes example of opting out to preserve the status quo. Meanwhile, the general pattern is that small numbers of already popular LEA schools have opted for GM status, thus raising concerns, in Kent, for example (*TES*, 19 June 1992), that the remaining county schools will be 'creamed', regardless of whether or not the GM schools actually introduce selection.

Support for opting out has been very patchy, concentrated mainly in Conservative areas (*The Times*, 13 July 1992), and the relatively small number of schools balloting for GM status in the wake of the 1992 general election led to the publication of a White Paper designed to accelerate the process (DES, 1992). This document envisaged in excess of 4,000 opted-out schools by April 1995 (compared with 280 out of 23,000 in 1992), with secondary schools – some of which may be backed by industrial sponsors –'specialising' in a particular curriculum area, such as science, music, modern languages or technology. 'Such specialisation', the document argues, 'liberates the talents of pupils' (ibid., pp. 43–4).

It is, however, unlikely that specialisation can be achieved without selection in a fiercely competitive climate, and it seems likely that the effect of further legislation will be to legitimise the already hierarchical structure of schools which has resulted from the policy initiatives of the past decade. Magnet schools, City Technology Colleges and the newly envisaged 'Technology Schools' may become the élitist successors to grammar and technical schools by receiving priority funding direct from the central government. LEAs would then be left to operate what might be seen as 'second division' schools, probably including schools for pupils with special educational needs.

Significantly, comprehensive education is not mentioned in the White Paper (except in a brief historical introduction), but by pointing out on the opening page that most schools already set or stream their students and that many have developed high reputations for particular subjects, it implies that they would provide good foundations for magnet schools. These recent developments thus provide many reasons to suspect that, within the next 20 years, historians of education may refer to 'the comprehensive era' as a decade or two of experimentation that was not particularly successful. Given the erratic path followed by the comprehensive school movement thus far, however, it is difficult to discern a very clear view of its future.

CONCLUDING SUMMARY

This historical survey has shown that the process of comprehensive reorganisation in England and Wales went through several phases over a long period of time. It was carried through in the context of assumptions and constraints associated with a decentralised system in which LEAs had scope to implement change, as well as to respond in a variety of ways to central government initiatives. This decentralised system was eventually threatened by the gradual and reluctant shift of Labour governments towards introducing legislation to force comprehensive reorganisation, despite the progress already made. The actual moves that served to reduce the power and responsibilities of LEAs were taken by Conservative administrations, but the earlier Labour initiatives had set the stage for those actions. Ironically, when, during the 1980s, the move towards central government dominance came, it served the opposite purpose from that intended by Labour. It was used to support the Conservative administration's efforts to restore mechanisms of differentiation in secondary education.

The movement to comprehensive reorganisation was, as we have seen, affected by various developments common to all LEAs – the undermining of tripartism with the failure to establish technical schools, the growing community dissatisfaction with the 11+ selection procedure, the persistence of the demand for comprehensive schooling among sections of the Labour movement, and the growth in political support for the comprehensive principle by Labour, culminating in the publication of Circular 10/65. Other important developments after 1965 were the raising of the school-leaving age (in 1974), and the growing popularity of the idea of the middle school, both of which made tiered schemes of reorganisation more viable. At the same time, all LEAs had to contend with vested interests and the emotional loyalty attached to existing grammar schools, although the strength of that loyalty varied widely.

Nevertheless, there was considerable room for manoeuvre, and much variation among LEAs over the *timing* of reorganisation, the *manner* in which it was carried through and the *type of scheme* that was favoured. To better understand the dynamics of the process of educational change, it is necessary therefore to reconstruct what happened at the local level and to study the particular mix of influences which shaped the pattern of change. We turn to these matters in the chapters that follow.

NOTES

1. After his death, some of Burt's research was exposed as fraudulent by the American psychologist, Leon Kamin, and his biographer, Leslie Hearnshaw. Besides statistical impossibilities appearing in Burt's work, Kamin claimed that Burt had invented the identities of co-authors and research assistants. However, two books published in 1991, *The Burt Affair* by Robert Joynson and *Science, Ideology and*

the Media by Ronald Fletcher, both claim to vindicate Burt, at least in part, which has led to calls for a public enquiry.

2. There is a copy of the Green Book in the PRO ED 136/214.
3. BP MS 660/54947, Boyle to John Vaizey, 17 Dec. 1974.
4. BP MS 660/25225, transcript of a television party political broadcast by Boyle and his Parliamentary Secretary, Christopher Chataway, MP, 1 May 1963.
5. BP MS 660/25217, briefing paper by Boyle, headed 'Prime Minister', 3 July 1963.
6. BP MS 660/25197, Boyle to Simon Wingfield Digby, MP, 4 March 1964. Boyle suggests that the remark was made by Wilson the previous year when addressing a CASE meeting.
7. AEC papers, E62, press release of a speech by Crosland, 29 May 1965.
8. BP MS 660/25510, Boyle to John Wells, MP, 11 Nov. 1965.
9. Ibid., MS 660/25520, Boyle to Dr Terry Thomas, 1 Dec. 1965.
10. AEC papers, E62, press release of a speech by Heath to the Conservative National Advisory Committee on Education, 17 June 1967.
11. BP MS 660/25948, Barber to Boyle, 11 March 1968.
12. AEC papers, A1113, Keith Robinson, CEO, Southport to Alexander, 17 March 1969.
13. Ibid., Mrs B. Bicknell, Chairman, Bournemouth Education Committee to Alexander, 28 Nov. 1969.
14. Ibid., Alexander to Robinson, 27 Oct. 1969.
15. Ibid., E62, press release of a speech by Wilson to the Huyton Teachers' Association, 21 Nov. 1969.
16. Ibid., A1113, memorandum on the Bill by Alexander, dated 4 March 1970. He forwarded his observations to a number of individuals and educational bodies.
17. Ibid., Alexander to Short, 28 April 1970.
18. Ibid., Short to Alexander, 26 March 1970.
19. Ibid., Short to Alexander, 4 May 1970.
20. CASE papers, MSS 236/3, local files, Helen Wickham, Hon. Secretary, Eccles, Swinton and Pendlebury branch, to Barbara Bullivant, Secretary, CASE executive, 10 Oct. 1970.
21. Ibid., AGM minutes, 26–27 Sept. 1970.
22. Ibid., local files, Joan Sallis, *An Account of the Campaign against Selection at 11 + in Richmond-upon-Thames*.
23. AEC papers, A1113, J.R.G. Tomlinson, Director of Education, Cheshire to Alexander, 10 Sept. 1973.
24. Ibid., Alexander to Mulley, 27 Feb. 1976.
25. Ibid.
26. Ibid.
27. Ibid., Mulley to Alexander, 17 March 1976.

3

The Ten Case Studies of Local Education Authorities

Chapter 2 has provided an overview of the historical process of movement towards comprehensive secondary education in England and Wales during the 1960s and 1970s. It has also suggested some of the kinds of factors that possibly explain the variation among LEAs in the ways they responded to this movement, both before and after Circular 10/65 was issued. Throughout this book we pay particular attention to that variation in response and its antecedents and consequences. There was so much variation, in fact, that no overall analysis can adequately represent it. It is fair to say that each LEA represents a unique combination of factors, and the specific combination needs to be examined if the actions taken by any given LEA are to be fully understood.

The rest of this book is devoted to reporting our attempts to come to terms with the tension between our wish to understand this highly varied set of conditions and actions and our desire to make some general sense out of the variation. We use detailed qualitative methods to examine ten particular LEAs in order to obtain a better grasp of the dynamics involved in producing so much variation. The results of that analysis are presented in Chapters 4 to 8. We also attempt to derive from those detailed case studies some general image of the process of movement towards comprehensive education during the critical period of change. That general image, presented in Chapter 9, is then used to guide our quantitative analyses of the full range of LEAs presented in Chapters 10 to 12.

RATIONALE FOR CHOOSING THE CASE STUDY LEAs

It is important to review briefly how we came to choose the ten LEAs for in-depth study. The selection is not random, nor do we suggest that these authorities are fully representative of English and Welsh LEAs during the period under review. Bearing in mind our stated objective to complement historical information with statistical data about schools and children from the National Child Development Study, we have deliberately chosen to study LEAs which had, to a considerable degree, 'gone comprehensive' by 1974. In no simple sense, therefore, is it the case that the ten LEAs we have chosen are truly representative of the national picture, although they do represent some of the varied approaches LEAs took to comprehensive reorganisation.

There were very few local authorities that had failed to establish at least one comprehensive school by 1974, but a few did nevertheless exist. Some were 'recalcitrant' authorities, intent on resistance to the comprehensive principle, and, as such, clearly represented a significant *impediment* to change. Since the qualitative aspect of this study seeks to examine the processes and effects of the introduction of comprehensive education, no very useful information can be obtained from those recalcitrant authorities, so they are not represented in our case study analysis. However, it should be noted that 'recalcitrance' alone does not explain why some authorities had still not moved towards comprehensive education by 1974. Other impediments, such as financial constraints affecting school accommodation, delayed otherwise enthusiastic LEAs from taking tangible effective action.

The ten LEAs we selected for in-depth study, and which will be discussed in detail in the following chapters, are:

London	Leicestershire
Manchester	West Riding of Yorkshire
Bristol	West Sussex
Leeds	Glamorgan
Stoke-on-Trent	Northumberland.

Although these ten LEAs are all examples of authorities that had achieved partial or total comprehensivisation by 1974, consideration was given in making our selection to the diversity of conditions and experiences that helped to shape the specific form of reorganisation adopted and the pace at which it occurred. A preliminary survey of some authorities' contrasting experiences of reorganisation informed the selection of ten LEA case studies, which provide a basis for comparisons and contrasts.

Our criteria of selection included the socioeconomic conditions in the LEA, geographical location, political control, particular highly visible personnel involved, and the type of comprehensive scheme adopted. We will briefly discuss the importance of each of these and show how our ten selected LEAs varied according to these selection criteria.

Socioeconomic Factors

The inner London boroughs displayed extremes of prosperity and hardship, with, for example, Kensington and Chelsea's affluence contrasting sharply with the poverty of Tower Hamlets or Hackney. The Inner London Education Authority (the ILEA took over the education powers of the London County Council [LCC] in 1965) was the largest LEA in the country, and also the biggest-spending authority. Employment in the capital's service sector predominated over manufacturing, and schools contained relatively high proportions of children from non-manual families.

Manchester and Leeds are both examples of large, northern, industrial cities, which were in decline by the 1960s. The academic performance of Leeds children was high, however, compared with the other nine case-study LEAs. As university cities, both Manchester and Leeds contained influential middle-class populations and a growing service sector, but they had experienced significant structural unemployment. Manchester was renowned for its prestigious direct grant schools, including Manchester Grammar School, and around ten per cent of Manchester children (around double the national average) attended non-LEA schools.

Bristol, another university city which had formerly been Britain's second busiest port, had similarly seen a decline in its traditional maritime and import–export industries, but had fared reasonably well in the post-war years, thanks to new employment opportunities in the aircraft and chemical industries. Bristol had a large number of private and charitably endowed direct grant schools, including Clifton College. Although the social backgrounds of Bristol children were unusually mixed, data from 1974 indicate that a rather large proportion of Bristol's secondary students attended independent schools (about 15 per cent). All three of these cities were characterised by large, post-war council housing estates.

Stoke-on-Trent was still a small, thriving industrial centre in the 1960s and 1970s, famous for its production of high-quality pottery. Working-class families predominated and, perhaps because of good employment prospects, typical academic achievements were not particularly impressive.

The remaining five LEAs included in our study were counties, although they varied in the degree to which agriculture was the predominant economic base. Northumberland was a mainly agricultural county, though a relatively prosperous one. A legacy of feudalism

49

still prevailed, with long-established county families tending to dominate the patterns of land-ownership and office-holding. To a lesser extent, this was also true of Leicestershire and West Sussex, which were both predominantly rural counties, with only light industry. Although agriculture was the most important source of employment in large parts of both counties, the West Sussex service sector was of overwhelming importance. Many workers commuted to London, and average earnings compared favourably with other areas of the country. Glamorgan and the West Riding of Yorkshire are examples of county LEAs where industry also had a significant presence. The woollen industry remained an important source of employment in the West Riding, whereas much employment in Glamorgan had traditionally been provided by the coal-mining industry. Although the number of pits in South Wales had declined significantly in the post-war years, light manufacturing had grown to complement the established iron and steel industries on the coalfield fringes. Glamorgan schools contained low proportions of children from non-manual families, and typical earnings were low.

Many of the early advocates of comprehensive education had advanced the idea that the abolition of selection could and *should* be used as a vehicle for social engineering. If we accept the view that comprehensive education was promoted by those with an egalitarian agenda, we might expect that it was a more attractive proposition – and would be introduced more rapidly – in underprivileged areas, and that there would be a greater tendency to resist it in more prosperous parts of the country. As we shall see, although some of the evidence is in line with that expectation, it is not wholly consistent.

Geographical Factors

The areas of investigation in this book do not include either Northern Ireland or Scotland. Wales is represented in our ten case-study LEAs by Glamorgan, one of the five county LEAs (the others being Leicestershire, Northumberland, West Sussex and the West Riding). The selection of these five gives a broad regional spread of county LEAs, ranging from Wales in the west, to the north, north-east, the east Midlands and south-east of England.

The remaining five LEAs (London, Manchester, Leeds, Bristol and Stoke-on-Trent) are English cities, located respectively in the southeast, north-west, north, south-west and the Midlands. In terms of population size, they vary markedly, with London being by far the largest and Stoke-on-Trent (itself an amalgam of six small towns) the smallest.

It was hoped that these geographical factors, together with the socio-economic factors, would help us to identify any critical differences along the rural–urban, rich–poor, and industrial–agricultural–commercial dimensions which affected the process of change to comprehensive education. As we shall see, some of these dimensions appear to have affected the process in rather unexpected ways.

Political Control

An effort was made to ensure that the ten case-study LEAs reflected a measure of political diversity. This permitted us to consider the questions of whether comprehensive education was the subject of greater political influence in the cities and urbanised counties, and whether it was a wholly Labour-led reorganisation movement.

Of our ten LEAs, Leicestershire and Glamorgan were the only authorities in which political control rested with one party (with the Conservatives and Labour, respectively) throughout the 1960s and early 1970s. However, one might legitimately add West Sussex to this list, bearing in mind that before 1967, when local Conservatives gained control of the County Council, power had rested with like-minded Independents.

Considerable continuity may also be observed elsewhere. Except for the period 1967–70, when control of the ILEA passed to the Conservatives, London was Labour-controlled throughout the period under review. Similarly, Manchester, Bristol, Leeds and Stoke-on-Trent were Labour-controlled except during the years 1967–71, 1967–72, 1968–72 and 1970–72, respectively. Strong, organised – though not always united – and well-informed Labour groups were a feature of each of the four large cities included in our case studies. Independents and Conservatives were not purely a feature of rural politics, however, as Bristol's 'Citizen Party' demonstrates.

Politics was more fluid in the West Riding and Northumberland than in most LEAs. In both instances, Labour lost overall control in 1967, heralding uneasy, yet long-lasting coalitions with Conservatives and Independents, respectively.

It is often suggested that comprehensive education was – and is – a purely Socialist phenomenon. Chapter 2 has shown the limitations of that notion, pointing to the important contributions of national Conservative politicians such as Sir Edward Boyle in advancing non-selective schooling. Chapter 2 has also shown that, although many

Conservative-controlled LEAs were reluctant to destroy grammar schools which, for decades – even centuries – had maintained high academic standards, they were often attracted to 'tiered' comprehensive school schemes which reorientated existing grammar schools, sometimes in only limited ways. The case-study approach allows us to examine in some depth how political control was associated with comprehensivisation.

Personnel Factors

There is clearly an overlap between personnel factors, political control and the type of comprehensive scheme adopted (discussed below). It was often alleged during the 1960s that the reorganisation process in particular LEAs was dominated by the thinking or actions of particular individuals or groups. The LEA case-study approach is especially useful in providing the opportunity to examine the importance of key individuals in the educational decision-making process, and to assess the extent to which the opinions of the wider community were effectively taken into account. A change of local council control naturally precipitated a change of personnel on the Education Committee. But to what extent did the reorganisation of secondary schooling in particular areas represent the accomplishment of particular individuals or community groups?

Reference has already been made in Chapter 2 to several studies which have examined the development of a comprehensive schools policy in one – or exceptionally more than one – area. Commentators such as Ribbins and Brown (1979), James (1980) and Fearn (1980, 1983 and 1989) have usefully analysed some of these studies and have highlighted the important influence which local politicians (such as the Chair of the Education Committee) or the Chief Education Officer (CEO) sometimes exerted over educational policy-making.

Personnel considerations were not, by any means, the major factor affecting the choice of case-study LEAs. However, the high profile which the CEOs of Leicestershire and the West Riding enjoyed during the 1960s made these counties interesting selections which invite comparison. We were equally aware of the prominence of particular local Labour politicians in promoting comprehensive schooling in London and Manchester. Also, the suggestion that a Conservative Chairman of Education exercised considerable influence over the rather liberal reorganisation scheme finally adopted in Leeds (Fenwick and Woodthorpe, 1980) added to the reasons for including that authority among our ten case studies.

Type of Comprehensive Scheme Adopted

London, Manchester, Bristol, Leeds and Glamorgan all established at least one early (ages 11–18) comprehensive school, as did West Sussex in the New Town area of Crawley. However, as dissatisfaction with selective schooling grew during the post-war years, a number of alternative models of comprehensive education emerged. As has been indicated already in Chapter 2, the apparent orthodoxy that comprehensive schools necessarily had to be large, 'all-through' institutions was challenged by developments in Leicestershire (which introduced the two-tier model, with children changing schools at 11 and 14) and in the West Riding. In the latter county, the CEO successfully exerted pressure on the Ministry of Education to waive the rule, dating back to the 1944 Education Act, which required transfer at age 11. Middle schools were to prove particularly popular in the wake of the 1967 Plowden Report, and this development is reflected in our selection of case-study LEAs. Middle and upper comprehensive schools were adopted for all or part of the administrative unit in West Sussex, Northumberland, Leeds and Stoke-on-Trent, although absolute uniformity was exceptional. Even if uniformity was considered desirable, it was not always possible, often because of the unwillingness of central government to pay for the replacement of buildings considered to be serviceable.

In many instances, political or administrative pragmatism lay behind the type of organisation adopted by particular LEAs. Rarely, it appears, did educational considerations dominate the thinking, even of CEOs. Leicestershire and the West Riding were honourable exceptions to this general observation, as was Stoke-on-Trent. Indeed, Stoke-on-Trent is of particular interest as the first English or Welsh LEA to establish a purpose-built sixth-form college, carefully modelled on the principle of the American junior college. Stoke also, it might be argued, took the question of research into possible comprehensive school structures and organisation more seriously than any other provincial authority.

Although all of these ten LEAs were active in the comprehensive reorganisation movement, they invite comparison with each other with respect to the timing and the pace of change they made. For example, the process of introducing comprehensive schools in London began almost 20 years in advance of the 1965 Circular, yet by the late 1960s, when a majority of reorganising LEAs were most active, the momentum in the capital had been lost. Leicestershire's pioneering county-wide scheme was, meanwhile, completely operational by the end of the 1960s. As 'early' providers of significant numbers of comprehensives, London and Leicestershire are counter-balanced in our sample by Northumberland, which had not established a single comprehensive school before 1970 and was still in the process of going comprehensive in 1974.

Reorganisation was also delayed in Leeds, which introduced its city-wide comprehensive scheme in 1972. Stoke-on-Trent's comprehensive scheme, operational from 1970, was also comparatively late, though this did not reflect any lack of conviction about comprehensive schools. In each of the remaining case-study LEAs (Bristol, Manchester, Glamorgan, West Sussex and the West Riding), limited pre-Circular 10/65 comprehensive developments are discernible, but their energies demonstrably increased after 1965.

METHODOLOGY

Ideally, a study of the introduction of comprehensive education in Great Britain would seek to make extensive use of central government records. We would expect these to detail, among other matters, the development and execution of central and local educational policy, and to throw light upon the relationships between ministers of the government and civil servants at the DES. Like all students of recent British history, we share the frustrations of not being able to consult files, many of which are, already – tantalisingly – listed at the Public Record Office in London. The thirty-year rule prevents access to Ministry of Education and DES files, including (presumably) correspondence and memoranda relating to every English and Welsh LEA, as well as evidence about the development of central government policy.

Chapter 2 indicates the extent to which, in the post-war era, various Ministers and Secretaries of State for Education and Science – sometimes even within the same political party – differed in their attitudes towards comprehensive education. However, in assembling that information, we have necessarily been heavily dependent upon secondary sources, including political biographies and autobiographies interpreting the national trend towards comprehensive education.

In conducting the LEA case studies, we have been fortunate in securing a high degree of co-operation from county archivists, current and former educational administrators and teachers who worked in

LEA schools during the period under review. A small number of studies, investigating local comprehensive reorganisation, have been of assistance. For example, an unpublished doctoral thesis (Rigby, 1975) undoubtedly increased our understanding of why West Sussex's hybrid comprehensive scheme evolved, and published articles on the Leeds (Fenwick and Woodthorpe, 1980) and Manchester (Fiske, 1982) comprehensive experiences threw valuable light on the complex political situations which governed the pace of change in those cities. All of these sources are acknowledged in the chapters that follow. Most of the information we assembled, however, was derived from field visits to each of the ten selected areas. The minute books of Education Committee and sub-committee meetings, together with a limited amount of surviving correspondence and memoranda from the 1960s and 1970s, have provided useful pointers towards what we will refer to as *impediments* and *enablers* to comprehensivisation. Regrettably, as far as the period under review is concerned, local newspaper article indexes are almost wholly lacking, but the discovery of significant dates, such as council meetings and school openings did guide us to some illuminating local press material. Our investigation into the comprehensive issue in Stoke-on-Trent, for example, was particularly assisted by an examination of press coverage. Indeed, the local evening newspaper's keen interest in the subject throughout the 1960s illustrates that, as an influential, opinion-shaping force in a comparatively insular community, the local press itself can often be an impediment or an enabler.

Only in one case-study area did we experience a general unwillingness on the part of current educational administrators – whose present heavy workload, we should acknowledge, can rarely allow the contemplation of the past – to co-operate with our research. It is unfortunate that this LEA was Glamorgan, our only Welsh authority. The reasons for denying us access to LEA records were never made entirely clear. Fortunately, information from other sources compensated, to a large degree, for the paucity of information gathered on a field visit to Cardiff. We are generally satisfied that our research gives adequate attention to the Welsh experience of comprehensive education which was, as indicated in Chapter 2, of pioneering importance.

The types of data mentioned above were supplemented by interviews and correspondence with former administrators. Much useful information was gleaned from the local press, back numbers of the *TES*, and other educational journals. Finally, we have made extensive use of non-LEA archive materials. By examining the papers of individuals, teacher unions and pro-comprehensive pressure groups, we have gained further insights into the processes of change in some of our LEA case-study areas. For example, Manchester reference library holds a unique collection of Lady (Shena) Simon's papers which reveal the hopes, anxieties and frustrations of a determined and influential advocate of Manchester comprehensive schools. The records of the AAM (deposited at the Warwick University Modern Records Centre) contain a useful file of papers specifically about reorganisation in Glamorgan, and the CASE archives (also at Warwick) extensively document efforts to reorganise secondary schooling in London and Leeds during the 1960s and early 1970s.

GROUPING THE CASE STUDIES

For convenience and to conserve space, we have found it useful to group some of the case studies where it is felt that the processes of comprehensive reorganisation were similar. This has enabled us to develop a number of contrasting models.

By any measure, the case of London is exceptional, and we have described its extended period of active consideration of and conflict over methods of school reorganisation in Chapter 4. Although London is clearly a unique case, some of the features of the London experience were common in all large urban areas. Chapter 5 reviews the other three large urban cases we have studied (Manchester, Bristol and Leeds) and shows that there were both common urban themes and special conditions in each of these cities.

Although Stoke-on-Trent was also an urban LEA, it was much smaller than any of the other four. It is included in our study and discussed separately in Chapter 6 largely because of its very unusual approach to comprehensive reorganisation and the special nature of the plan it adopted: uniform organisation of secondary schools for ages 12 to 16, followed by transfer to a sixth-form college. Leicester-shire and the West Riding were county LEAs, but their primary features of interest here were the kinds of reorganisation plans they adopted and the processes through which these came into being. As we indicate in Chapter 7, although they originally approached the issue of reorganisation with entirely different orientations, the reorganised systems developed were surprisingly similar.

Finally, we discuss the other three county LEAs (Glamorgan, West Sussex, and Northumberland) in Chapter 8. Although they differ in important ways among themselves, they typify the relatively gradual approach to reorganisation taken in many LEAs. The reasons for the gradualness varied, sometimes arising out of internal divisions, sometimes the result of restricted resources, but none of these LEAs was a leader in the comprehensive reorganisation movement. In that respect, they may be more *typical* of the English and Welsh LEAs than were those more innovative LEAs such as Stoke-on-Trent or Leicestershire.

A detailed discussion of these four types of LEAs follows in Chapters 4 to 8, and some concluding remarks about our findings are offered in Chapter 9, where we attempt to relate these case studies to the general national processes discussed in Chapter 2. A major theme that pervades this entire review is the high degree of local influence on the reorganisation process, and there was a great deal of variation in the forms of the comprehensive schools that were established. That variation, in turn, raises further questions about the possibility of systematic reasons for, and identifiable effects of, the varied forms of the new comprehensives. We turn to those questions in Chapters 10 to 12.

4

The Evolutionary Capital Experience: London

Any analysis of the local dynamics of reorganisation from selective to comprehensive secondary schools must include an examination of the case of London. Not only is (and was) London the nation's largest city and the capital, it also epitomised many of the major forces affecting the course of the comprehensive school movement. Our extended discussion of London also reflects some of the city's special qualities, however. It was one of the very first local authorities to establish comprehensive schools, and one in which ideological and political factors were of major importance. It was especially 'visible' to the central government agencies involved, and what happened in the capital has been more fully documented – by historians, politicians and the press – than is the case anywhere else. It is thus appropriate to begin our series of case studies with London.

THE 1947 PLAN

More than 20 years before the publication of Labour's 1965 Circular, London was contemplating a city-wide network of comprehensive schools. Indeed, even before the ink was dry on the pages of the 1944 Education Act, the London County Council (LCC) had received, and adopted as policy, what has been described as an 'epoch-making' report (Rubinstein 1979, p. 164) which challenged the general principle of selective secondary schooling. The LCC maintained that differentiated secondary schools would give some schools an inferior status in the eyes of parents, and that 'comprehensive high schools' were the fairest means of securing for all pupils 'equal opportunity for physical, intellectual, social and spiritual development'.[1] With the enactment of the 1944 Education Bill, which required every English and Welsh LEA to submit a long-term educational development plan, came the opportunity for progressive authorities to challenge the assumed orthodoxy of tripartism.

It is significant that London and Coventry, the two cities which suffered most during the wartime Luftwaffe attacks were the most prominent English cities to contemplate comprehensives in the immediate post-war period.[2] A great deal of rebuilding was needed in both cities, and it was rational to plan for new schools and for major rebuilding of housing areas at the same time. New schools did not necessarily mean comprehensive schools, though.

The push for comprehensives in the capital was indisputably political, although the educational arguments for abandoning selection had been spelled out in a much-publicised policy document (Cole, n.d.). While the idea of the multilateral – or comprehensive – school had been promoted by enthusiasts within the Labour movement since the 1920s, no national policy had emerged. Yet, at the grass-roots level, within London, a group of radical and talented Labour activists grasped the opportunity to advance the cause of non-selection (Rubinstein, 1979, p. 162).

Having been briefed by his Education Committee, it fell to the LCC's Education Officer, Sir Graham Savage, and his assistant to visit the Ministry of Education in March 1946. They explained the authority's plans for two distinct types of non-selective secondary school: the full comprehensive school, of around 2,000 pupils and the 'county complement', accommodating around 1,500. The latter were to be 'complementary in organisation and educational provision' to the voluntary (church-run) grammar schools, which typically had around 500 on the roll. Three months later, Savage wrote to the ministry seeking permission to submit a development plan to create 65 comprehensives, of which 33 would contain in excess of 2,000 pupils.[3]

The authority were evidently optimistic that the post-war Labour government would encourage alternatives to tripartism and look favourably upon the comprehensive school. Initially, this view seemed well-founded, with the suggestion that the Minister of Education, Ellen Wilkinson, 'would not be indisposed to consider proposals for comprehensive high schools and groups on their merits'.[4] The authority was eager to begin the process of change as soon as possible, but others interpreted this as impatience. A relatively modest proposal in the late spring of 1946 to create five community comprehensive schools was attacked by one HMI, who noted: 'I feel that the whole business is being rushed without giving the scheme the thought it deserves and I fear that with this hand to mouth planning we shall not get anything better than we have at present'.[5] The suggestion that the conservatism of Wilkinson and her successor, George Tomlinson, stunted the growth of the comprehensive school movement by 20 years (Rubinstein, 1979,

p. 161) has been challenged (Hughes, 1979, pp. 157–60; Redcliffe-Maud, 1981, p. 57). However, it is significant that when it became clear that the LCC was determined to press ahead with the development of a city-wide comprehensive schools plan, the Ministry of Education received a deputation from the London Head Teachers' Association.[6] The organisation was representative of grammar school interests and was predictably hostile to the notion of comprehensive education.

The LCC's official development plan, the 253-page *London School Plan*, was published the following year (LCC, 1947). A total of 103 'comprehensive school units', consisting of 67 comprehensive schools and 36 county complements was now the target, though no time-scale was laid down for completion. Given the immense complexities of educational planning in London, this was inevitable. Quite apart from questions of if, when and how much central government money would become available to build new and replacement London schools, there existed a large number of (selective) denominational and direct-grant schools, their status protected by legislation, and also of independent schools. These, too, contributed to the difficulty of producing a workable plan.

This situation illustrates a number of important and unique features of the London experience. First, because there was so little foreseeable likelihood of translating theoretical planning into practice, London's development plan was bound to be as much a statement of political polemic as of educational intent. Although committed Labour activists requested the availability of necessary resources to establish a city-wide, non-selective plan, they did not do so with any realistic expectation of success, nor did they ultimately accept that equal opportunities for all children could be created by resources alone. But if the London School Plan was couched in rhetoric, so were many of the responses to it. In contrast to the general experience outside the capital, those who condemned plans for universal comprehensive education in London often did so in the spirit of political cut and thrust, rather than out of any serious conviction that the Labour plan, as it stood, was achievable.

Realistically, a piecemeal movement towards comprehensive education over decades was the best that the London Labour Party could hope for, and by 1947 the authority had already embarked upon small-scale change. With ministerial approval, eight interim 'experimental' comprehensives were established between 1946 and 1949, by combining pre-war senior and central school buildings (Simon, 1991, p. 171). This suggests that there existed within the ministry a curiosity to test the multilateral idea in the capital, without allowing critics to suggest that the city's best secondary school traditions were in jeopardy. Although these schools were very different from the kind of comprehensives envisaged in the 1947 plan, W.F. Houghton, the LCC Education Officer, was to reflect in 1961 that: 'these schools blazed a trail which has become a broad highway, and under conditions of great difficulty and in the face of some hostility they carried out pioneer work of the utmost value' (LCC, 1961, p. 14). In addition to the anticipated educational and ideological opposition to the plan from London's grammar school heads, much of this 'hostility' was political. In a confidential 1947 briefing paper to Conservative members of the LCC Education Committee, Dame Catherine Fulford, the opposition leader, condemned the dogmatic tone of the London School Plan, which approached 'the Hitler state'.[7]

Happily for the Conservatives, the post-war economic situation determined that there was no danger that the development plan would be quickly implemented, although they were not slow to make political capital by playing upon the electorate's fear that long-established grammar schools were under threat. In other ways, however, it might be suggested that the Conservative defence of tripartism was not as robust as expected. Fulford's memorandum acknowledged the existence of 'defects' in the educational system and, somewhat surprisingly, one of the objections which she advised colleagues to stress was the fact that 'many generations of children will suffer by the unavoidable delay in completing the Plan'.[8] George Tomlinson's reaction to the London School Plan was one of caution, rather than hostility.

Predictably, the anticipated size of the LCC comprehensives was a point of contention. Ministerial Circular 144 (1947) had recommended that the minimum size of a comprehensive school should be 10- or 11-form entry (accommodating in excess of 1,500 children). Small schools, Tomlinson believed, would find it difficult to provide grammar and technical courses or to sustain sixth forms. While most of the proposed LCC comprehensives were 13-form entry, some were as small as five-form entry, and the ministry advised reconsideration.[9] The authority's 'interim' arrangements to group existing schools as comprehensive units were also challenged. Somewhat ambiguously, it was suggested that 'if in a particular district the grouped system is likely to have to subsist for an indefinite period, the Minister suggests that it would be well to contemplate some form of organisation other than the comprehensive school system. But the Minister thinks that it might well be preferable to have a system of grouped schools the virtue of which, as a solution to the problem at issue, would lie, not in any particular merits, but in the fact that it was regarded as a stage on the way to the system of comprehensive schools.'[10]

Even if he was disappointed by the lukewarm response of the ministry, Education Officer Savage acknowledged the drawbacks of interim planning. For the time being, the authority resolved to monitor carefully the experiences of the eight recently established interim schools, at the same time recognising that they could not be seen as genuine 'pilot' comprehensives. Savage acknowledged that the exercise 'would not provide any permanent solution which must await the provision of proper buildings for the new Comprehensive High Schools'.[11] In fact, no purpose-built comprehensive school for London opened until 1954, and even then, due to unprecedented central government interference, its intake was far from truly *comprehensive*.

EXPERIMENTATION, EXPANSION AND CONTROVERSY, 1949–65

In the eyes of many advocates of multilateral education, the post-war Labour government had been a great disappointment. Indeed, the Fabian Society, an organisation at the heart of the Labour movement, condemned 'the failure of the Labour Party to get real support for its policy apart from votes at conferences' (Fabian Society Research Series, 1949). When, therefore, on 27 September 1949, George Tomlinson approved the LCC's proposal to build the capital's first purpose-built comprehensive school in Greenwich, this was widely greeted as a limited but important step forward. It was to be named Kidbrooke School and, upon the closure of five existing schools (two technical, two secondary modern and Eltham Hill Girls' Grammar School) would accommodate 2,000 girls. However, the Conservative Party's general election victory of 1951 cast a shadow on the proposal. The new Education Minister, Florence Horsbrugh, was an unapologetic opponent of comprehensive education. Flying in the face of the 1947 circular's recommendations that effective comprehensive schools should be large, Horsbrugh announced to her Conservative Party conference audience of 1952 that she saw 'no educational advantage in the comprehensive schools that could possibly outweigh the disadvantages in connection with their enormous size' (*Education*, 17 October 1952, p. 513). Her pronouncements rejuvenated disillusioned Conservative members of the LCC Education Committee, one of whom had complained that to question the ruling party's policy 'is considered near-blasphemy by the devoted and selfless members of the Labour Party who control London's education and have controlled it since 1934' (Connell, 1953, pp. 294–5).

Unhappy that the proposed establishment of Kidbrooke involved the closure of a grammar school, Horsbrugh intervened directly by requiring the LCC to issue formal notices of closure for the five schools concerned, thereby initiating a public debate about a policy matter which had long since seemed resolved. Moreover, shortly afterwards, she took the extraordinary step of urging a London Conservative Women's Conference to organise protests against the closure of existing schools (Simon, 1991, pp. 171–2). The *TES*, under the editorship of a new, fiercely anti-comprehensive editor, Walter James, sided with the minister and attacked the national Labour leadership in the post-war years for being 'drawn by their rank and file into a policy for destroying, in the grammar schools, the one proved and solid element in the English system' (*TES*, 9 October 1953).

There followed over the next few months several strong and well-publicised objections from the London grammar schools' lobby. Having stage-managed, at least to some degree, this preservationist activity, Horsbrugh stepped forward, in March 1954, as the self-appointed champion of the grammar schools. Eltham Hill School would not, she announced, close after all. Her actions were anathema to many, including Sir William Alexander, Secretary of the Association of Education Committees, though he was not, at this time, a supporter of the comprehensive school. In an editorial for his association's journal, he wrote: 'in approving the proposal to provide the Kidbrooke School with 2,000 places it is surely reasonable that the Ministry ascertained from where the children would come. In particular, they should have been quite clear that the opening of Kidbrooke School would involve the closure of one or more grammar schools.' Despite the estimated £600,000 of public money which had been spent on building and equipping Kidbrooke as a fully comprehensive school, Alexander argued, it could not now be regarded as such. Worse still, Horsbrugh's decision might establish a precedent for 'destroying the autonomy of Local Education Authorities in determining the appropriate use of school accommodation in their area and the best plan for the organisation of secondary education.' (*Education*, 12 March 1954, p. 432). Other similar ministerial decisions followed, and Horsbrugh left office in October 1954, without having approved the establishment of a single London comprehensive which involved the closure of a grammar school (Simon, 1991, p. 172). Nevertheless, the process of comprehensivisation proceeded apace during the second half of the decade. New schools – both full comprehensives and county comple- ments – emerged both in purpose-built accommodation and in the premises of amalgamated schools. Sensitive to the feelings which Horsbrugh had stirred up, the LCC Education Committee had promised that governors, heads and staffs of schools earmarked for closure would be consulted before irrevocable decisions were taken. A senior officer, usually W.F. Houghton, the Deputy Education Officer, attended a large number of such schools' governing body meetings during this period.[12] Enthusiasts recognised the importance of promoting the image of the comprehensive schools in order to appease the doubts of those who feared that the authority was moving too fast. In 1958, one headmaster of a London comprehensive contri- buted a glowing progress report on the implementation of the London School Plan for *Forum*, a newly established journal – co-edited by Brian Simon – which specifically sought to promote new educational trends (King, 1958, pp. 6–9). Publicity was specifically – and deliberately – given to five 'showpiece' comprehensives which had formerly been grammar schools,[13] but a more substantial evaluation was deemed necessary if critics of the comprehensive initiative were to be silenced.

In the autumn of 1959, the authority's Chief Inspector, Dr L.W. Payling, conducted a large-scale investigation into the performance of 16 of the authority's comprehensive schools. This could only take the form of an interim evaluation when it was published in 1961, since even those Kidbrooke girls who had entered at 11+ in 1954 and proceeded into the sixth form had yet to sit their A-Level examina- tions. This report, simply entitled *London Comprehensive Schools*, noted diversity in curriculum and pastoral matters but also identified significant continuity from the selective system as far as setting and streaming practices were concerned.

It is hard to escape the conclusion that the *raison d'être* for the pamphlet was to endorse optimistically the capital's comprehensive schools, in which a pupil 'can feel the stimulus of achievement at his [sic] true level' (LCC, 1961, p. 71). Differences between the grammar school and comprehensive education were deliberately marginalised, and *London Comprehensive Schools* is an early example of how the term 'comprehensive' was fudged, or – to use John Elliott's term – 'grammarised' (quoted in Chitty, 1989, p. 40). The report's findings pointed to the conclusion that within a school styled *comprehensive*, classroom activities need not be all-embracing. Indeed, it suggested that in a subject such as English, abler students might be asked to write an essay on 'the delights of motoring', while the 'less intellectual' would be stimulated by 'motor-cycles and scooters are a menace – do you agree with this point of view?' (LCC, 1961, p. 35). The suggestion was clear: academic differentiation within the comprehensive school was *desirable*:

> None of the schools bases its organisation upon the impracticable assumption that teaching groups covering the whole range of ability are suitable or desirable. All recognise that it is desirable to devise groupings that will enable children to work at their own pace with opportunities for give and take between teacher and taught (LCC, 1961, p. 32).

By 1961, when *London Comprehensive Schools* was published, 59 London schools were, theoretically, comprehensive (including the less-than-satisfactory 'county complement' units), leading Robin Pedley, a founding editor of *Forum*, to declare that 'the example of London shines like a beacon'. However, Pedley regretted that the London experience had done nothing to dissipate public reservations about large schools and that 'the bogey of size was fastened to the whole comprehensive school movement' (Pedley, 1962, p. 4). The authority proudly boasted that 53.4 per cent of London children attended a comprehensive school (LCC, 1961, p. 15). But statistics can be, and were, deceptive. Very few, if any, of the London comprehensives could genuinely claim to accommodate children from the full ability spectrum. Quite apart from London's large numbers of independent schools, 21 county grammar schools, 41 county secondary moderns, together with more than 50 voluntary grammar schools still remained. One commentator felt that London had done well 'in spite of ministerial discouragement', but noted that parents' inclinations were usually still to try to get their children into grammar schools (Simon, 1962, p.72).

There was, undoubtedly, a basis on which to build for the future, but the LCC Education Committee (still Labour-controlled) recognised by the early 1960s that the 1947 London School Plan was now out-of-date and in need of significant revision for two important reasons. First, the plan had envisaged a substantially higher school population in the capital than there actually was; secondary school rolls had peaked in 1960, and the decline offered an opportunity to vacate older, unsatisfactory accommodation. Second, the authority had, by this time, entered into negotiations with the denominational authorities with a view to encouraging them to participate in a revised comprehensive scheme (LCC, 1961, p. 15).

It fell to the new Education Officer, W.F. Houghton, to revise the 1947 plan in the light of the authority's anticipated future needs. His 1962 *London School Review* reaffirmed the commitment to comprehensive schooling, but with fewer and, in many cases, smaller schools than had been envisaged after the war. With no prospect of Treasury money for new, purpose-built schools, further progress towards achieving a city-wide network of comprehensive schools was contingent upon school closures and amalgamations. The political climate did not favour rapid change either. The early 1960s saw a number of large, urban, Labour-controlled authorities, including Manchester and Bristol (see Chapter 5), as well as Liverpool and Birmingham, unveil sweeping plans for comprehensive schools. Now that the national Labour leadership was belatedly formulating a policy for universal comprehensive education, questions of reorganisation invariably became politicised and attracted frenzied, often hostile, media coverage. In some ways, the unique set of impediments which determined the slow pace of change in London may be seen as advantageous. The inability of the Education Committee to act upon Houghton's plan without initiating a wide-ranging round of consultations determined that the authority was incapable of the kind of public relations blunders which undoubtedly occurred in some of the larger provincial cities. Even when the LCC finally decided, in 1964, to replace the 11+ examination by a combination of teacher assessment and parental choice, the *TES* wryly noted the 'basic irony that while London's policy would abandon selection, London's mixture of schools must make it go on' (*TES*, 28 February 1964). Sporadic efforts to persuade the controlling bodies of London's voluntary status schools to abandon selection continued, but more pressing still was the question of incorporating the remaining county selective schools. With clear indications now emerging from the newly installed Labour government that there would be a national drive for comprehensivisation, a new round of consultations, based on Houghton's 1962 paper, was scheduled to begin at the start of 1965. London's experience of amalgamations during this period does not appear to be markedly different from other reorganising authorities. Secondary modern school heads, staff and governors generally saw amalgamation as a means of improving their status and preserving teaching jobs, whereas grammar school representatives expressed fears about the possible loss of academic standards and long-standing traditions. However, just as the amalgamation discussions were about to begin, national press coverage of the so-called 'Kidbrooke affair' and 'Risinghill controversy' shifted attention away from purely local and institutional considerations.

In December 1964, Miss Joyce Lang, a music teacher from Kidbrooke School told *The Times* and the *Daily Telegraph* that ten years of comprehensive education at the school had been a failure. Children of higher ability, she claimed, did not pull up those from a poor home background, who formed a 'difficult element'. The LCC attracted much unwelcome media publicity by suggesting that Miss Lang should reconsider her position within the school, and, over the following two weeks, Walter James cited the school several times in *TES* editorials which sought to prove a causal link between unsegregated schooling and poor disciplinary standards (*TES*, 1 and 8 January 1965). Local Conservative politicians also seized the opportunity to exploit the school's growing notoriety, including John Selwyn Gummer, the local prospective Conservative parliamentary candidate, who attacked the authority for having 'slapped down' Miss Lang (*The Teacher*, 19 February 1965).

Across the river, in Islington, media interest had also been aroused by reports of disciplinary problems at Risinghill School, a purpose-built comprehensive (though, in reality, a poorly designed school with a secondary modern intake), which had opened in 1960. After the number of children on the Risinghill roll had peaked at 1,240 in 1961, parents had increasingly opted to send their children elsewhere (Berg, 1968; Weeks, 1986, pp. 118–19 and 133). The LCC considered that closing the school at the end of the 1964–65 school year might be the most effective means of damage control. Vacating the Risinghill premises offered an opportunity for Starcross, a nearby split-site comprehensive to become unified. The headmistress of Starcross was not, initially, enthusiastic about this proposed change, fearing problems resulting from Risinghill's 'difficult building, crushing neighbourhood problems, bad reputation and poor quality intake',[14] but the transfer was later adjudged to have been successful. The authority's sense of injustice is perhaps understandable. There had been little press coverage of notably successful London comprehensives, including Abbey Wood, Tulse Hill, Vauxhall Manor and Woodberry Down, not all of which were created in auspicious circumstances, yet Kidbrooke and Risinghill were frequently being held up as examples of how comprehensive education was failing, by people with no direct experience of this type of school. In an effort to counter the damaging anti-comprehensive publicity which Kidbrooke and Risinghill had generated, the LCC organised an open day for the press and public at eight of its showpiece comprehensives (including Risinghill) in early January 1965 (*The Teacher*, 15 January 1965). However, this cosmetic exercise could not conceal the tense atmosphere in which the new round of negotiations with staff and governors in schools proposed for amalgamation took place. Those opposed to the loss of further London grammar schools had gained new reserves of strength as a result of the authority's recent discomforts.

The proposed amalgamation of Barnsbury Secondary Boys' School with Highbury Boys' Grammar School provided a new focus for the debate. The retirement of Highbury's head, together with the impending closure of Laycock School, a nearby secondary modern, seemed to offer the authority an ideal opportunity for Highbury and Barnsbury to combine as an eight-form comprehensive school.[15] With no immediate prospects of capital funds for a new building, it would – like so many other comprehensives created by 'the "London" method' (O'Connell, 1970, p. 54) – inevitably be a split-site school, but the curriculum and pastoral advantages were perceived to outweigh this handicap.

Sir William Houghton, who remained as Education Officer when the education powers of the LCC were transferred to the Inner London Education Authority (ILEA) on 1 April 1965, despatched his Deputy, Dr Eric Briault, to persuade the two schools' governors that the proposals were sound. Briault stressed that the plans amounted to nothing new, since as long ago as 1947 the *London School Plan* had envisaged a boys' comprehensive school for the area. He also attempted to allay fears of staff redundancies. Evidence from the five former county grammar schools which had been enlarged into comprehensives was, he pointed out, encouraging, with an increasing proportion of pupils opting to stay on into the sixth form. Moreover, parents who remained unconvinced about the merits of comprehensive education for their sons would be able to apply for places at one of the two remaining Islington grammar schools.

Perhaps predictably, the heads and staff of Barnsbury and Laycock Schools were enthusiastic about the proposals, but the head and staff of the grammar school were not. Highbury's governors were equally divided on the question of amalgamation, but their chairman used his casting vote to approve the plan.[16] A petition, hostile to the proposals, from the Highbury Parents' Association was received, but did not prevent the ILEA Education Committee from approving the plan on

12 May 1965.[17] The newly formed Highbury Grove Comprehensive School opened under the headship of Dr Rhodes Boyson in September 1967, and its initial success was reflected in the title of Boyson's book about the school, *Oversubscribed* (Boyson, 1974). His enthusiasm for the comprehensive principle later waned, however, and as a Conservative MP in the mid-1970s, Boyson contributed to a new wave of *Black Papers* (Cox and Boyson, 1975 and 1977).

Other amalgamations raised similar issues, and, indeed, brought similar responses from the parties concerned, but the new Secretary of State, Anthony Crosland, was by now attempting to accelerate the national trend towards comprehensive education, precipitating, in some instances, premature retirements. According to Houghton, one headmaster bluntly advised him that 'he had been appointed, and would retire, as head of a grammar school'.[18] Grammar-school staffs and parents who doubted the efficacy of combining pupils of widely differing aptitudes and abilities were countered by ILEA predictions of wider educational opportunities for all children within larger and better-equipped schools.

The ILEA interpreted Circular 10/65, published in July 1965, as a belated but welcome vindication of London's comprehensive schools policy over the previous 20 years. Moreover, it was well-known that Crosland favoured the 11–18 'all-through' comprehensive school model, to which the authority had remained steadfastly committed since the 1940s. Despite the emergence of alternative systems such as those being implemented in Leicestershire and parts of the West Riding (see Chapter 7), the ILEA remained of the opinion that 11–18 schools provided 'the simplest and best solution' to the question of reorganisation.[19] In the long run, however, as we shall see, the authority's unwillingness to contemplate exceptions to this policy commitment was a source of weakness, rather than strength.

MOMENTUM SUSTAINED, 1965–70

The ILEA Education Committee looked to Sir William Houghton to draw up a response to Circular 10/65, and he set to work on a further revision of the 1962 proposals. Inevitably, this involved further controversial closures and redesignations. Renewed efforts were to be made to secure the participation of the voluntary schools' boards or commissions, with discussions 'on a confidential basis and on the clear understanding that there is no commitment on either side'.[20]

The complexities of administrative planning which had affected the 1947 and 1962 proposals remained, complicated further by new and important demographic movements (discussed more fully below), and when Houghton presented a discussion paper to the ILEA Schools Planning Sub-Committee in June 1966, his preface warned that 'no tidy uniform scheme of organisation is practicable', and that, despite the authority's stated preference for 11–18 schools, practical difficulties would prevent this in a number of cases.[21] Several broad guiding principles had been observed in devising the plan, which included maintaining a balance between boys' and girls' places, and providing a reasonable opportunity for London parents to send their children to a single-sex, rather than a mixed school. Opportunities for denominational education were also to be safeguarded, and reorganisations were to be designed to cause the minimum disturbance to staff (avoiding the unnecessary displacement of head teachers), parents and children. A radical scheme for extending comprehensive education across the city's ten divisional areas then followed. No longer was the huge comprehensive school of 1,500 or 2,000 pupils a prerequisite; experience over the previous ten years, during which there had been a significant improvement in the staying-on rate, had shown that schools with six to eight form-entries made sixth forms viable. However, in some areas the prospects of implementing proposals within the foreseeable period seemed better than others. In Camden, the City of Westminster and Hackney, for example, the proposed comprehensive schools could proceed without further amalgamations, being subject only to further building work. But in Southwark and Lewisham, by contrast, several potentially controversial amalgamations would be required in order to implement the plan.[22] There was little progress to report on the discussions between the ILEA and the voluntary authorities, which still controlled seven inner London grammar schools, and the chair of the General Purposes Sub-Committee was forced to concede that: 'While the grammar schools still exist the comprehensive schools are prevented from having a fully balanced intake and this varies from area to area.'[23] With hindsight, a later Education Officer of the ILEA suggested that 'this calling of so many schools "comprehensive", reflecting their aspirations rather than their actual circumstances, did more harm than good to the prospect of winning wholehearted public support for a fully comprehensive system' (Newsam, n.d., p. 11).

The ILEA was anxious that its formal response to Circular 10/65 be seen to have been the subject of public discussion before it was submitted to the DES. A series of 42 public meetings, with a total attendance of more than 19,000 parents, were held between December 1966 and February of the following year, making this the largest consultation process undertaken by any LEA during the period. Aspirations to 'grammarise' the comprehensives were again evident from the remarks of Education Committee members. It was suggested that 'comprehensive schools with the benefit of a grammar school nucleus'[24] were more likely to achieve high levels of success quickly, and the promise was made that children in a comprehensive school 'will receive an education no less effective than if the school had remained grammar'.[25] The real value served by this consultation exercise is debatable, but the suggestion that the ILEA had no intentions of modifying its plans was countered by a reminder that the public would have an opportunity to judge the scheme in May at the GLC elections, a confident boast which the speaker may have had cause to regret after the election result.[26] Houghton's proposals were approved by the Education Committee and forwarded to the DES at the end of February 1967. To support the plan and, no doubt with the proximity of the forthcoming local elections in mind, this was adjudged to be an appropriate time to issue an updated version of *London Comprehensive Schools*, which had first appeared in 1961. In *London Comprehensive Schools, 1966*, Houghton described the evolution of a policy which was 'no longer experimental' (ILEA, 1967, p. 11). The effective deployment of staffing and facilities in large comprehensive schools had, it was claimed, afforded wider subject opportunities, while the introduction of the CSE examination[27] had enabled more children to leave school with some qualifications. Comprehensive schools had made a 'decisive contribution' by promoting social mixing and by encouraging children to shoulder responsibilities. Perhaps most important of all, statistics showed that many 11+ failures had gone on to be successful at O-Level and A-Level in London comprehensives (ILEA, 1967, pp. 47, 54–5, 59, 102). Press reviews of the pamphlet were generally encouraging, but the limited selection of schools included in the study was queried by the *Guardian* newspaper, which ventured to suggest that electoral considerations had helped to shape the contents of the report:

> The Conservatives, who protest that the report is one-sided, have got a case ... Some of the smaller comprehensive schools, working in two sets of buildings with a comparatively small range of entry, simply do not compare with some of the bigger, better,

newer schools named in the report. The progress made in London as a whole may be satisfactory, the good schools may be very good indeed, but what about the gap between the good and the indifferent? The ILEA would have done better to admit that it was wide (*Guardian*, 15 February 1967).

In fact, secondary school reorganisation was not highlighted as a major feature during the campaign preceding the May elections (*Comprehensive Education*, 6, 1967, p. 1) which saw London Conservatives triumph for the first time since the 1930s. As ever, the newly constituted ILEA was operating under conditions of severe financial stringency, and even if a reversal of the comprehensive initiative to date had been suggested – which it was not – it could not possibly have been afforded. Instead, the Conservatives' prime educational objective was to preserve those remaining grammar schools that were not scheduled for imminent redesignation. This was, in the words of one commentator, 'the price of the reorganisation of the rest' (Weeks, 1986, p. 33).

Consistent with the actions of other newly elected local Conservative administrations, including Manchester (see Chapter 5), the ILEA response to Circular 10/65 was immediately withdrawn for further consideration. Acting on the instructions of his new political masters, a revised, more moderate plan, looking ahead no further than 1975, was prepared by Education Officer Houghton. Christopher Chataway, the new ILEA leader, revealed that the immediate educational priorities would address primary, rather than secondary education,[28] a policy which conveniently seemed to secure the future of the capital's remaining grammar schools. This policy, which opponents claimed would 'destroy comprehensive education in London',[29] was condemned by teachers, some of whom were disillusioned that almost 20 per cent of London children still received some form of selective education (McCarthy, 1968, pp. 25–7).

Chataway did not profess outright opposition to comprehensive schools, but articulated the objective of improving their *quality*, rather than quantity. 'We are reducing the grammar schools as fast as is consistent with producing good comprehensives', he told an audience in June 1968, but 'lame duck comprehensive schools' would not be tolerated. Greater consistency between the comprehensives would be achieved, he also contended, by discontinuing the practice of placing 40 per cent of primary school pupils in the top ability band. This had led to grammar schools and the better-known comprehensives quickly filling their intake numbers with a disproportionately high number of brighter children, to the disadvantage of other comprehensives (*TES*, 21 June 1968).

The DES response to the revised plan made it clear that the earlier Labour proposals were preferred. Although Crosland was prepared to approve the plan 'in principle', it was suggested that the ILEA should attempt to amalgamate two pairs of boys' schools. Two grammar schools, the Bec County Grammar and St. Marylebone Grammar, could be brought into the comprehensive scheme through amalgamation, respectively with Hillcroft Comprehensive and Rutherford Comprehensive.[30] The ILEA was unmoved, however. A resolution of October 1968 acknowledged that 'conflicting views' had been expressed, but that since 'a majority of staff at two schools and a substantial majority of the staff at a third have all strongly advised the Authority against amalgamation' the *status quo* would be preserved.[31] Crosland had also recommended the merger of Rosa Bassett County Girls' Grammar School with Ensham Girls' School, three-quarters of a mile away, but again the authority stated that no net educational gain could result, given the distance between the two sites.[32]

During this period of Conservative control of the ILEA (1967–70) further schools described as *comprehensive* were created, but, significantly, all the approved amalgamations involved only secondary moderns and existing comprehensives, *not* grammar schools. When a series of further possible amalgamations (involving grammar schools), resulting from unexpected demographic changes, came before the Schools Sub-committee in February 1969, the authority again rejected the proposals, although it was conceded that the separate schools should work in 'close association'.[33]

In late 1969 it looked for a time as if the ILEA's hand might be forced by Secretary of State Ted Short's proposed legislation to end all selection for secondary education, but the Bill was lost when Parliament was dissolved for a June general election, the following year. The London Labour Party had, by this time, already been restored to power, complete with an ILEA team whose collective educational knowledge has been described as 'astounding' (Newsam, 1983, p. 21), but in the country at large the optimism of the previous decade had given way to real doubts about the comprehensive principle. The first *Black Paper* (Cox and Dyson, 1969) appeared in March 1969, marking the beginning of a period when 'Old Right' educational policies gave way to the 'New Right' of greater centralised control of schools (Chitty, 1989, pp. 49–52). With the return of a national Conservative government in 1970, pledged to remove the obligations which Circular 10/65 placed upon LEAs, the next four years were to prove difficult for the ILEA. In particular, they were characterised by a series of clashes with the new Secretary of State, Margaret Thatcher.

IMPASSE AND ACHIEVEMENT: 1970–77

Margaret Thatcher's decision to issue Circular 10/70 was welcomed by London Conservatives, by this time the opposition party on the ILEA's Education Committee. But when a Tory member of the Schools Sub-committee enquired of the new Chairman, Canon Harvey Hinds, whether the Secretary of State's circular would precipitate a change of ILEA policy, he received a combative reply:

> No, there is no cause to reconsider our decision. According to the circular issued today withdrawing circular 10/65 – I quote: 'authorities will now be freer to determine the shape of secondary provision in their areas. The Secretary of State for Education and Science will expect educational considerations in general, local needs, and wishes in particular and the wide use of resources to be the main principles determining the local pattern.' As these have always been the majority party's principles we expect no difficulty in obtaining the Secretary of State's agreement to the necessary variations in the plan prepared by the party opposite, which in many respects singularly failed to meet these criteria.[34]

The favoured model of reorganisation in the capital still (unnecessarily) exclusively involved 11–18 comprehensives. 'Politically and educationally', it has been suggested, 'the ILEA of the early 1970s was still deeply influenced by the vision embodied in the 1947 London School Plan' (Newsam, n.d., p. 11).

As far as the new circular's emphasis upon obtaining the wishes of parents was concerned, Hinds maintained that the consultation process which the ILEA had undertaken in 1966–67 had already met this condition. At the same meeting, Ashley Bramall, the new leader of the authority, announced that the ILEA would not be taking up its quota of free places in London day independent and direct-grant schools.[35] The soundness of this decision might be queried, since the net effect was to make the direct-grant schools, which Thatcher pledged to defend in her first speech as Minister to the Party conference, even more selective. The Secretary of State also announced that, in view of the fact that primary schooling would top the government's education agenda for the 1970s, all building grants for secondary schools, other than those earmarked to meet the raising of the school leaving age to 16, were to be limited to cases where 'roofs over heads' was at stake (*Daily Telegraph*, 8 October 1970). This, in the words of Hinds, threatened to put the ILEA 'out of business for ten years as far as improving any secondary schools in London is concerned' (Simon, 1991, p. 421). A deputation, led by Bramall, met Thatcher in early March 1971, and asked her to extend the authority's building programme and allow completion of minor works, which now faced the axe. However, there was evidently no meeting of minds.[36] Signs of disillusionment which London teachers felt about the impasse situation again surfaced. In May 1971, The *Sunday Times* carried a feature reporting that the staff of Vauxhall Manor School, a comprehensive which had pioneered unstreaming, were prepared to quit because of the authority's inability to carry out a building programme which had been planned since 1958. It was now suggested that 1980 was the earliest date that work could begin (*Sunday Times*, 9 May 1971; see also Hoyles, 1970, pp. 39–52). Evidence supports the view that London's experienced comprehensive school teachers were, by this time, much in demand by provincial reorganising LEAs, and many sought new challenges which seemed to offer a greater prospect of success.[37] Among her other pronouncements, Thatcher, whose actions frequently reflected her legal training, indicated that she would discontinue the previous government's practice of giving administrative approval to non-statutory plans. In a letter to a CASE executive member, dated 6 August 1971, she explained:

> such 'decisions' had no legal significance and it had become quite clear that the practice of approving these non-statutory plans, which set out authorities' broad schemes for reorganising an area, had tended to create confusion about the statutory procedure under Section 13 of the Education Act 1944 (as amended).[38]

However, individual proposals to create new comprehensive schools proved no more attractive to the Secretary of State than large-scale plans. One such proposition which she refused to sanction was to replace the Thomas Calton Secondary Modern School in Peckham, at that time spread over five sites, with a purpose-built comprehensive. The local AASE condemned the Secretary of State's decision, observing that 'by her inflexible attitude towards the rebuilding of old secondary schools (an attitude which, on the face of it, looks simply

75

like a device for slowing down the rate of comprehensive reorganisation in the country), Mrs Thatcher has set back the most exciting prospective development in London's secondary education'.[39] Bramall's efforts to arrange a further ILEA deputation to discuss the decision with Mrs Thatcher were unsuccessful, and her suggestion of a meeting with a junior minister proved unacceptable to the authority which refused to be 'fobbed off with someone else'. Thatcher's attitude, Bramall concluded, 'reflects her determination to do nothing for secondary schools in Victorian buildings'.[40]

In spite of these less than propitious circumstances, the ILEA still felt that authority-wide planning was essential to the achievement of equitable schooling in every district. A new review, which was eventually to produce three *Green Papers* entitled *Planning for 1980*, had begun in July 1971. The task ahead was still formidable. At the end of the year, the inner London AASE took stock of the situation, estimating that 15 per cent of children in the ILEA area still attended selective grammar schools:

> at present there are 59 grammar schools within the ILEA area – 12 of which are county grammar schools, but six of these are scheduled for amalgamation or closure. The few remaining 'county' grammar schools are what might be described as the 'hard core' cases such as Clapham County and St Marylebone Grammar Schools where parental opposition is strong and vociferous. With sympathy for their cause coming from the DES, it is difficult for ILEA to push them any further. ILEA's position is made the more difficult by the total cut back on money for secondary school rebuilding and improvement. Not only does this mean that there is no hope at present of rehousing 'comprehensives' which are in unsuitable buildings, but it also means that there is no means of easing the process of amalgamation by offering new buildings.[41]

Inability to proceed further with comprehensive plans had now, the paper suggested, reached a crisis point. Teachers were impatient and disillusioned, while parents were confused. It continued:

> some of the comprehensive schools do get their 'fair quota' of entrants who span the full range of abilities, but many, particularly those who had no grammar school unit in the original amalgamation, fail to get anything like their full quota of the top ability group, and instead get an undue proportion of pupils in

the middle and lower ability groups. For this reason, these schools cannot be directly compared with old grammar schools. Yet the public will insist upon making such comparisons – 'if they are so much better, then why don't they get better 'O' and 'A'-Level results than the grammar schools?' is a common comment. In vain does one point out that many of the very pupils who 'clock up' vast scores at 'O' and 'A'-Level are still at grammar schools. Criticisms like these are sapping the morale of both Heads and teachers, many of whom were appointed in the mid-1960s with the promise and prospect of a full comprehensive system in London. They feel that they are now battling against the odds – as indeed some of them are – and there now seems no prospect of the odds changing in their favour to any marked degree. It is no wonder that many of the younger staff are looking to promotion not within London, but to the increasingly attractive pastures which are growing up in counties such as Leicestershire, Nottinghamshire and Hampshire which are introducing comprehensive schemes.[42]

The first ILEA *Green Paper*, covering the north-east London boroughs of Hackney and Tower Hamlets, appeared in 1972 (ILEA, 1972), with a foreword by Dr Eric Briault, Houghton's successor as Education Officer. Further documents, covering north and north-west London and south and south-west London appeared the following year (ILEA, 1973a and 1973b). The introduction – common to each of the three divisional reports – restated some familiar themes:

> ... the main objective of the whole review is to make plans to achieve a complete system of fully comprehensive schools as quickly as possible ... A complete system of fully comprehensive schools means that there can be no place in our long-term plans for selective schools (ILEA, 1972, pp. 2–3).

Consistent with the authority's previous policy documents, the *Green Papers* envisaged both the elimination and the amalgamation of very small schools, including the voluntary grammar schools. However, as Sir Peter Newsam (who arrived in London as Briault's Deputy in 1972) has recalled, the proposals ran into several 'insuperable problems', of which the first was:

> ... that practically no one was prepared to believe in the fall in the secondary school population that the statistics predicted. Even those who did believe in it thought others would go to the

wall. Less well supported schools looked about themselves and found comfort in plans for a new housing estate or some such chimera (Newsam, n.d., p. 11).

Heads, teachers, governors and parents all found it difficult to swallow the bitter pills of closure or amalgamation, and, with a sympathetic Secretary of State at the DES, many were prepared to fight. Though opposition ILEA members, claiming the existence of a link between comprehensive education, truancy and violence, accused Labour of 'a campaign of secrecy' regarding its plans for the future of London's remaining grammar schools,[43] there was very little more, in reality, that Bramall and his colleagues could do. Only the governors of the voluntary schools, Newsam has observed, '... could propose changes of the kind envisaged in the Green Papers', and decisions about the closure of county or voluntary schools rested with the Secretary of State (ibid., n.d., pp. 11–12).

Mrs Thatcher turned down another attempt by the ILEA to amalgamate St Marylebone Grammar School with Rutherford County Secondary School on the grounds that this would create 'administrative and organisational difficulties' and thereby disadvantage children. Similarly, she moved to block the closure of the Strand County Grammar School in 1973, citing the strength of parental opposition to the ILEA proposal.[44] In a 1983 speech, Sir Peter Newsam recalled the effects of some of the demographic and ethnic movements upon London schooling more closely, suggesting that as many as 500,000 skilled workers, together with their above-average performing children had moved out of London from the mid-1960s, while

> ... into the empty spaces ... came families from overseas. The numbers coming in were fewer than those leaving and, a factor of permanent significance, with those leaving went the jobs that had previously given the inner areas of the city much of their economic strength (Newsam, 1983, p. 3).

Given the fact that there were already surplus places in London secondary schools, and that these figures were likely to continue to rise steadily, it was recognised that no realistic case could be made for additional building funds. In Peckham, for example, it was estimated that, by 1980, there would be provision for over 22,000 places, but a demand for only 16,500 (ILEA, 1973b, pp. 10–11). There appeared every reason for the ILEA to suppose (reluctantly) that most of the selective schools would remain in business – stable, well-staffed and full to capacity. It was also clear that those comprehensives which had worked hard to establish strong academic reputations could remain full only by attracting proportionately more of a declining supply of the most able children. If this were the case, in what sense could other non-selective schools genuinely claim to be *comprehensive*? Many London secondary schools seemed destined to plunge into 'an irreversible downward spiral', and 'efforts being made to improve this or that feature of the system were ... no better than rearranging the deckchairs on the *Titanic*' (Newsam, 1983, p. 6). Racial tensions had already led to isolated ugly incidents in some London schools and, looking ahead to 1980, it seemed possible that many schools would be seen as either 'black' or 'white'.

The way ahead, Newsam reasoned, was to abandon the authority's exclusive attraction to the 11–18 comprehensive school:

> too many leading politicians, on the best professional advice, had proclaimed the virtues of these schools and denied that there was any valid alternative to them ... But the only way of ending selection and avoiding the iceberg was to rethink the nature of the comprehensive school. The test of a responsible authority, in such a situation, is to eat its words. There were some tantrums and flying crockery but, in the end and just in time, that is what the ILEA did. (Newsam, 1983, p. 9)

The inner London AASE had suggested the introduction of a middle-school system for part, or even all, of the ILEA area in October 1972, but this was immediately dismissed on the grounds of cost and likely opposition from the teaching organisations.[45] A division within County Hall was, by now, becoming evident. Briault and the ILEA Chief Inspector, Dr Michael Birchenough, retained a preference for large, all-through comprehensives, while Newsam, drawing upon his own experience in the West Riding, advanced the case for smaller schools and more flexible patterns of organisation (Maclure, 1990, pp. 210–11).

Briault and Bramall found it impossible to resist increasingly voiced demands for flexibility. According to Maclure, two prominent ILEA members, Caroline Benn and Tyrrell Burgess, were particularly influential in this regard. He identifies Highbury Hill Girls' Grammar School's offer to drop its selective entry in return for a guarantee from the ILEA that it would not be pressured to merge with Highbury Grove as an important 'turning-point' (Maclure, 1990, p. 122). This school became a three form-entry 'mini-comprehensive' (Newsam, n.d., p. 13) and opened the door for further pragmatic solutions to reduce selection in the capital. During the *Green Paper* discussions, a majority of Islington head teachers on an *ad hoc* committee had formed the conclusion that, in view of the high proportions of disadvantaged children in their catchments, either a Leicestershire-style 11–14 and 14–18 organisation or a sixth-form college, serving 11–16 feeder schools, was a more practical solution than 'all-through' secondary education (ILEA, 1973a, pp. 12–13). The Islington Sixth Form Centre owes its origins to this new thinking.

A period of notable progress followed, during which a number of other grammar schools opted to follow Highbury Hill's lead, resulting in the announcement in March 1975 that, from September 1977, the ILEA would only be prepared to maintain schools which accepted a full ability range. Abandoning selection, of course, did not guarantee the operation of a fully *comprehensive* system; with so many independent schools and London's diverse (though segregated) socioeconomic composition, this was never a realisable objective, in any case. Yet, Newsam had good reason to refer to this period of change as a 'Revolution by Consent':

> ... between 1975 and 1977, 39 Section 13 Notices to cease to maintain or change the character of 48 schools were issued by the Authority. To fewer than half of these Public Notices were there objections in the form laid down by statute, namely by ten or more local government electors or by Borough Councils (Newsam, n.d., p. 13).

Active reorganisation continued for many years. Maclure records that 37 grammar schools became comprehensives in 1977, although four others opted instead to become independent. Moreover, 'between 1977 and 1989, 20 schools closed; 63 schools were merged in 36 amalgamations; nine turned into 11–16 schools; 41 were cut down in size; and two single-sex schools changed to become mixed schools without amalgamation, as did others as a result of mergers' (Maclure, 1990, p. 224).

The decade of the 1980s was a period of increasing difficulties, both internally and in the relations between the ILEA and central government. The ILEA lived in the shadow of the axe after a 1983 White Paper foreshadowed the abolition of Metropolitan Authorities. Abolition eventually occurred on 31 March 1990, and the schools, colleges and services of the authority were handed over to the 12, politically diverse inner London boroughs and the City. There remain continuing difficulties of reorganisation in the mid-1990s.

VIEWING LONDON IN CONTEXT

The experience of London during the years of comprehensive reorganisation was both typical and utterly unique. It was typical in the kinds of issues being faced and in many of the forces that affected the actions taken. There were strong political and ideological forces moving the LCC and ILEA towards comprehensive reorganisation, but there was also strong resistance, heavily influenced by the loyalties many felt to the grammar schools. These same contending forces were at play in many of the other LEAs; for example, the questions of whether 'creaming' made it impossible to have a 'real' comprehensive school, how to fit comprehensive schools into buildings previously used in the selective system, and whether middle schools or sixth-form colleges should be considered. Shifting relations with central government, which we have just reviewed, were also observable in many other LEAs, as was the case for particular individuals to influence strongly the course of events. London was unique in the magnitude of its problems, however. Massive bomb damage and the need to rebuild whole areas, comparable in size with many other authorities, presented difficulties not faced elsewhere and gave impetus to early consideration of comprehensive schools. The large number of independent schools and well-established grammar schools provided the opposition to comprehensivisation with an exceptionally strong base. Equally importantly, London was the 'home' of the central government, and any actions taken by the LCC and ILEA occurred under the close scrutiny of a series of changing administrations. Finally, London was also the centre of the communications industry. The LEA's actions were thus constantly being observed and reported on by newspapers, radio and television. Through these media, other parts of the country were bound to be influenced by what happened in London. Many of the factors that were at play in the case of London will be encountered again as we review our other nine focal LEAs. In most of those LEAs, however, we will also find special forces operating that served to shape the comprehensive movement in ways not found elsewhere. We turn first to three LEAs, Manchester, Bristol and Leeds, that were most similar to London in that they were large urban settings. Then, in Chapters 5 to 8 we discuss other LEAs in less urban settings and those which made particularly unusual or important contributions to the movement.

NOTES

1. GLRO (Northampton Road repository), LCC Education Committee Minutes, 19 July 1944.
2. It should not be forgotten, however, that around the same time in Wales, Anglesey, a predominantly rural LEA, also unveiled ambitious plans for comprehensive schools on the grounds that they were cost-effective, as well as educationally desirable.
3. PRO ED 152/105 Savage to G.G. Williams, 28 June 1946. This file also contains a memorandum of the meeting between Savage, his deputy Dr A.G. Hughes and ministry officials on 21 March 1946.
4. Ibid., G.W.W. Browne to Savage, 6 Aug. 1946.
5. Ibid., comments by HMI J.W. Ireland, 1 June 1946.
6. Ibid., memorandum dated 27 May 1946.
7. GLRO (Northampton Road respository), EO/PS/1/141, papers of Alderman Martin Parr, 1946–53, 'Note on the London School Plan, 1947' by Catherine Fulford.
8. Ibid.
9. PRO ED 152/107, R. Morrison to Savage, 7 Jan. 1949. Earlier drafts of the letter are in the same file. ED 152/108 contains objections to the London School Plan by various school governing bodies. The most frequent complaints were of 'insufficient particulars' or concerned the 'proposed remodelling' of their schools.
10. Ibid.
11. Ibid., memorandum of a meeting between Savage, Hughes and ministerial officials, led by G.N. Flemming, 11 July 1949.
12. GLRO (Temple House repository), ILEA/DO3/1 boxes 4 and 7, School Governing Body minutes.
13. The schools, with their accommodation details and dates of opening, were: Holloway (1,350 boys, 1955); Mayfield (2,130 girls, 1955); Parliament Hill (1,350 girls, 1956); Sydenham (1,650 girls, 1956) and Wandsworth (2,130 boys, 1956).
14. GLRO ILEA/DO3/1 box 21, Starcross School governors' minutes, 4 Dec. 1964.
15. ILEA Paper 73, 1 March 1965, presented to the Schools Planning sub-committee meeting of 8 March 1965. A full set of ILEA Education Committee and sub-committee minutes are housed at the GLRO Temple House repository.
16. ILEA Paper 163, 2 April 1965, presented to the Schools Planning sub-committee meeting of 8 April 1965.
17. Education Committee minutes, 12 May 1965.
18. ILEA Paper 245, 'Future of Henry Thornton and Aristotle Schools, Lambeth and Tennyson School, Wandsworth', 21 June 1965, presented to the Schools Planning sub-committee meeting, 29 June 1965.
19. Schools sub-committee minutes, 18 May 1965.
20. Ibid., 13 Jan. 1966.
21. ILEA Paper 608, 'The Organisation of Secondary Education: Circular 10/65', presented to the Schools Planning sub-committee, 16 June 1966.
22. We should remember, however, that despite significant petitioning by LEAs the central government had specifically refused to grant additional funding to enable

authorities to establish more comprehensive schools.

23. Education Committee minutes, 6 July 1966, comment by Mrs I. Chaplin.
24. Appendix to Schools Planning sub-committee minutes, comment by Mrs I.L. Phillips at Hammersmith County School, 5 Jan. 1967.
25. Ibid., comment by Mr L. Sherman at the Congress Hall, 16 Jan. 1967.
26. Ibid., comment by Mrs I. Chaplin at Archway Central Hall, 17 Jan. 1967.
27. Under the selective system following the Second World War, it was assumed that only those at grammar schools would take examinations leading to nationally recognised certification. These were the General Certificate of Education (GCE) examinations, 'Ordinary' (O-Levels) at age 16 and 'Advanced' (A-Levels) at age 18. No comparable form of certification was available for those attending secondary modern schools. Dissatisfaction with this lack of certification was one of the forces behind the comprehensive movement. The same pressure led some secondary modern schools to provide opportunities for O-Level examination entry, but this was not a widespread pattern. The CSE (Certificate of Secondary Education) examinations were introduced to offer secondary modern school students some kind of certification. Although less valued than the GCE examinations, they provided an important goal and valuable credential for students outside the grammar schools.
28. Education Committee minutes, 18 Oct. 1967.
29. From a statement by the staff at Wandsworth School, reported in *Forum*, 11, 1 (1968), p. 18.
30. Schools sub-committee minutes, 3 Oct. 1968.
31. Ibid.
32. Ibid.
33. Ibid., 20 Feb. 1969.
34. Education Committee minutes, 1 July 1970.
35. Ibid.
36. Schools sub-committee minutes, 18 March 1971.
37. University of Warwick Modern Records Centre, CASE archives, MSS 236/3, Inner London AASE file, paper by Margaret Sharp entitled 'Middle and Upper Schools – A Possible Solution to Some of London's Secondary School Problems', Dec. 1971.
38. Ibid., 'Other bodies' box 2, Thatcher to John Allard (CASE Executive member), 6 Aug. 1971.
39. Ibid., Sydenham AASE file, Oct. 1971 *Newsletter*.
40. Education Committee minutes, 8 Dec. 1971.
41. CASE archives MSS 236/3, Inner London AASE file, as Note 37.
42. Ibid.
43. Education Committee minutes, 28 June 1972.
44. Ibid., 31 Jan. 1973.
45. Ibid., 25 Oct. 1972.

5

The Urban, Political Reorganisation: Manchester, Bristol and Leeds

Like London, the cities of Manchester, Bristol and Leeds had strong local Labour Party organisations, which actively promoted comprehensive education. The experience of London and these three cities provides strong support for the argument that the comprehensive movement was an urban movement, led by the Labour Party. As we have seen in Chapter 2, and as will be shown in later chapters, however, that is not the whole story, even though it is an important part of it. There was even a good deal of variation among the four major urban LEAs we have studied in detail, and that variation becomes apparent in what follows.

EARLY MOVES: 1946–63

As early as 1947, the Manchester Education Committee submitted a Development Plan to the Ministry of Education which was deliberately non-committal about the long-term future of secondary education in the city. The following year, W.O. Lester Smith (CEO 1930–49) confided to Ministry of Education officials that a number of local Labour councillors were enthusiastic about the principle of multi-lateralism.[1] In what appeared to be an expression of that enthusiasm, Manchester LEA designated one school (Yew Tree, in North Wythenshawe) simply as a *secondary*, rather than a *secondary modern* school, and GCE examination courses were offered there. The Yew Tree school quickly gained a good academic reputation, but its uncertain status was the subject of a destructive 1952 HMI report. It is not clear whether Lester Smith actually supported comprehensive reorganisation (Fiske, 1982, p. 13), but the HMI report served to confirm the adherence of Norman Fisher, Lester Smith's successor, to tripartism.[2]

By contrast, Harold Sylvester, who had been appointed as Bristol's CEO in 1942 at the age of 35, and who held the position for the next quarter of a century, strongly supported multilateral education. Doubts about the secondary modern school's ability to command parity of esteem with grammar and technical schools surfaced soon after the 1944 Education Act was passed, and Bristol's Development Plan of 1946 was deliberately *bipartite*, rather than *tripartite*. Within three years, however, Sylvester was pressing the Education Committee Labour group to view this as a second-best solution. As in London, extensive wartime bomb damage in Bristol offered an opportunity to consider future housing and schooling developments simultaneously, and the minutes of a 1949 meeting record that it was decided 'to ask the CEO to prepare a draft report to Council based on his plan for comprehensive schools; if this were defeated to press for Grammar schools and Technical-Modern Schools as a foundation on which to build'.[3]

Clearly then, the dynamics of early comprehensive developments in Bristol were quite different from those of Manchester. In Manchester, the ideology of Socialist politicians did little to challenge the scepticism of the LEA administrators, but in Bristol, it was the CEO himself who should be seen as the progenitor of educational radicalism. These are examples of a general pattern, which we will note further in this and later chapters, in which the personnel responsible for developing or administering reorganisation policy within an LEA often served as *enablers* of or *impediments* to progress.

Exact details of Sylvester's proposals have not survived, but it is clear that his proposed scheme was considered controversial, even by some Socialist councillors. A city-wide plan for comprehensive schools was narrowly rejected by a full Council vote,[4] but there was interest in the idea of developing comprehensive schools for new housing estates planned for the outskirts of the city. A new Development Plan of 1951 was intentionally not specific about how secondary education should be organised, but the acquisition of several 30-, 40- and 50-acre sites, adjacent to new housing on the fringes of the city, indicated the authority's determination to launch a series of *experimental* comprehensive schools (Sylvester, 1965, p. 12). This new type of school, egalitarians argued, was the key to securing a democratic community within the city. In May 1953, after retaining control of the City Council at the polls, the Labour group audaciously declared their objective 'to transform the educational system of Bristol from an instrument perpetuating class divisions and class distinctions into an instrument for promoting social unity'.[5]

The following year saw Labour return to power in Manchester.

Encouraged by the victory, Councillor Lady [Shena] Simon of Wythenshawe, a radical figure who helped formulate the Labour group's comprehensive education policy for nearly three decades, urged the city to 'take her place again with those LEAs who are trying out multilateral and comprehensive schools'.[6] Within months, Lady Simon had co-ordinated fact-finding visits to schools in Coventry and London (Fiske, 1982, p. 14), and had identified three possible sites for an experimental Manchester comprehensive.[7] However, Lady Simon was frustrated by CEO Norman Fisher's disinclination to support alternatives to tripartism.

In a letter written in the wake of Fisher's departure to take up a post with the National Coal Board, Lady Simon highlighted the fact that although local democratic processes determined that CEOs were the servants of elected Education Committees, personal preferences and prejudices were not always set aside. The question of who succeeded Fisher, she reminded a colleague, was crucial to the question of implementing the Council's most recently declared objective to establish three comprehensives in the Wythenshawe area of Manchester:

> The Chief official ought to be prepared to carry out whatever policy the committee decided upon, but we have had recent experience of how, without apparent opposition – the official can obstruct. It would be disastrous if whoever is chosen, is chosen on a party vote. It will also, I am afraid, affect applicants for headships. If we advertise the three as comprehensive schools, and appoint on that basis, and if then, in one or two years' time – before the full intake has been absorbed, two of the schools are changed into selective ones, the position of the heads will be very difficult – their salaries probably reduced ...[8]

These hopes were to be frustrated on two accounts. First, the new CEO, John Elliot, was no more sympathetic towards comprehensive schools than his two immediate predecessors had been. It has been generously suggested by Dudley Fiske, Elliot's successor, that this was because he 'took great pride in the tripartite system ... that he had helped to create and in which he himself had taught', and Elliot's visits (with senior colleagues) to LEAs which had introduced a measure of comprehensive education 'did not convince them that the advantages of alternative systems would justify the considerable dislocation caused by change' (Fiske, 1982, pp. 14–15).

A further blow was dealt when the proposal for three comprehensives was blocked by Sir David Eccles, the Conservative Minister of

Education, in July 1955, on the grounds that it would involve the destruction of existing grammar schools, and because one of the proposed schools would be based on two sites, half a mile apart.[9] Lady Simon immediately identified the inconsistency between this ministerial decision and the government's decision to approve plans for a comprehensive school in the West Riding with sites separated by a distance of two miles. Anxious that Manchester should not be denied 'the opportunity to experiment',[10] she assembled and briefed a delegation of Education Committee members, but their visit to the ministry failed to persuade Eccles to reconsider.

The only tangible step towards the realisation of a non-selective pattern of education for Manchester between 1955 and 1963, a period when 'there was a lot of debate, a lot of work, but not much progress' (Fiske, 1982, p.15), was the official designation of the Yew Tree School as a *comprehensive* in 1962. The lack of progress is partly explained by the fact that comprehensive education was still a vexed issue for the Manchester Labour Party, whose 'parlous state' caused Lady Simon fleetingly to consider retirement from political life.[11]

During these years of inertia in Manchester, there was important progress in Bristol. Three new *experimental* schools, serving new housing estates, opened in 1954. They were variously known as *bilateral* schools, *mixed* schools, and *schools with grammar and modern streams*, but not comprehensive schools. It has been observed that these schools served working-class communities with relatively few education-conscious parents (Keen, 1965, p. 23), but the conservatism of Labour councillors favoured experimentation, rather than wholesale change. Although an early interest in comprehensive education had been demonstrated, Bristol LEA's most immediate challenge lay in meeting the 1944 Act's stipulation that authorities should replace all-age schools with separate primary and secondary institutions. This process was not completed in Bristol until 1958, so the reorganisation of secondary education was necessarily a subsidiary issue during these years. This naturally proved frustrating for the head teachers of the new secondary schools, who, on more than one occasion, represented the view to Education Committee members that central Bristol's grammar, direct-grant and independent schools deprived them of more able pupils.[12]

The doubts about comprehensive schools which existed within the local Labour parties of Bristol and Manchester may also be observed elsewhere. In Leeds, another city which the Socialists had gained in the 1953 local elections, it has been observed that the 'widespread theoretical commitment masked scepticism amongst leading Labour councillors that anything but the slowest progress was either practicable or acceptable' (Fenwick and Woodthorpe, 1980, p. 21). No radical schemes involving grammar school closures were put forward before the end of the 1950s, but a purpose-built boys' comprehensive, serving a new housing estate in east Leeds opened in 1956, to be followed, two years later, by the redesignation of a secondary modern school in the south of the city.[13] Encouraged by these developments, the Leeds Labour Party began to confront the question of comprehensive education with more enthusiasm towards the end of the decade.

The 1959 New Year Message by the national party leader, Hugh Gaitskell (a Leeds MP), called for the abolition of the 11+ examination, and later in the year another of the city's Socialist MPs, Michael Stewart (then Labour's chief spokesman on education), reportedly told the Leeds Fabian Society that 'the answer to the 11+ is a comprehensive system of secondary education'. Concrete policy commitments were nevertheless slow to materialise. A further purpose-built secondary school, serving new housing in south Leeds opened in 1961. The Chairman of the Education Committee used this opportunity to declare publicly that comprehensive schools would become 'a way of life' in Leeds, but this masked private reservations about the speed at which a city-wide plan could be introduced (Fenwick and Woodthorpe, 1980, pp. 21–2).

CHANGE OF PACE, 1963–65

Surveying the history of comprehensive education, Brian Simon has argued that 1963, two years before the issue of Tony Crosland's circular, was 'the crucial moment of change' (Simon, 1991, p. 271). That year saw the 'break-out' from the chains of tripartism by a group of large, urban LEAs, which sought to reorganise the whole of their administrative area along comprehensive lines. This marked the end of the experimental phase for comprehensive education. Tripartism and selection were no longer *de rigueur*. Evidence to support this thesis may be found in each of the three cities discussed in this chapter. It has been observed that 1963 was the year in which 'things began to move' in Manchester (Fiske, 1982, p. 15), and important developments in Leeds and Bristol are also identifiable.

In May 1963, after a break of three years, Labour returned to power in Bristol, having spent their period out of office developing a more coherent policy towards comprehensive education. Confident that Bristol's experimental schools had been successful, Labour now sought to discontinue the 11+ examination at the earliest opportunity. However, as so often at this time, the political desire to increase the number of designated comprehensives was stronger than the tendency to scrutinise the expected nature of the intake in these schools.

This was a period when flawed logic was in abundance. For example, in 1962, the Bristol Labour Party announced that, if re-elected, they would immediately upgrade secondary modern schools and rename them comprehensives. This misleadingly suggested that comprehensives and grammars were compatible alternatives, a notion which the local evening newspaper found heartening in a supportive editorial:

> the outstanding feature of the future policy is that parents have freedom of choice. Seven out of every ten Bristol parents still prefer their children to go to a grammar school, but there can be no denying, in the light of experience, that comprehensive schools are a success.
>
> (*Bristol Evening Post*, 30 March, 1962).

After Labour's victory in Bristol, reality dawned, and all thoughts of grammar and comprehensive schools co-existing in the longer term were quickly dismissed. Although actual council proposals took some months to emerge, the Education Labour Group, under the chairmanship of the Reverend Frederick Vyvyan-Jones, quickly resolved that each district of the city – not just the areas of new housing – should be served by a comprehensive school. Where new buildings could not be rapidly erected, two or more existing school buildings would be linked. It was also confirmed that the authority would discontinue its traditional practice of taking up places in Bristol's direct-grant schools.[14] There appeared to be solid grounds for optimism. The number of Bristol comprehensives had risen steadily since 1954 (when the first three opened), yet this development had largely been inconspicuous, since the new schools served areas of new housing on the fringes of the city.

The 1960s also saw the Manchester Labour Party's policy towards comprehensive education become less ambiguous than it had been during the previous decade. A new pro-comprehensive chairman of the Education Committee, Frank Hatton, took office in 1962. He was determined that CEO Elliot's lack of enthusiasm should not be an impediment to reorganisation. Without troubling Elliot for his view, Manchester City Council dramatically passed a resolution in July

1963, calling on the Education Committee to submit, within six months, detailed proposals to convert county secondary schools 'to a wholly comprehensive system' (Fiske, 1982, p. 15). Broad indications of an interim plan for a mixture of all-through and two-tier comprehensives followed in November, but the LEA's efforts to keep secret the finer details until teacher associations had been consulted were thwarted by newspaper revelations (*TES*, 22 November 1963) which rallied the Conservative forces of opposition.

In contrast to Bristol, there was no suggestion, at this stage, of discontinuing the practice of purchasing places in Manchester's nine direct-grant schools (although this was a later feature). But other aspects of the interim plan were controversial, precipitating a clash between the CEO and his political masters. The question of *zoning* was one such issue. Elliot maintained that neighbourhood schools, as envisaged by the plan, were inappropriate, given that Manchester's grammar and technical schools drew children from all over the city, while the small, secondary modern schools had purely local catchment areas. Others represented the view that the modern schools were too small and ill-equipped to be easily amalgamated. These considerable objections, combined with an acceptance by Labour that its public relations and consultation procedures had not been well handled, forced the withdrawal of the proposals in April 1964.

In Leeds, the pace of change was slower, but by the end of 1963 the LEA had, at last, committed itself to abolishing the 11+. Although attracted to the idea of comprehensive education, the authority wished to effect change without attracting controversy. Caution was, therefore, the watchword. An interim plan was devised envisaging transfer at 13, but which also allowed for later transfer at 16 in those parts of the city where small school buildings could not easily be extended to accommodate the full 13 to 18 range. An all-party working group was established to consider the plan.[15] Local press releases (*Yorkshire Post*, 19 November 1963), inviting the responses of parents and teachers to comment on the proposal, prevented allegations of secrecy.

Although such care was commendable, in retrospect it might be argued that these were not the ingredients most likely to produce a workable scheme. The spirit of compromise gave rise to a confusing proposal to introduce a network of two-tier secondary schools, while retaining existing grammar schools as an alternative to the senior high schools. This would not create satisfactory *comprehensive* schools, as the local CASE group (which favoured *all-through* comprehensives created through amalgamations) pointed out in a memorandum to the

LEA. In middle-class neighbourhoods, they argued, almost all parents would opt for a grammar-school education for their children, making selection unavoidable. Moreover, they maintained that grammar schools and senior high comprehensives could not happily co-exist, since facilities, equipment and staffing ratios would be relatively inferior in the latter type of school:

> the senior high schools will scarcely avoid being much inferior to the present secondary modern schools. Their pupils will enter at a physically developed age ... Their pupils seem likely to suffer as much, if not more, from the parental disinterest that has placed them there as many present secondary modern pupils suffer from their rejection by the present 11+ selection system. It does not seem likely that a two-year school of unselected children, without sixth forms, will attract many teachers from choice, or open genuine opportunities for the transfer of pupils to grammar schools at 16.[16]

The working party's moderate, but confused recommendations also came under fire from local Conservatives, who particularly disliked the 'transit camp' 11–13 school proposals. Their support for alternative transfer procedures to replace the 11+ examination was growing, yet bipartism, they suggested, was working rather better than their political opponents credited:

> we believe that Socialist politicians should recognise the good work done by Secondary Modern Schools, and stop running them down.[17]

Having witnessed this less than enthusiastic reception for its interim scheme proposals, the Leeds working party reconvened towards the end of 1963 to consider the various representations which had been made.

Of the three LEAs discussed here, the strongest working association between the CEO and Education Committee was to be found in Bristol. This was a clear case of an enabler which promoted reorganisation. Another enabling factor, which hastened reform was the co-operation received from teachers in the city. At the end of 1963, it was announced that the official teachers' consultative body had agreed that long-term educational planning should be geared towards the establishment of a fully comprehensive scheme.[18] This was a helpful move, but the 'long-term' might be interpreted as meaning almost anything. Even the Education Committee's own Development Plan

Sub-committee was, by this time, cautiously suggesting that Bristol's grammar schools could not be phased out before 1971.

As far as Sylvester and Vyvyan-Jones were concerned, the gradual introduction of more comprehensives was an illusory option, since it would involve proposing more building projects than the Ministry of Education could be realistically expected to approve. Accordingly, in March 1964, the reorganisation sub-committee was requested to approve an additional plan which would permit comprehensive schools to operate as soon as possible. Fourteen city comprehensives were already operating, without controversy by this time, accommodating 60 per cent of Bristol's LEA-maintained secondary school population. The rapid extension of the plan to cover the established neighbourhoods of the city was essential, it was maintained, if equality of opportunity was to prevail.[19] Reflecting, in 1965, upon the authority's decision not to wait for new building funds to become available, Sylvester wrote:

> ... the hard facts are that the long term plan might take anything from 10 to 15 years to complete. The advocates of the more completely comprehensive plan therefore felt that some further progress must be made towards the objectives which they had in mind, even in the short term (Sylvester, 1965, p. 15).

Two months after Labour had strengthened its control of the City Council in the May 1964 elections, Vyvyan-Jones called a press conference at which he dramatically announced that the 11+ examination would be held for the final time in 1965, facilitating the extension of comprehensive education to central Bristol. Grammar schools would become amalgamated to form interim split-site comprehensives, which would operate a zoning system to allocate children to their neighbourhood school. What interested the press and media more, however, was the announcement that the Council would abandon the practice of buying places in Bristol's seven direct-grant schools when reorganisation occurred in 1965 (subject to DES approval). Although the *Evening Post* attacked the 'intellectual vandalism' perpetrated by the authority (*TES*, 3 July 1964), others were delighted that, at last, city comprehensive schools could look forward to a more representative intake of pupils. One delighted comprehensive school headmaster reported to his professional association that:

> the decision not to take up places at Direct Grant schools means, of course, that the comprehensive schools will get more of

the complete intellectual range rather than under the present situation in which it is rare for us in the Comprehensive Schools to obtain any student in the top ten percentile range.[20]

The following months were characterised by innumerable heated political debates and petitions fuelling – and fuelled by – the ferocious anti-comprehensive stance of the *Bristol Evening Post*, which published a variety of damaging rumours and misrepresentations relating to the Bristol Labour Party. Indeed, it was suggested that the City Council's ratification of the short-term plan in October 1964, just two days before Harold Wilson's Labour Party swept to a convincing general election victory, cost Labour two 'safe' Bristol seats (*TES*, 23 October 1964, letter by C.T. Sandford). One recurring allegation – that the quota of 'free' places in the direct-grant schools would disappear altogether as a consequence of the LEA's stated policy – was wholly false, but, according to the local CASE branch, many of those who signed the petitions of the self-styled Secondary Education Defence Association and the Joint Action Defence Committee were unaware of this. The actions of such groups, which generated both local and national media coverage 'successfully diverted most people's attention from all other aspects of the Plan than that of the future of the Grammar Schools'.[21] The authority was forced on to the defensive, even contemplating the organisation of a 'comprehensive schools week', during which heads could publicise their schools, preferably on television.[22]

Perhaps the most often-repeated and adhesive charge which was laid against Bristol LEA during the autumn of 1964 was that its consultation procedures had been inadequate. On 27 November the Secretary of State, Michael Stewart, who was in the process of considering his response to the authority's proposals, told the House of Commons that Bristol 'could have taken more and earlier steps' to gather local opinions (although there was no statutory duty to take soundings).[23] The criticism was justified to some extent. Not everyone warmed to Vyvyan-Jones's brusque style of presentation, and too much political invective characterised Education Committee members' defences of the scheme. Stewart's criticisms were carefully noted by other reorganising authorities (though not, apparently, in Manchester, as will be discussed below). The implication seemed clear: if the government was not satisfied that reorganisation schemes accurately reflected community feelings, or if it was suspected that political motives outweighed educational ones, DES approval would not be forthcoming.

However, as CEO Harold Sylvester observed in 1965, one of the difficulties of holding public meetings would have been 'to try to ascertain the extent to which people attending the meeting really represented the majority view among parents' (Sylvester, 1965, p. 18). Assessing the typicality of views represented by Bristol's several articulate, well-organised and media-aware anti-comprehensive groups would have been nearly impossible. It should also be remembered that local and national elections gave parents the opportunity to judge the politicians, while access to the press offered both individuals and groups the opportunity to discuss and appraise policy matters. Nor should we overlook the fact that groups of teachers, parents, governors and politicians were not mutually exclusive in their membership.

Perhaps surprisingly, in view of the criticisms which had forced the abandonment of its earlier scheme, the charge of inadequate consultation was again levied when Manchester's reconstituted reorganisation sub-committee, chaired by John Elliot, reported in November 1964. Some city head teachers again complained that they had not been adequately informed of the recommendations (broadly similar to the previous ones), contemplating a mixture of all-through and two-tier comprehensives, with a sixth-form college serving small feeder schools in one district. The proposals were not well-received either by LEA administrators or the Manchester Labour Group, who continued to prefer the uniform all-through comprehensive scheme (Fiske, 1982, p. 23).

As far as the Education Chairman, Frank Hatton, was concerned, Elliot had failed in what was his final chance to work in partnership with the Labour Group. Hatton, together with his political allies Norman Morris (a university lecturer) and Maurice Pariser (a solicitor), therefore unilaterally sketched out the broad outline of a scheme, to which Elliot was required to add details.

The decision to dispense with traditional committee and sub-committee structures inevitably prompted the charge that the guidelines produced by the triumvirate were 'more the result of successful pressure grouping than the will of a city' (*TES*, 28 May 1965), but it is clear that the ideological clash between Manchester's Socialist council leaders and its preservationist CEO had produced a stalemate. In June 1965 a detailed plan appeared, allegedly prepared by Elliot 'almost at the dictation of Mr Hatton and against his own advice' (*Guardian*, 22 June 1965). The 11+ examination was to be held for the last time in 1966, and in September of the following year 29 comprehensives would open. Of these, 23 were to be 11–18 schools (including a number of split-site schools on two or three sites), and the remaining six comprehensives were to be formed by grouping 'junior' and 'senior' high schools, with pupils transferring at the age of 14. Less than a year after Michael Stewart had censured Bristol, Hatton correctly gambled that Stewart's successor, Tony Crosland (a known advocate of all-through comprehensives who was working on a circular to hasten LEA compliance in ending selection), would agree that Manchester's extra-ordinary local circumstances necessitated a heavy-handed approach.

In some ways, this reorganisation plan, which bore the fingerprints of Labour politicians, drew rather less contempt from the opposition than might have been expected. The Conservative spokesperson, Dr Kathleen Ollerenshaw, a well-known and respected educationist and *TES* columnist, did compare Hatton's scheme unfavourably with one proposed by Elliot, which would have initially placed 76 per cent of Manchester secondary school children in comprehensives, permitting 'a process of learning by experience how best to organise schools in Manchester on comprehensive lines without making an all-out plunge into the unknown, in unsuitable conditions'. Norman Morris, how-ever, dismissed Elliot's preferred solution as one which sought to preserve 'all the nice, suburban middle-class grammar schools in south Manchester' (*Guardian*, 22 June 1965). Elliot's only contribution to the debate was to muse ambiguously that he had never questioned the right of education committees to instruct him. But the *TES* was scathing of Labour's *fait accompli*, noting that, at the Education Committee's June meeting, 'Dr Ollerenshaw was heard out, as she was bound to be, with that bored patience only possible to those who are sure of getting their own way no matter what anybody says' (*TES*, 26 June 1965). The Manchester plan was duly adopted as council policy and forwarded to the DES for consideration, just a few days before the publication of Circular 10/65 in July 1965.

By this time, preparations were well under way in Bristol for the launch of its newly approved plan for neighbourhood comprehensives, due to operate throughout most of the city from September. DES objections were confined to the *presentation* rather than the content of the proposals, yet serious consideration of the merits of the plan was still sidelined by the continuing controversy concerning the position of the direct-grant schools and the status of the maintained grammar schools. The most significant hostility again came from the *Bristol Evening Post*, which, in June, carried a commissioned – and devastating – assessment of the Bristol plan by Professor Boris Ford, Dean of the School of Educational Studies at the University of Sussex. The 'Ford

Report', as it became known locally, argued that neighbourhood schools were likely to *prevent*, rather than enhance a diversity in intake, and that Bristol 'has gone forward with astonishingly little detailed study, research experiment, testing and redesigning which would have seemed essential in so large a project' (*Bristol Evening Post*, 23 June 1965). However, it is unlikely that, just over two months before the plan was due to come into operation, either Professor Ford or the *Evening Post* had any real expectation of persuading the authority to reconsider, nor indeed did they. At its next meeting, the Education Committee 'noted' the appearance of the Ford Report,[24] and hastily moved on to the business of implementing the scheme, which, owing to financial and other impediments, had been subject to minor modifications. Two-tier secondary schools (rather than 11–18 institutions) were to be a feature of the eastern side of Bristol from September 1965, but more disappointing for Labour was the need to retain selective schooling in the central areas of the city.

POLITICS AND REORGANISATION: CIRCULAR 10/65

Circular 10/65 was, of course, a non-statutory directive, making it inevitable that some authorities would not respond positively or, indeed, would not respond at all. Equally inevitably, given that at the time of the circular's appearance the vast majority of LEAs were Labour-controlled (Simon, 1991, pp. 284–5), some opposition parties at the local level were bound to resist plans for comprehensive reorganisation. This appears to have been a particularly urban phenomenon, where education debates were rather more politicised than was the general experience in the shires.

Labour's political opponents in Bristol, the Citizen Party – nominally independent, but Conservative in all but name – were quick to capitalise upon the ambiguity which had been exposed by central Bristol remaining selective. The Citizens said that, if they were elected, they would repurchase places in the seven direct-grant schools, and saw no reason why the surviving grammar schools should not co-exist alongside comprehensives, offering places on a competitive basis to every Bristol child, rather than just drawing upon the local catchment area.

Supporters of comprehensive education debated whether Labour's 1965 circular was well-advised in *requesting*, rather than requiring, LEAs to submit reorganisation plans. Pressure from the backbenches of his own party forced Secretary of State Crosland to consider, in 1966, whether to legislate in order to protect the national government's education policy from the uncertainties of local democracy. However, this option was passed over in favour of allowing enthusiastic LEAs with acceptable reorganisation proposals to lead by example. According to one (anonymous) officer of the Manchester LEA (an authority that had opted for the Secretary of State's preferred model of 11–18 schools), 'Crosland needed some LEAs to show comprehensive reorganisation could be done', and, indeed, offered a financial 'sweetener' to ease administrative costs (quoted in Ranson, 1990, p. 49).[25]

Having received DES approval for the Hatton plan in June 1966, Manchester was able to embark upon a 14-month period of preparation. The rapidity with which the plan was drawn up, adopted as council policy, submitted to and approved by the DES is remarkable, and illustrates the extent to which the educational objectives of Socialist central and local governments had converged by the mid-1960s. Altogether, there had been an interval of just 13 months between the first revelation of Councillor Hatton's proposals and their acceptance by the Secretary of State.

Rapid progress in Manchester contrasted sharply with the situation in Leeds, where, despite the existence of similar ideological objectives, progress was faltering owing to an intractable impediment. Though the Labour-controlled City Council accepted the long-term desirability of establishing all-through comprehensives, they were faced with the constraints of utilising existing (invariably small) secondary school buildings. It was with reluctance that the Labour Chairman of Education, Councillor Josh Walsh, backed a two-tier interim scheme, which had been recommended by the reorganisation working party in June 1965 (*TES*, 19 June 1965).[26] This appeared to him to offer the only prospect of abandoning the 11+ within the foreseeable future. But powerful representations by the NUT, the Headmasters' Association and the local CASE branch forced the Education Committee to reconsider the case for all-through schools, which had been widely preferred by other large, urban authorities.

The working party was reconvened with a brief to produce a scheme which included 11–18 comprehensive schools wherever feasible, and to identify two-tier solutions elsewhere. Tiered reorganisation models, of the kind mentioned in Circular 10/65 (which took account of a number of the administrative and logistical impediments which were present in Leeds) were clearly not admired by Walsh or his colleagues.

They found it difficult to contemplate the *comprehensive school* as anything other than an 11–18 institution. The working party's final report of May 1966 was, as a consequence, backward-looking and non-uniform. It anticipated the introduction of an interim plan in 1968, when 50 per cent of Leeds secondary school children would be accommodated either in one of the city's existing 11–18 comprehensives or in all-through schools created as a result of mergers. A two-tier system, with transfer at 13, would operate elsewhere, but this feature would gradually be eroded to produce uniformity by 1981. It was further announced that the denominational authorities had agreed to draw up proposals consistent with those of the LEA,[27] and that the practice of taking up places in the local direct-grant schools would cease once reorganisation had been effected. Since there were only two such schools in Leeds, this decision caused comparatively few ripples.

Leeds also contrasts with Bristol and Manchester on the question of consultation and accountability. Having devised its proposed scheme, the Leeds Education Committee moved swiftly to print and distribute an explanatory pamphlet for parents of children likely to be affected by reorganisation,[28] and in the autumn of 1966 embarked upon a series of 22 public meetings across the city. There is no evidence of co-ordinated opposition to comprehensive schools, either from parent action groups or the local press (as had been the case in both Manchester and, particularly, Bristol), but the public forums were not altogether comfortable affairs for the LEA. Fears were expressed about the two-tier system, and the relatively ill-equipped junior high schools' abilities to attract top quality teachers. Although they acknowledged that the LEA was 'sincerely concerned about the difficulties these schools will face', Leeds AASE, which supported the interim plan as a kind of necessary evil, ominously warned that 'no precise plans for overcoming them have been made'.[29]

COUNTER-REFORMATION AVERTED

The positions that these three Socialist-controlled, pro-comprehensive, urban authorities had reached by the spring of 1967, when Labour lost control in each of the cities, invite comparison. Bristol was, by this time, as comprehensive as it could hope to be, given, first, that financial impediments prevented the replacement or modification of the four grammar schools in the central area of the city, and, second, that a relatively high proportion of Bristol children were outside the LEA-maintained sector in independent or direct-grant schools. Bristol's opposition Citizen Party was, however, publicly committed to revitalising grammar schools (thus relegating comprehensives to the status of *de facto* secondary moderns). In Manchester, the Education Committee's plans were also being challenged by local Conservatives, while the Leeds Labour Party was in the even more unhappy position of still awaiting a decision regarding the acceptability of its imperfect plan.

The Conservative election victories in Manchester, Leeds and Bristol were all convincing, and (as in other English and Welsh large cities) speculation focused upon the prospect of a reversal of comprehensivisation. The change of political control in cities which, like London and Liverpool, as well as Bristol and Manchester, were pioneering a full-scale comprehensive reorganisation, ensured that 'if there was a real, popular movement in support of the divided system, now was the time for it to exert its power' (Simon, 1991, p. 294). The fact that the Conservatives *did not* seek to put the clock back in Manchester, Bristol or Leeds (or elsewhere, in fact) deserves careful consideration.

As expected, Bristol's newly installed Conservative (or Citizen) administration quickly moved to take up places in the city's seven direct-grant schools once again,[30] but the experience of almost two years of operating a comprehensive system throughout most of the city had apparently changed perceptions about the desirability of reintroducing selection at 11+. Bristol Conservatives actually began several building projects, which permitted the *reduction* of selective schools in the central districts during the years 1967–70. During the same years, Manchester Conservatives demonstrated unexpectedly protective instincts towards their comprehensive inheritance.

Interestingly, Norman Reece, Bristol's Chairman of Education, was privately reported to have said that to revert to selection would be tantamount to 'committing political suicide'.[31] This was the very same view expressed by Dame Kathleen Ollerenshaw, Manchester's new Chairman of Education. For years, she had publicly opposed the principle of comprehensive education, but was now forced reluctantly to concede that public support for LEA selective schools had all but disappeared. Manchester's secondary school reorganisation therefore occurred, on schedule, at the beginning of September 1967, when the new chairman philosophically reflected that the preservationists' cause was lost:

all notices of closure were meticulously posted and adequate time given for public protests ... By March 1967 heads of the reorganised schools had already been appointed and the forms on which choice of schools were to be made had been distributed to parents. Before the 1967 May elections most senior members of staffs had been appointed to the new schools. The Conservatives now have a majority of one on the Education Committee. To reverse plans between June and September, even if this had been possible legally which it was not, would have piled chaos upon chaos and would not have been in the best interests of the children.[32]

Ollerenshaw now believed that the main objective should be to maintain high academic standards in the comprehensives, as well as bolstering those remaining selective elements outside the LEA system (including the High School of Art and Music, the direct-grant schools and those denominational institutions which had opted to retain their former admissions policies).

This raises an important point, particularly applicable to both Bristol and Manchester, where comparatively large numbers of schools controlled by bodies other than the LEA continued to operate. In both these cities, parents who objected to the reorganisation of secondary education had the opportunity to remove their children from the maintained education sector and send them to one of the direct-grant, independent or aided schools. In Bristol, it has been suggested that, after the initial furore of 1965, reorganisation was uncontentious:

> the acceptance of comprehension may be partly due to the proved value of the comprehensives themselves, partly due to the presence of Clifton College[33] and seven direct grant schools, which gave a fair alternative choice to comprehension.
>
> (Brace, 1971, p. 135)

The continuing existence of *alternatives* to comprehensive education, even for parents of modest means, may help to explain why incoming Conservative administrations in Manchester, Bristol and elsewhere encountered no significant demands to put the clock back in favour of a grammar school revival in 1967. It is likely that at least some of those parents who had resisted comprehensive reorganisation in the early- and mid-1960s no longer had vested interests in the policy decisions of the LEA, having sent their children to be educated elsewhere. Another likely explanation, identified by Ollerenshaw, was the fact that 'parents and public – not to mention teachers – are fed up with upheaval'.[34]

Thus, 1967 marks another watershed in the history of comprehensive education. It had been arrived at in part because Conservatives had realised that 'going comprehensive' did not necessarily imply the creation of vast, impersonal, undisciplined, unstreamed and socially-engineered institutions. Secretary of State Crosland's endorsement of several alternative reorganisation models, together with his approval of certain LEAs' notoriously *uncomprehensive* reorganisation plans (Simon, 1991, p. 282) and the Plowden Report's support for middle-school schemes, ensured that, in a typically British way, comprehensive education shifted from being a term of narrow interpretation to one which suggested flexibility.

Manchester and Bristol had both started (and, in the latter case, largely completed) their reorganisations at a time before this new order had emerged. This was not true, however, of Leeds where, in May 1967, the local Conservative Party assumed council control for the first time since 1953. The decision of Leeds Conservatives to withdraw their predecessors' reorganisation plan, which was still being considered by the DES, came as no surprise. It appeared that the LEA would settle for the contradictory compromise option of gradually upgrading secondary moderns to comprehensive status, while still retaining the city's grammar schools (albeit with selection decided by *guided parental choice*, rather than examination).[35] But the autumn of 1967 witnessed a surprising development, when the LEA unveiled an imaginative proposal for a three-tier system of comprehensive schools. It was, in fact, rather more forward-looking and radical than anything that had emerged during the long years of Labour control, when idealism had been more in evidence than pragmatism. The scheme, which leaned heavily upon the experience of parts of the neighbouring West Riding (see Chapter 7), the pioneer of 9–13 middle schools, was largely the work of two men; the Chairman of the Education Committee, Patrick Crotty, and CEO John Taylor (a more progressive figure than his predecessor and namesake, George).

The widespread popularity of tiered reorganisation schemes in Tory-controlled LEAs during the late 1960s suggests that Crotty's admiration for comprehensive education was far from unique, but middle-school schemes had hitherto widely been considered as being more appropriate to shire counties and smaller urban districts than to large cities. Crotty succeeded in winning over inexperienced Tory colleagues on the Education Committee, persuasively arguing that the plan merely involved a modest *reorientation* of grammars to become upper-tier schools (Fenwick and Woodthorpe, 1980, pp. 24–5).

The prospect of abolishing selection without requiring existing grammar schools to close, amalgamate or lose their responsibilities for preparing students for public examinations and university was irresistibly appealing to many Tory-controlled LEAs at this time, and also attracted the party leader, Edward Heath and the Shadow Education Minister, Sir Edward Boyle (Crook, 1993, pp. 56–8). Moreover, this was a solution for which Leeds' existing small schools would be ideal enablers, facilitating change, rather than the impediments which they had long seemed to be. Every existing grammar school (plus a small number of the better-equipped secondary moderns) would become an upper-tier school with (generally) existing primary schools and secondary moderns becoming the lower- and middle-tier schools, respectively.

The Crotty–Taylor plan quickly generated interest, but the deliberate style of local government in Leeds, which tended to militate against rapid educational change, determined that it was not until January 1970 that the plan was forwarded to the DES for approval. In the meantime, there was a period of consultation which was less token than that pursued in either Manchester or Bristol. Again, this appears to be consistent with the notion that the process of educational policy-making was not politicallydriven to the same extent in Leeds as in the other two cities. Both Labour (in 1966) and the Conservatives (in 1969–70) sought the opinions of Leeds' teachers and administrators, as well as organising public forums, before submitting their reorganisation plans. However, this concern for good public relations and procedural propriety had a cost in terms of time. Almost five years elapsed between the announcement and the implementation of the Leeds plan, contrasting markedly with the situation in Manchester, where Councillor Hatton's proposals had progressed from the idea stage to reality in less than two years.

The national political context in which the Leeds plan was considered also differed from that which had prevailed during the 1960s. It has been amusingly recalled that, when an early summer general election was called in 1970, Alderman Crotty became so anxious that the plan would be rejected by Margaret Thatcher (who was poised to become Secretary of State in the event of a Conservative victory), that he 'repeatedly pestered' Secretary of State Edward Short and his minister Alice Bacon, by telephoning them daily at the Department and at their private homes (Fenwick and Woodthorpe, 1980, p. 25).

Once installed as Secretary of State, Thatcher admitted to reservations about the 'totally comprehensive' nature of the Leeds scheme, a description which apparently also alarmed a number of Crotty's Council colleagues, who had been unaware that the plan was so far-reaching (Fenwick and Woodthorpe, 1980, pp. 26–7). Permission to reorganise was reluctantly given, although, ironically, as in Manchester five years earlier, the task of overseeing reorganisation in September 1972 did not fall to the party which had developed the proposals. Labour won back control of the City Council in May of that year, and chose only to amend the plan to the extent of removing the element of co-operation with the direct-grant schools, which had been formerly included as a minor concession to those who opposed total comprehensivisation.

POINTS OF COMPARISON

By way of summary, three brief observations are offered, based on the content of this chapter. First, it may be observed that, in purely chronological terms, the transition to comprehensive education in Leeds (in 1972) was slower than either Bristol's (1965) or Manchester's (1967). However, any tendency to dismiss Leeds as a laggard authority must be countered by recalling that in September 1972 the city introduced an absolute and uniform comprehensive scheme which did not include any split-site schools. This happened, it might be noted, at a time when, despite Bristol's early and highly publicised rejection of selection, grammar and secondary modern schools were still operating in the north-central and eastern areas of that city. In fact, the complete reorganisation of the Bristol LEA had not been completed before its education powers were assumed by Avon County Council in 1974. Although the eastern division did eventually go comprehensive in 1973, Secretary of State Margaret Thatcher (1970–74) rejected building plans which would have permitted the extension of comprehensive education in the north-central area, and also used her Section 13 powers to prevent the reorganisation of the city's Roman Catholic schools.[36]

Clearly, Leeds was able to implement such a far-reaching reorganisation only because of the new reorganisation options which existed after 1965. If the city had effected a change to comprehensive education earlier, it would have been restricted to a Manchester-style solution, with 'linked' schools, often considerable distances apart.

Of the three cities, therefore, it was Leeds which achieved the more

103

complete and satisfactory reorganisation. Despite leading the 'break-out' (Simon, 1991, pp. 271–82) of local authorities away from selection during the early- and mid-1960s, Bristol and Manchester could only contemplate going comprehensive in terms of creating all-through schools. Leeds, on the other hand, was an unwitting beneficiary of a changing climate which saw a reappraisal of traditional notions of the comprehensive school. The key enabling factor for Leeds, it might be argued, was the waiving of transfer at 11. The three-tier system was the least controversial method of going comprehensive, since it made efficient use of existing school buildings and did not involve the controversial closure or amalgamation of grammar schools.

Second, it is interesting to note that Bristol, Manchester and Leeds each consciously opted for an *instant* rather than a piecemeal reorganisation. Each also sought to impose a uniform pattern of secondary school throughout their administrative unit. The overnight reorganisation appealed to those who argued that the co-existence of selective and comprehensive schools within an LEA, even for a temporary period, was damaging, and that reorganisation should be all or nothing to guard against the possibility of piecemeal expansion plans being subverted by unpredictable impediments, such as political change and the withdrawal of anticipated financial support. This type of reasoning appears to have been particularly prevalent in (though not exclusive to) urban authorities, where contrasting or unequal neighbourhood educational facilities might be seen as harder to justify than temporary variations in a shire county's educational provision.

Third, each of the LEAs discussed here reflects the idea that, despite the checks and balances of English and Welsh local democracy (designed to promote consultation and collective decision-making), individuals often played key roles in determining LEA reorganisation policy. Harold Sylvester, Bristol's long-serving CEO, for example, emerges as a key enabler. Sylvester was resolutely determined that tripartism was wrong, at a time (the late 1940s) when it was unfashionable, even in Socialist circles, to attack the post-war orthodoxy. Without him, there is reason to suppose that Bristol would neither have launched experimental comprehensives nor effected the reorganisation of its remaining selective schools as early as 1965. As a CEO who formed a strong and productive working relationship with his Education Chairmen, Sylvester contrasts markedly with George Taylor of Leeds and Norman Fisher and John Elliot of Manchester, whose preservationist tendencies at times acted as an unwelcome brake upon the aspirations of local politicians.

The independent actions of these individuals produced outcomes that sometimes violated the stereotypical view of the relationship between party political affiliations and comprehensivisation. Education chairmen and other local politicians did not always conveniently fit their expected roles as enablers of or impediments to change.

It is true that political support for comprehensive schools came first, and most consistently, from local Labour politicians, such as Lady [Shena] Simon and Frank Hatton (Manchester), R. St John Reade and the Rev. Frederick Vyvyan-Jones (Bristol). But, it was Conservative politicians in all three cities, after 1967, whose actions ensured that comprehensive reorganisation was not reversed or averted. In particular, Patrick Crotty (Leeds), a maverick Conservative Chairman of Education, emerges as a key enabler. Not only was Crotty the author of the Leeds scheme, he was also its saviour since, by the early summer of 1970, he was 'desperately trying to and succeeding in steering his reorganisation scheme clear of an incoming Conservative Secretary of State' (Fenwick and Woodthorpe, 1980, p. 27).

NOTES

1. PRO 152/328, memorandum of a meeting at the ministry, 27 July 1948.
2. MCL, M301/2/2/17, Papers of Alderman Sir Maurice Pariser, Lady Simon to Pariser, 19 May 1954.
3. BRO, Education Committee Labour Group minutes, 15 July 1949.
4. Ibid., 6 Sept. 1949.
5. Ibid., 21 May 1952.
6. MCL, M301/2/2/17, Pariser Papers, Lady Simon to Pariser, 19 May 1954.
7. Ibid., 3 Nov. 1954.
8. Ibid., 7 March 1955.
9. Ibid., 1 Sept. 1955.
10. Ibid., 13 October 1955.
11. MCL, MS14 addl./4/25/1, Lady Simon Papers, Joan Simon, *Shena Simon: Feminist and Educationalist* (privately printed, 1986), p. 23.
12. BRO, Education Committee Labour Group minutes, 20 July and 12 Oct. 1956.
13. LCA, *Report of the City Council on Education for the year ended 31 July 1958*, p. 18. The document appears as an appendix to the 1958 Education Committee minutes.
14. BRO, Education Committee Labour Group minutes, 12 June 1963 and 5 Sept. 1963.
15. LCA, Education Department files (Accession), 3560, 2/2, *Reorganisation of Secondary Education in Leeds: a memorandum considered by the Committee* (Nov. 1963); Education Committee minutes, 27 Nov. 1963.
16. WUMRC, CASE archives, MSS 236/3, Leeds AASE file, *The Future of Secondary organisation in Leeds*, n.d.
17. LCA, 3560, 2/2, *Draft Policy Statement on Educational Reorganisation by the Leeds City Council Conservative Group*, n.d.
18. BRO, Education Committee Labour Group minutes, 30 Dec. 1963.

19. A further three comprehensive schools opened in September 1964, raising the proportion of Bristol secondary school children in comprehensives to 64 per cent.
20. WUMRC, MSS 58/6, Incorporated Association of Head Masters archives, H.W. Simmons, Head of Bedminster Down Comprehensive School, Bristol to E.H. Goddard, Acting Secretary, IAHM, 6 July 1964.
21. WUMRC, MSS 236/3, CASE archives, Bristol AASE file, *The Bristol Plan for the Organisation of Secondary Education*, November 1964.
22. BRO, Education Committee Labour Group minutes, 4 Nov. 1964.
23. Specifically, Stewart's concern centred upon the apparent lack of parental consultation, but the report in *Hansard* (27 Nov. 1964, col. 1792, para. 1) increased the authority's discomfort by mistakenly printing 'teachers' instead of 'parents'.
24. BRO, Education Committee minutes, 24 June 1965.
25. If it is true that Manchester received preferential funding, it was rather less conspicuous than this comment might lead us to believe, since no new, purpose-built comprehensives were established in Manchester. Some of these schools 'were no better than four-form entry secondary moderns with extensions to make them non-selective added in a single building operation' (Fiske, 1982, p. 16).
26. LCA, 3560, 2/2, Reorganisation of Secondary Education Sub-Committee minutes, 15 Sept. 1965.
27. ULBL, AEC archives, E74, statement by the Ripon Diocesan Education Committee (1966).
28. LCA, 3560, 2/2, City of Leeds Education Department, *From Eleven-Plus to Comprehensive: A Guide to the Reorganisation of Secondary Education in Leeds*, July 1966.
29. WUMRC, Mss 236/3, Leeds AASE *Newsletter* VII (Oct. 1966).
30. BRO, Education Committee minutes, 25 May 1967.
31. BP, MS 660/25899, Papers of Lord Boyle, Boyle to William Whitelaw, Opposition Chief Whip, 16 Nov. 1967.
32. Ibid., MS 660/25855, Statement by the Chairman on the Reorganisation of Secondary Schools in Manchester, Oct. 1967, enclosed with letter from Ollerenshaw to Boyle, (?) Sept. 1967. See also Simon, 1991, p. 295.
33. Clifton College was, and is, possibly the most famous of Bristol's independent sector schools.
34. Ibid., letter.
35. WUMRC, Mss 236/3, Leeds AASE memorandum, *Some Questions about the Conservative Proposals for Secondary Education in Leeds*, June 1967.
36. BRO, Secondary Education Sub-Committee minutes, 19 July 1971 and 18 Sept. 1973.

6

A Calculated Educational Reorganisation: Stoke-on-Trent

The small working-class Midlands city of Stoke-on-Trent would appear to be, at first sight, an unlikely pioneer of educational innovation. However, it was the first English LEA to establish a system of city-wide middle schools of the type recommended in the Plowden Report of 1967, and the first to establish a purpose-built sixth-form college. Such innovation thus makes Stoke-on-Trent an important case study for historians of comprehensive reorganisation.

'THE EARLY STAGES'

Formed from an alliance of the six towns of Tunstall, Burslem, Hanley, Fenton, Longton and Stoke, located on the North Staffordshire coalfield, the city has been the home of the English pottery industry since the eighteenth century. Although the number of workers employed in the coal-mining and pottery industries had declined significantly by 1945, compensating employment opportunities arose in new, smaller industries, including glazing, engineering, electrical goods, vehicle components and chemicals.

The post-war industrial growth of the area was complemented by educational developments. In 1949, the newly established University College of North Staffordshire, based in Stoke's neighbouring town of Newcastle-under-Lyme, was granted a charter allowing it to award its own degrees, rather than being restricted to preparing students for external University of London awards. Shortly after this, in 1951, the appointment of Henry Dibden, a young and highly able Chief Education Officer for Stoke, marked the beginning of a long period of planning for the reorganisation of secondary schools within the authority. Dibden was to remain at the helm until the authority's education powers were assumed by Staffordshire County Council in 1974.

By 1955, members of the solidly Labour Stoke-on-Trent Education Committee had begun to voice serious reservations about the tripartite system which, they believed, militated against 'late developers'. In July of that year, Dibden prepared a report at the request of the Committee, suggesting that the city could introduce a measure of comprehensive reorganisation. The CEO's thinking reflected the widespread belief that comprehensive schools had to be huge institutions if they were to include facilities which were comparable with the grammar and technical schools and offer courses as varied as those available in the secondary moderns. As Dibden later recalled, however, there were concerns about following the example of authorities such as London and Coventry, which had established 'experimental' comprehensives. It was recognised that so long as the 11+ examination continued to operate and grammar schools remained in existence, any comprehensive school would be deprived of a significant proportion of more able pupils:

> ... the clamour to build one comprehensive school as an experiment had to be countered by the argument that if you are going comprehensive you should go completely or not at all; that by its very nature the comprehensive will not harmonise with other forms (Dibden, 1965, p. 67).

In spite of these potential disadvantages, the Education Committee remained determined that its commitment to the principle of comprehensive education should be reflected in the authority's future building programme. At the end of October 1965, it was decided that a new comprehensive school should be erected at Bentilee, and Blurton Secondary Modern School should become comprehensive after an extension had been built. Both schools, it was maintained, should have a technical orientation.[1] A special sub-committee was established to draw up detailed plans, but their over-zealous efforts to ensure that parental wishes were accommodated stretched notions of *comprehensiveness* beyond credulity. It was proposed that mechanisms should permit the transfer of children from Blurton to a grammar school both at 13+ and at the sixth-form stage, and Bentilee would have a 'grammar stream' which would also be open to those outside the normal catchment area.[2]

In their efforts to offend nobody, the Education Committee's extraordinary proposals achieved precisely the opposite effect. However, reservations about the content of the plan were secondary to the 'storm of criticism' (Dibden, 1965, p. 68) concerning the lack of teacher consultation involved in the planning process. A series of protests by teachers, parents and the press resulted in the total with-drawal of the plan (O'Rourke, 1978, p. 44).

This setback did nothing to dent the Education Committee's resolve to widen opportunities for secondary school children to follow examination courses. As the former Chairman of the Education Committee put it, too many youngsters sought 'to follow their parents into pits and pots at the earliest opportunity'.[3] With fewer than 15 per cent of Stoke children typically proceeding to a grammar or technical school, there was great pressure on places in these institutions. A timely, but short-term remedy seemed to arise out of the Conservative government's White Paper of 1958 (Ministry of Education 1958) which high-lighted the need to raise the status of secondary modern schools in the light of technological advances (Simon, 1991, pp. 203–4). In September 1959, six secondary moderns each accepted a selective intake of 30 pupils who would, for the first time in Stoke, follow GCE O-Level courses in these schools, henceforth to be known as *junior highs* (Dibden, 1965, p. 68).

Having initiated this relatively uncontroversial experiment, it was anticipated that, in due course, a high proportion of the new intake would seek to transfer to a school offering A-Level courses, and that provision would have to be made to accommodate these children. The authority decided to redesignate Longton school, which was being built as a four-form entry boys' grammar school, as a three-form entry co-educational grammar school, with provision for a sixth form of 360, equivalent to the total number of pupils in the rest of the school. The Ministry of Education was not uncritical of this proposal, but 'grumblingly agreed' (Dibden, 1965, p. 68) to permit pupils from the junior high schools who stayed on after the minimum leaving age to join regular sixth-formers (who had passed the 11+ exam) at Longton in September 1963 (City of Stoke-on-Trent Education Committee, 1964, p. 102).

This innovation was regarded as an important, but *experimental* step towards widening educational opportunities. The long-term aim remained the establishment of a city-wide network of comprehensive schools. Stoke-on-Trent had not suffered severe wartime bomb damage, however, and there was little prospect of obtaining the necessary funds for new buildings. All-through comprehensive schools could only be created through amalgamations, a prospect which the Education Committee found neither practicable nor desirable. In any case, by the early 1960s the orthodox view that a comprehensive school had to be a large institution with in excess of 1,000 pupils on the roll was increasingly being challenged by educationists and administrators alike.

The adoption of the 'Leicestershire plan' (see Chapter 7) was considered to be an attractive option by some, because it seemed to offer the prospect of better staying-on rates and would keep opposition from the pro-grammar schools lobby to a minimum. Doubts remained, however, about the cost-effectiveness of having a sixth form in every upper school and about the motivation of children who remained in the high school for their final year (rather than transferring to an upper school). Additionally, there were concerns that higher parental aspirations would ensure that middle-class children would be more likely to transfer to the upper school. In a solidly working-class area with low achievement and staying-on rates such as Stoke-on-Trent, it is easy to see why this negative aspect of the Leicestershire plan weighed heavily. There was, however, a further alternative, to which CEO Dibden and the Education Committee were greatly attracted, particularly in view of the anticipated developments at Longton High School. This was the so-called Croydon plan (Donnison, Chapman *et al.*, 1965, pp. 201–29), which contemplated a single sixth-form college, serving a network of 11–16 non-selective schools throughout the city.

At the beginning of 1963, Bob Cant, the Chairman of the Education Committee, prepared a memorandum for his fellow committee members. He reported that he had been trying to familiarise himself with developments in the educational systems of western Europe, the USSR and the United States, and that he had concluded that the most innovative developments in education for 16–18-year-olds were occurring in the 'junior colleges' of the United States. Such institutions, Cant maintained, represented a stepping stone between broad, general secondary education and higher education.

In order to investigate more thoroughly the possible application of these ideas in Stoke-on-Trent, Cant proposed that he and CEO Dibden should undertake an eight-week study tour of the USA. The costs of the proposed visit, he argued, would be easily justifiable in terms of the amount of information which the investigation would yield.[4] As a lecturer at the University College of North Staffordshire (soon to become the University of Keele), Cant valued the importance of research, and, as an economist, he particularly understood that a cost-benefit analysis could usefully inform future discussions about reorganisation and building costs. His motives were not universally understood, however.

The Education Committee resolved to accept Cant's proposal, but the local evening newspaper was less than enthusiastic, giving sympathetic coverage to the Conservative opposition spokesman's view that the visit would serve no purpose, except to waste an estimated £1,200 of ratepayers' money (Stoke-on-Trent *Evening Sentinel*, 31 January 1963). A savage editorial by the newspaper, entitled 'Is this journey necessary?', observed that the Education Committee 'have shown themselves to be insensitive to local public and professional criticism of the pattern of educational reorganisation which they are imposing on the city', and concluded: 'the education authority have not advanced any convincing reason why this journey is necessary. It should be called off' (*Evening Sentinel*, 1 February 1963).

The objections went unheeded and Dibden and Cant's visit went ahead in the spring of 1963.

FROM 'AMERICAN JOURNEY' TO PLOWDEN, 1963-67

The local controversy surrounding the study tour did have the effect of prompting a decision that a detailed report on the visit should be prepared. The outcome was *American Journey* (Stoke-on-Trent City Council, 1963), an impressive 80-page booklet which describes in detail discussions with American government representatives, academics, teachers and administrators during Dibden and Cant's whistle-stop coast-to-coast tour. In addition to observations and recommendations about organisational matters, the booklet also included observations on pedagogy and learning resources. These included far-sighted ideas about the possible applications of closed circuit television, teaching machines and language laboratories. Recommendations regarding aspects of school design, assessment, pastoral care and timetabling were also included, and, as an English LEA document from the early 1960s, *American Journey* is uniquely forward-looking. It was to become widely read by academics, local politicians and education administrators. The report confirmed the authority's desire to establish a Croydon-style sixth-form college, a scheme which was, as the Education Committee's annual report for 1963 acknowledged, much misunderstood:

> as a new and unknown factor and, because, unlike the Leicester-shire plan it involves the complete disappearance of the Grammar Schools, the concept of the 'Junior College' has been the most bitterly opposed ...
> (City of Stoke-on-Trent Education Committee, 1964, p. 107).

111

The Chairman of the Education Committee remained resolute, maintaining in a speech to the North Staffordshire Trades Council that 'if it calls for great changes and upsets a number of people, that is the price we must pay for what we believe is educational progress' (*Evening Sentinel*, 9 April 1964). What was needed, the Education Committee concluded, was a greater articulation of the advantages of the sixth-form college. A break at age 16 would be beneficial, it was argued, in that it would tend to reduce the 'post O-Level neurosis' and would improve staying-on rates. Mindful of the opportunity to establish links with the newly designated University of Keele, it was also argued that such a college would place sixth-form students in an adult learning environment where they could experience lectures, seminars and independent study (City of Stoke-on-Trent Education Committee, 1964, p. 108).

Meanwhile, Dibden, the CEO, devised a plan to enlarge a number of existing LEA schools, bringing them up to six-form entry (except for the denominational schools). The rebuilding programme was to permit older, pre-1910 premises to be evacuated, leaving 23 11–16 high schools in place of 40 existing secondary modern, technical and grammar schools (Education Committee, 1964, pp. 110–12). Earlier thoughts of developing Longton School into the sixth-form college had, since the American visit, been abandoned in favour of the more ambitious objective of creating the country's first purpose-built sixth-form college.

The plan was finalised and forwarded to Whitehall shortly before the end of 1963. Edward Boyle, the Conservative Minister of Education, and an enthusiast for tiered comprehensive school schemes (Crook, 1993) quickly approved the idea of the sixth-form college in principle, but the Ministry reserved judgement on the 11–16 high schools (City of Stoke-on-Trent Education Committee, 1965, p. 13). It was during this period of uncertainty for Stoke that the Ministry of Education was administratively reshaped to become the DES. As it was headed by Secretary of State Quintin Hogg, with Boyle and Lord Newton as junior ministers, the *Evening Sentinel* wryly remarked that the fate of Stoke's scheme now lay in the hands of three old Etonians. Boyle, it was reported, had recently told a prospective Conservative parliamentary candidate for the city that he had 'approved nothing', and the newspaper assured opponents of the plan that 'the field is still open for debate' (*Evening Sentinel*, 10 April 1964).

It was, in fact, another 12 months – by which time Harold Wilson's Labour administration was in power – before the DES finally notified the authority that the 1966–67 building programme would make provision for a new sixth-form college, though for only 750 students rather than 1,250, as stated in the LEA submission. Once again, judgement was reserved on the remainder of the plan, but the *Evening Sentinel* glumly predicted that it was just a matter of time before approval was gained for the 11–16 feeder schools. Bob Cant, the Labour Chairman of Education (and shortly to become MP for Stoke Central), was elated, attributing the success to 'the careful thought which has gone into the preparation of our plan over the past ten years'. By contrast, a Conservative spokesman lamented, 'it means the end of the grammar school system. This is a black day' (*Evening Sentinel*, 23 April 1965).

Three days later, an *Evening Sentinel* editorial urged the local pro-grammar school lobby to accept that 'the game is lost' and that 'it would seem pointless to prolong the agony indefinitely'. Conciliation was still tinged with bitterness, however. The newspaper gave no recognition to the educational merits of the scheme proposed. The fact of the matter, it concluded, was that 'a radically ideological authority' had been 'backed up by the government in power' (*Evening Sentinel*, 26 April 1965).

By this time, a suitable location for the sixth-form college had at last been found, and arrangements were made for a compulsory purchase order for the Fenton Manor site.[5] Much national interest focused on developments in Stoke. Although a small number of other authorities had followed the Croydon reorganisation model, there was, as yet, no purpose-built sixth-form college in England or Wales. The model was by no means universally admired, even among devotees of comprehensive education. Bob Cant, perhaps surprisingly, did not altogether disagree with critics who suggested that the Croydon scheme merely served to *postpone* selection from 11 to 16, and that sixth-form colleges were 'exclusive academic hothouses'. His defence was that:

> ... whilst children in this country are faced with the 'crunch' of external examinations from the age of 16 years onwards, we need to tailor our school system to the realities of the situation.
>
> (*Forum*, 7, 3, 1965, p. 94, letter by Cant)

Within weeks of learning that the sixth-form college could be built, the authority's aspirations were dealt a blow when the DES informed them that their 11–16 school arrangements were unacceptable. Momentarily this decision threatened to abruptly reverse the careful course towards a comprehensive system which the LEA had been following for more than a decade, but two factors were to simplify the task of revising the scheme.

First, in July 1965, Secretary of State Anthony Crosland issued Circular 10/65, which included in an Appendix six possible reorganisation models. As a progressive authority, Stoke was already familiar with all but the most recent of these, namely the three-tier middle-school system, which was being introduced in parts of the West Riding (see Chapter 7). With comparatively inexpensive modifications, Stoke's small school buildings seemed to lend themselves to such a scheme. The second factor that helped to resolve Stoke's dilemma was the fact that, by 1966 it had become clear that Lady Plowden's Committee on Primary Education was attracted to the middle-school idea. In fact, the Stoke-on-Trent Education Committee was to anticipate the 1967 Plowden recommendation that 8 and 12 should be the ages of transfer in their revised proposals of November 1966. The cost-effectiveness of the plan guaranteed its acceptability; just four secondary schools required new annexes in order to facilitate the change (Stoke-on-Trent Education Committee 1974, p. 17).

REORGANISATION COMPLETED

The 5–8, 8–12, 12–16 and sixth-form college plan was formally sanctioned by the DES in August 1967, leaving the authority with the question of whether to 'phase in' the plan at the lower age range or to wait until the sixth-form college building work had been completed. The latter course of action was decided upon, in order to minimise the disruption to children in city schools. By deciding to wait until September 1970 before operating the reorganisation plan, the LEA also allowed itself time to discuss the potentially difficult question of how the city's denominational schools would fit into the proposed scheme. In the light of negotiations with the authority, these schools opted for consistency with the city plan by taking in pupils at age 12, though the two Catholic schools also opted to keep their sixth forms.

The scheduled completion of the new college seemed to be threatened in early 1968, when it was announced that the raising of the school-leaving age to 16 would be postponed for a further three years. The crisis was averted, however, when a city deputation to the DES secured a promise that Stoke would receive the financial assistance which had been anticipated. Ironically, by the time the plan was implemented in September 1970, Labour was out of office, both nationally and locally. As reorganisation approached, there is evidence of some school zoning disputes between parents and the authority (see, for example, *Evening Sentinel*, 14 March 1970), but the opening of the newly erected college was apparently eagerly anticipated by this stage.

When Prime Minister Wilson (performing one of his final public duties before losing office) opened the college in April, he may have had cause to regret his government's decision to limit student places to 750. There were already 900 enrolments for the autumn term, clear evidence of popularity which may help to explain why the new Conservative Education Chairman's promise to re-examine the city's comprehensive system attracted little support. This was certainly the view of Jack Ashley, prospective MP for Stoke South, who warned during the general election campaign that: 'any attempt to turn this Labour achievement into a Tory white elephant will be fiercely resisted by the people of this city' (*Evening Sentinel*, 4 June 1970).

The sixth-form college was a comparatively small component in the large reorganisation which occurred in September, but as the first purpose-built sixth-form college, offering brand new facilities, it is easy to understand why this aspect of the plan attracted most of the publicity. Characteristics of the building revealed the extent to which a number of the more affordable recommendations of *American Journey* had been implemented. In addition to a large, well-stocked library and individual study carrels, there were lecture theatres, open-plan science areas and common rooms. By the standards of school buildings of the time, these were indeed innovative features. More than 30 GCE A-Level subjects were offered to the ablest 16-year-olds, determining that the curriculum attracted at least as much attention as the facilities (Bright, 1972, pp. 22–3).

STEADY COMMITMENT

By the end of the 1960s, advocates of comprehensive education, especially within the parliamentary Labour Party, were sometimes prone to assume that the absence of comprehensive schools within an LEA was indicative of defiance towards the terms of Circular 10/65. This kind of frustrated reasoning undoubtedly influenced Secretary of State Edward Short's decision to frame his Education Bill of 1969. However, the delay in implementing the Stoke scheme cannot be explained by recalcitrance. Beginning soon after the Second World War, there was an unwavering thrust towards comprehensive re-organisation. The delay in implementing the Stoke scheme was due to cautious planning and an uncommon attention to the pedagogical, as well as the organisational aspects of going comprehensive. The prosecution of the Croydon scheme was not the result of an arbitrary decision, but was arrived at after a great deal of discussion and research into alternative models. Able policy-shapers (particularly CEO Henry Dibden and Bob Cant, Stoke's Education Committee Chairman during the early and mid-1960s), good relations with the voluntary school providers, realistic timetables and, after initial difficulties in the late 1950s, co-operation from teacher associations, all helped to facilitate the transition to comprehensive education in Stoke-on-Trent. In many ways, this might be represented as an ideal example of how to go about reorganising an educational system. Whatever one's view of the *form* taken by the reorganisation, the *process* by which it was carried out must be admired.

NOTES

1. Stoke-on-Trent Education Committee minutes, 26 Oct. 1955. The minutes are now housed at the Staffordshire County Council Education Offices, Stoke-on-Trent.
2. Secondary Education and the Comprehensive School sub-committee minutes, 16 Nov. 1955.
3. Letter from Bob Cant to David Crook, 25 Nov. 1991.
4. The full text of the memorandum appears in an appendix to *American Journey: A Report on the Visit to the United States of America, April–June 1963, by the Chairman of the Education Committee and the Chief Education Officer, Stoke-on-Trent with comment and recommendations* (Stoke-on-Trent City Council, 1963), pp. 78–80.
5. Education Committee minutes, 28 April 1965.

7

The Innovative County Experience: Leicestershire and the West Riding of Yorkshire

These two county LEAs are widely credited with introducing school reorganisation methods that served to break the impasse faced by those who desired comprehensive reorganisation but were unable to fit all-through schools into buildings designed to serve the selective system. Although these two LEAs developed systems that were similar in many ways, the motivation that lay behind the innovations and the routes followed in evolving the organisational pattern adopted were quite different.

IN SEARCH OF ALTERNATIVES TO TRIPARTISM, 1946–57

So strongly was the doctrine of tripartism pushed by Labour's post-war Education Ministers, Ellen Wilkinson and George Tomlinson, that few LEAs were bold enough to contemplate dissent from the prevailing orthodoxy when preparing their development plans for primary and secondary education. To fly directly in the face of ministerial 'guidance' was hardly an option for a majority of LEAs, but this did not prevent authorities as diverse as Middlesex, the North Riding, Anglesey and London from submitting radical plans for complete or near-complete comprehensivisation. Their successes were mixed. The acceptance of Anglesey's complete reorganisation represented perhaps the greatest *coup* for comprehensive supporters, but even this demonstration that the ministry was supportive towards a policy of developing multilateral schools in rural areas stemmed from *economic*, rather than educational, thinking (Simon, 1991, pp. 104–9).

There is some evidence to suggest that Labour's approach to secure as much tripartite uniformity as possible was resented, not only by radical LEAs whose comprehensive aspirations were denied, but also by some which opposed the forces of centralism impinging upon policy-making at the local level. The notion that children could be allocated to grammar, technical or modern schools that actually enjoyed a parity of esteem was also questioned. One of the most troublesome features of tripartism was the assumption that an 11-year-old's technical aptitudes could be discerned, something which was denied by the most distinguished psychologists and academic experts of the time (Clegg, 1965, p. 75).

A 1947 survey of 54 LEA development plans revealed that more than half were seeking at least a measure of organisational flexibility through the establishment of at least one multilateral or bilateral school (Simon, 1991, p. 107). While it is sometimes assumed that progressive educational attitudes were confined to urban, Labour-controlled areas, this was not so. In Yorkshire, for example, 'a comprehensively-minded Conservative West Riding Committee vigorously opposed the tripartite views of the ... Labour Government' (Clegg, 1965, p. 75). In 1948, the West Riding Education Committee published a development plan which proposed both to develop a number of comprehensives and to abandon the notion of creating specialist technical institutions.

George Tomlinson, the Labour Education Minister, did not stand in the way of the West Riding Education Committee's proposed conversion of a pre-war secondary modern school at Mytholmroyd, primarily because of the school's rural location. In 1950, this school, Calder High, became the county's first nominal comprehensive (Gosden and Sharp, 1978, p. 179), but the term *comprehensive* was hardly appropriate in view of the limited nature of this experiment.

Leading the demands for more radical change in the West Riding was Alec Clegg (CEO, 1945–74), who was, by the early 1950s, becoming increasingly convinced that no meaningful distinctions could be made in terms of intellectual ability between grammar school pupils who had narrowly passed the 11+ and the borderline secondary modern 'failures'. The division was especially unsatisfactory in the south of the county, he reasoned, where pressure on grammar schools was greatest and just 12 per cent of 11-year-olds obtained a place. This prompted an interesting experiment in 1952, when Clegg and the Education Committee supported the initiative of a number of secondary modern heads, allowing them to enter pupils for GCE O-Level examinations in a limited range of subjects (Gosden and Sharp, 1978, p. 175). However, political instability during the decade of the 1950s determined that these early efforts to ameliorate the effects of selection were not a prelude to any sudden abandonment of selection in the West Riding.

Although Clegg was successful, in 1952, in convincing W.M. Hyman, the new Labour Chairman of the Education Committee, that three purpose-built comprehensive schools should be established in the Colne Valley, Penistone and Tadcaster districts, the plans seemed doomed by the return of a Conservative administration three years later. During their 1955 election campaign, local Conservatives (whose previous interest in comprehensive schools had apparently faded) attacked their opponents' intentions of 'wiping out' eight existing grammar schools to facilitate the introduction of the three proposed comprehensive schools. But once in office, preservationist hostility was tempered. A spirit of compromise, permitting the operation of the scheme, prevailed at a meeting in May 1955 attended by Clegg and J. Fuller Smith, the Conservative Education Chairman. Although it has been suggested that personal tensions existed between these two key figures, it was nevertheless agreed 'that the three projected comprehensives should be watched carefully but given every chance to succeed' (Gosden and Sharp, 1978, pp. 178–81).

This was, according to Clegg, a 'noble gesture' on Fuller Smith's part, permitting the Colne Valley comprehensive school to open on schedule in 1956, with the other two following two years later. However, approval was only secured in return for an exacting agreement that, in future, the establishment of comprehensive schools would not involve the closure or redesignation of existing grammar schools, and could only be contemplated in areas of the county where there was no grammar school (Gosden and Sharp, 1978, p. 181). The terms of this contract determined that two further comprehensives, approved by West Riding Conservatives for Elland and Settle during the years 1956–58, were comprehensive only in terms of aspiration, and not intake.

Despite their attachment to grammar schools, the Conservative Education Committee did concede that existing methods of selecting pupils at age 11 were unreliable. This led to the 1955 adoption of an experimental scheme in the Thorne district, whereby teacher assessment replaced formal selection tests. The Thorne scheme was quickly extended by West Riding Tories to the Batley district, and thereafter to the traditionally Conservative areas of Cleckheaton and Ripon, after Labour returned to power in 1958. However, Councillor Hyman, who returned as Education Chairman, feared that the Thorne scheme might be seen as a substitute for, rather than a progression towards, comprehensivisation.[1] That fear appeared to be justified, given the significant degree of interest demonstrated by LEAs that wished to soften selection procedures without committing themselves to comprehensive education.

A further alternative to 11+ selection manifested itself in a much smaller and less industrial county than the West Riding in 1957, when Stewart Mason (Director of Education for Leicestershire 1947–71) announced plans for a unique experiment in two county districts. Mason claimed that the idea for a two-tier secondary school scheme came to him in a 'blinding explosion' while he was shaving one morning in early 1957 (*Guardian*, 12 September 1978; Jones, 1988, p. 57). Actually, Robin Pedley, a Leicester University lecturer, had already articulated the same idea in lectures, seminars and at a meeting with the Education Minister, Sir David Eccles, one year earlier (Crook, 1992). Originally a supporter of selection at 11+, Mason became acutely aware, both as a CEO and as the parent of a child who was unsuccessful in the 11+ examination, of the distress which selection often provoked. He was later to reflect that, at the time the Leicestershire experiment was launched,

> a sense of success in a few was being paid for by a sense of failure in many; primary school friendships were severed, brothers and sisters artificially separated. A sense of social injustice was being engendered while reservoirs of talent were doomed to remain untapped. More and more people were coming to see that 11+ reflected an outmoded 'we/they' society (Mason, 1965, p. 52).

These sentiments closely echoed those of Alec Clegg, who shared Mason's interests in the arts and in the processes of education (Simon, 1991, pp. 355–6). Both were also passionate about the importance of high-quality primary education, and were motivated by a desire to remove 'the deadening backwash' (Mason, 1965, p. 52) of the 11+ which had an adverse impact upon the primary curriculum.

Constrained by the inability to bypass the 1944 provision requiring children to transfer from primary to secondary education at the age of 11, the options for change in Leicestershire were limited. Mason had no wish to destroy Leicestershire grammar schools, most of which had long traditions and excellent academic reputations, nor did he consider that huge 'all-through' comprehensive schools, of the kind that had been pioneered in London and elsewhere, were appropriate for a small rural county (Jones, 1988, pp. 56–7). However, as he later explained in a newspaper interview, 'instead of having the schools parallel, as it were, they could be placed one on top of the other' (*Guardian*, 12 September 1978).

Recollections of what happened next vary somewhat, although

there is no doubt that Mason moved with astonishing speed to devise some kind of experiment in non-selective schooling. A retrospective account of the Leicestershire Plan, written in 1965 by the Director himself, stressed the extent to which consultations with primary, secondary modern and grammar school head teachers were characterised by co-operation and a spirit of compromise, and that unanimous recommendations for a pilot scheme were forthcoming from each of these groups.

There is certainly no doubt that the secondary modern schools embraced the proposal and were anxious 'to have the opportunity of removing the stigma of failure from their schools' (Jones, 1988, p. 62). However, one former grammar school head has argued that the tactics used by Mason to achieve uniformity suggested the existence of a *fait accompli*, recalling that the proposal 'was just sprung upon us' (ibid., p. 61). Another head drove round to see every member of his staff personally on a Saturday morning so that their first knowledge of the proposed plan did not come from reading the local press (ibid.). Consultation of this kind would have been wholly inadequate in almost any other English or Welsh LEA, but the peculiarities of Leicestershire's lingering feudal system determined that, so long as administrators such as Mason enjoyed the personal support of key County Councillors, they could exercise extraordinary powers. This was to prove a significant enabler, which assisted the launch of the Leicestershire experiment and the subsequent extension of the county-wide plan.

Mason formed particularly strong alliances with Sir Robert Martin, chairman of both the Leicestershire County Council and the Education Committee, and his successor, Colonel Pen Lloyd. Martin, Jones speculates, may have longed for the county to re-establish its former reputation in the vanguard of forward-looking LEAs, which had endured during the long years of Sir William Brockington's Directorate, between 1903 and 1947. Pen Lloyd, on the other hand, was principally motivated by the desire to challenge the inherent unfairness of the 11+ examination (Jones, 1988, pp. 64–5).

Confident of support from Martin and Lloyd, and satisfied also that he now had a mandate from the county's teaching personnel, Mason drew up a memorandum for the County Council, entitled *The Organisation of Secondary Education in Leicestershire: Suggestions for a Limited Experiment*, requesting permission to pilot a two-tier secondary structure in the Hinckley and Oadby–Wigston districts, from September 1957.

This document listed several advantages in the proposed scheme. First, it directly addressed the increasingly voiced criticism that 11 (or, actually, 10½) was too early an age at which to determine a child's aptitudes. The Leicestershire experiment envisaged all children proceeding from the primary school to their local *high school*, where, upon reaching the age of 14, they could, if they and their parents so wished, transfer to a 14–18 *upper school* to study for GCE examinations. Those students not wishing to transfer would remain in the high school for their final year of compulsory schooling, before seeking employment. Second, calculations offered by the Assistant Director of Education (which assumed that 40 per cent of children would transfer from the high schools to the upper schools) suggested that both pilot districts could reorganise without any necessity for further building. A third advantage – perhaps the masterstroke – was that, by not requiring the grammar schools to amalgamate, close or lose examination work, reorganisation could be achieved without much controversy. Indeed, there was no expectation that these schools should even drop the title 'grammar', unless they so wished.

Significantly, the term 'comprehensive' was not once mentioned in the Director's memorandum. Indeed, two-tier secondary education, Mason skilfully argued, was a means of abolishing selection *without* going comprehensive:

> I believe that such a solution may be possible without wiping out, as the comprehensive system does, the secondary modern schools and the grammar schools but by modifying their function.
>
> (Quoted in Jones, 1989, p. 27)

The appeal of these arguments proved irresistible to County Councillors for whom 'Mason appeared to be promising grammar school education on demand in schools which would be of the acceptable size of 700 pupils' (ibid., p. 27) in the Hinckley and Oadby–Wigston areas. Permission was duly granted for an experiment, which began, as planned, in September 1957. Although one Ministry of Education official believed Mason to be less ambitious than his Education Committee, having no plans to widen the scope of the experiment 'until sufficient time has elapsed for a realistic evaluation of results',[2] this is not the view of Mason's biographer. Pointing to the absence of contingency plans in the event of failure, Donald Jones has observed that 'in Stewart Mason's mind at least, it was a permanent feature and not an experiment' (Jones, 1988, p. 67).

FINANCIAL AND POLITICAL IMPEDIMENTS, 1958–63

The introduction of the 1957 Leicestershire experiment aroused significant national attention. Not surprisingly, it did not go unnoticed in the West Riding where, after 1958, a new Labour administration was anxious to extend the benefits of comprehensive schools. Any comprehensive system for the county would need to utilise the relatively large numbers of small secondary schools, however. Since there was little support for further split-site 11–18 schools (largely on the grounds of transportation and safety), and there was no money for new buildings, a Leicestershire-style two-tier arrangement seemed to offer exciting possibilities for a workable solution.

CEO Alec Clegg disliked three particular aspects of the Leicestershire experiment, however. First, he opposed the retention of a *fast stream*, whereby a small percentage of pupils could transfer from the primary to the high school at age 10, rather than 11. Mason had incorporated that soon-to-be abandoned feature of the experiment as a sop to grammar-school conservatism. Second, Clegg rejected the notion of *guided parental choice* as the sole method of allocating children to upper schools, an arrangement which he felt would discriminate against working-class children from families where high educational aspirations were not the norm. Finally, Clegg felt that two years in the upper school was an insufficient period of preparation for O-Level examinations (Clegg, 1965, p. 76).

The political and administrative structure of the West Riding, where 20 divisional executives in seven county divisions plus the Excepted District of Keighley held sway over important policy matters, contrasted markedly with the simplicity of Leicestershire. Clegg did not possess the same extraordinary power or influence over committee structures that Stewart Mason was able to exercise. Furthermore, he was a more cautious figure. Initially, this aspect of his personality weakened his reputation with local politicians. After Labour's 1958 victory (with a majority of two), several divisional executives expressed frustration at Clegg's delay in responding to requests for comprehensive schemes. His reluctance to acknowledge that the Leicestershire approach was correct for the West Riding also placed a strain upon Clegg's relationship with certain Education Committee members, who had not warmed to his warning that 'it was idle to believe that a pattern of comprehensive schools will evolve within the next twenty-five years' (Gosden and Sharp, 1978, p. 184; quotation from a Policy and Finance Sub-committee memorandum of July 1958). Though some Labour members suspected the CEO of conservatism, this was actually wide of the mark: first, he felt that if the Authority was hurried, it was likely to produce bad schemes which could provide the opponents of comprehensives with just the ammunition they needed. Second, he was afraid that alarm would be caused among the grammar school teachers, and, in a time of teacher shortage, he placed particular importance upon the Authority retaining the services of good graduate staff. Third, and perhaps most important, he was determined to avoid a situation in which a multiplicity of small sixth forms were created. He argued that with a small sixth form it was not possible either to offer a full range of subjects or to attract well-qualified staff (Gosden and Sharp, 1978, p. 184).

Clegg's unwillingness to encourage what he considered to be an unsound reorganisation proposal from the Ecclesfield division, during the late summer of 1958, again raised the question in his critics' minds about how serious his reformist convictions were. It also indicated the need to clarify what, precisely, the obligations of the Director were with regard to the execution of reorganisation policy matters. A meeting between Clegg and W.M. Hyman, the Chairman of Education, helped to ease the strain, but Clegg was forced to concede that if a division decided to embark upon reorganisation, he was obliged to assist, regardless of his own particular recommendations.

The Ecclesfield proposals, which contemplated only *partial* comprehensivisation, were rejected by the ministry, but with Clegg's obligations towards the county divisions and excepted district now clear, four additional proposals to reorganise either exactly or approximately along Leicestershire lines, were forwarded to the LEA's Wakefield offices over the next four years.[3] The fine tuning of these proposals was delayed not by an absence of co-operation on Clegg's part, but rather because of a bleak financial outlook. Nevertheless, the widespread welcome which had been extended to the Leicestershire experiment, both in the national Conservative government's 1958 Education White Paper (Ministry of Education, 1958) and by comprehensive-minded LEAs, did nothing to alter Clegg's view that this model was an imperfect solution for any division of the West Riding.

The Leicestershire experiment had been operating for only seven terms before Stewart Mason approached the County Council's School Organisation and Staffing Committee (to which the full Education Committee was effectively subservient until the 1970s) with a request to extend the two-tier system to the Coalville area of the county, where extra classroom accommodation was needed. Mason persuasively argued at the committee's January 1959 meeting that the cost of providing extended accommodation to facilitate the operation of the scheme in that district was significantly cheaper than building a new secondary school, the only other alternative.[4] The following month, he went further, by circulating a memorandum which, though modestly entitled *Leicestershire Experiment – The Next Phase*, was radical in terms of its content. Both the high schools and the upper schools (or grammar schools as many were still called), he argued, had adapted admirably to their new roles, with transfer rates in the two pilot districts giving much cause for satisfaction.[5] The time had come, he continued, to consider extending the benefits of the scheme to the remainder of the county. After all, Leicestershire was blazing a trail for other LEAs to follow:

> Public reaction to the experiment had on the whole been exceptionally favourable, and it was encouraging to note that although the experiment had been under continuous and detailed scrutiny from other Authorities, and indeed other countries, no insuperable defect in its conception had yet been pointed out.[6]

This undoubtedly amounted to a powerful case for extending non-selection, but even so, when it is remembered that Leicestershire was a solidly Conservative-controlled County Council, the absence of criticism at the political level is remarkable, serving again to illustrate the extent to which educational affairs were uncoloured by political dogma. The fact that Mason enjoyed the support of County politicians at the highest level was undoubtedly an enabler which underpinned the School Organisation and Staffing Committee's February 1959 decision to recommend to the Education Committee that the Leicestershire 'experiment' should be known henceforth as 'the plan'. Moreover, it was determined that there should be rapid progress in implementing the uniform operation of the two-tier scheme. Most immediately, it was agreed that the plan could be extended to Birstall and Scraptoft, located to the north of the county town, with the Melton Mowbray district being identified as the next most likely area for extension.[7] Interestingly, consultations in the newly proposed plan areas began only *after* the Education Committee and County Council had already adopted the School Organisation and Staffing Committee's recommendations as policy, a situation which could not have been contemplated in almost any other English or Welsh LEA.

The absence of resistance at the political level was not mirrored at the grass-roots, however, where the opening of discussions led to protests from groups of grammar-school teachers and governors in Melton Mowbray and Ashby-de-la-Zouch, areas by this time officially scheduled to join the plan in 1962.[8] A petition from the Ashby Boys' School governors clearly illustrated the extent to which grammar school attachments remained stronger than any desire to participate in educational innovation:

> to ask the governors to sweep away an established grammar school which has been acclaimed successful over the centuries by all peoples and to agree to the substitution of a scheme which is as yet unproven, is to our view an invitation to a complete abdication of responsibility.[9]

This particular dispute was even the subject of a Whitehall deputation in the summer of 1960, but since, by this time, the projected introduction of the plan to the western side of the county had been postponed for the immediate future owing to inadequate finances, the discussions were somewhat theoretical. Mason, who was supposedly in attendance at the meeting as an 'observer', vigorously defended the proposals, yet was forced to concede that the Education Committee would reluctantly continue to operate a bipartite system in that part of the county if no satisfactory long-term solution could be found.[10]

In some ways, by the autumn of 1962, the Leicestershire plan had been disappointing, in spite of its promise. Since the launch of the pilot in 1957, only one further area had been incorporated into the plan, and Mason's impatience with the ministry was clear:

> when I first put this line of policy before the committee, there was no reason to suppose that we were going to be starved of our proper share of building allocations. Had we had a reasonable helping it would have been possible by now to have been operating the plan properly over two-thirds of the county, and have completed the whole operation by 1964. Whatever the reasons, it is a fact that the launching of the Leicestershire Plan has been followed by a quinquennium of building allocations to this county on such a lean scale as to constitute a clear injustice.[11]

An element of paranoia, it seems, was by this stage haunting the Director. Further progress, he argued, was imperative if the morale of those involved in the county education service was not to suffer. He left the School Organisation and Staffing Sub-Committee to ponder his understanding that:

the delay has not only been a source of intense frustration within the county but has led to rumours being spread about the county that the Education Authority is not really behind the Plan, that it is having second thoughts, that it has come up against serious snags, and so on.[12]

A sense of frustration also characterised the West Riding CEO at this time, where the impediment of insufficient financial resources had served to heighten tensions between Alec Clegg and his political masters. By 1962, Clegg had abandoned his former preference for the all-through comprehensive, which the West Riding had already introduced in several rural districts. Such schools were, he now accepted, too large and too impersonal. However, he remained resolute in his belief that the Leicestershire scheme, which was not truly comprehensive because of its reliance upon guided parental choice to determine the transfer of 14-year-olds, was not a desirable model. The biggest single barrier standing in the way of secondary reorganisation for the remainder of the West Riding, he concluded, was the stipulation laid down since 1944 that transfer from primary to secondary education should occur exclusively at the age of 11. But what, if not 11, *was* the ideal age of transfer? Clegg decided to consult a number of West Riding heads, inspectors and training college representatives, who overwhelmingly reported their preference for a break at age 13 (Clegg, 1965, p. 76). This evidence seemed to point towards support for a *three-tier* system of secondary education, an idea which had informally been advanced by a fellow CEO. Without demonstrating any firm commitment at this stage, Clegg decided to float the idea of children transferring schools at 9 and 13 in a letter to the Ministry of Education, dated May 1963 (Gosden and Sharp, 1978, pp. 187–8).

MOMENTUM INCREASED, 1963–65

The initial response of the ministry to Clegg's suggestion of a middle-school scheme was not promising, although there was no fundamental objection to the notion of an LEA forwarding proposals which by-passed transfer at 11. Clegg concluded that, if there was interest in such an arrangement among his county's divisional executives, it would be a question of persuading the minister to accommodate alternative schemes in due course. He therefore approached several comprehensive-minded divisions, and in October 1963 published a widely circulated memorandum (ensuring maximum press coverage) reporting that the Castleford, Hemsworth and Normanton districts all favoured reorganisation involving 5–9, 9–13 and 13–18 schools, and that two further districts, Craven and Keighley, were also considering the suggested scheme.[13] Such an arrangement would require a change in the law, however, something which Walter James, editor of the *TES*, counselled Sir Edward Boyle, the Conservative Minister of Education, against:

> these are clearly not irrevocable matters but they do affect school building and that involves public money. It is fair that the law should act as a break on too much chopping and changing.
>
> (*TES*, 11 October 1963)

Local authority pressure on the minister for a 'divine dispensation'[14] persisted throughout the remainder of 1963 and into the following year, when Boyle, on an official visit to the Don Valley, told Hyman's successor as Education Chairman, C.T. Broughton, that he hoped that legislation permitting middle-school reorganisation would soon be enacted (Gosden and Sharp, 1978, p. 189). True to his word, Boyle oversaw the drafting of a parliamentary Bill which was enacted shortly before the Conservative government lost power in October. Initially, provision was only made for a limited number of LEAs to develop such schemes, with the West Riding leading the way.

Consistent with Brian Simon's thesis that 1963 was 'the crucial moment of change' (Simon, 1991, p. 271), when comprehensive schools became a *permanent*, rather than an *experimental* feature of the English and Welsh educational system, the reorganisation aspirations of Leicestershire and the West Riding both received fresh impetus during that year. In Leicestershire, Stewart Mason's impassioned plea for further progress in implementing the Leicestershire plan resulted in the reorganisation of the Braunstone area in September 1963, followed by the two large eastern districts of Melton Mowbray–Bottesford and Market Harborough–Kibworth, 12 months later. In each of these districts, the LEA was able to effect reorganisation without incurring major building costs, an important enabler, in view of Mason's continuing disappointment with the level of ministerial capital grants. However, one grammar-school head teacher had reason to be grateful for the stop-go economic climate which had resulted in the postponement of plans to extend the scheme to Lutterworth and Enderby in 1964,[15] entertainingly recalling that:

teachers on the verge of retirement breathed a sigh of relief – has anyone ever assessed the strains imposed on those in their fifties? There was a little more time in which to introduce CSE courses in English, Mathematics and French into the old grammar school curriculum; there were a few more opportunities to appoint new staff with secondary modern or comprehensive experience; two more years in which the grammar school and secondary modern staffs could tentatively approach liaison by looking at one another's courses and introducing themselves to one another (in itself an unaccustomed adventure); two more years in which to draw on the limited experience of schools going through the same process. (Dodge, 1980, p. 89)

Meanwhile, in October 1964, the West Riding Education Committee approved the first three-tier plan, drawn up by the Hemsworth divisional executive, with Clegg's assistance.[16] However, the subsequent good news that the proposal was satisfactory to the DES was balanced by a setback for Clegg when the Castleford division unexpectedly shunned the three-tier model in favour of a Leicestershire-style reorganisation. This decision owed much, it has been suggested, to personality clashes between members of the district Labour Party and Broughton, the chairman of the Education Committee (Gosden and Sharp, 1978, p. 189). Nevertheless, by this time the middle-school option was arousing much interest, both in and beyond the West Riding, a point confirmed by its apposite inclusion in the appendix to Circular 10/65 in July 1965. Even though Secretary of State Crosland was still only prepared to support a limited number of middle-school reorganisation schemes, the importance of both Leicestershire and the West Riding in challenging the traditional conception of comprehensive education was clearly acknowledged in the circular's contents.

CIRCULAR 10/65 AND PRAGMATIC CHANGE

The complex mechanics of local government in the West Riding certainly provided a more challenging environment in which the CEO had to operate. This was in contrast to Leicestershire, where a working alliance with the most powerful gentry leaders permitted Stewart Mason, the Director of Education, an extraordinary degree of administrative freedom to plan and execute the reorganisation of secondary education. But, of course, the Leicestershire plan had never been presented as a means of establishing comprehensive education, and by 1965, with a national Labour government purporting to favour universal comprehensivisation, Stewart Mason was no longer the darling of progressive educationists. Reginald Prentice, Labour's Schools Minister, had warned, two months before the appearance of Circular 10/65, that, in the long term, Leicestershire's retention of a form of selection at 14 would be unacceptable to the government (*TES*, 7 May 1965).

The weaknesses of voluntary transfer had already become self-evident to Mason, both as a result of internal evidence, which suggested that the proportion of girls transferring to existing upper schools was relatively low,[17] and a Leicester University study, which seemed to highlight the importance which class factors played in pupil transfers. Figures for 1964, for example, showed that 85 per cent of children in the predominantly middle-class district of Oadby transferred to their local upper school, as against just 39 per cent in working-class Hinckley (*New Society*, 25 March 1965, p. 17).

Having deduced that Labour's circular would not indicate approval for the Leicestershire plan in an unamended form, Mason developed a pragmatic strategy aimed at achieving consistency with national policy. Labour's announced intention to raise the school-leaving age to 16 from 1970–71 offered a welcome opportunity to remove the anachronistic extra year in the high school for non-transferring pupils. Thus, it was agreed in 1966 that every pupil in a high school where transfer rates were already above 80 per cent should transfer at 14 to the upper school. This was viewed as the first of several stepping stones towards complete comprehensivisation, to be followed the next year by the – to some minds belated – decision officially to refer to all remaining schools which had retained the title 'grammar' as 'upper schools' (Jones, 1989, p. 32).

Transfer to the upper schools became universal in 1972–73, by which time the remaining bipartite districts of the county had entered the plan. The Soar Valley and Lutterworth–Enderby districts were reorganised in September 1967, with Coalville and Ashby following 12 months later. In the latter area, it is significant that the controversy which had greeted Mason's original proposals eight years earlier did not resurface. The one remaining element in the county jigsaw, Market Bosworth, was set in place in 1969, by which time a modification to the plan was being launched, involving the gradual introduction of transfer to the high school at the age of 10, rather than 11.

In Leicestershire, it might be observed, Circular 10/65 served more to highlight the need to introduce certain modifications to the county scheme, which was already well advanced, than to provide structural guidance. This contrasts with the position in the West Riding, where the Circular was a powerful enabling factor that either prompted or hastened reorganisation activity in most remaining county divisions. Although the middle-school preferences of CEO Clegg and Education Chairman Broughton were well known, it was left to the divisions to put forward individual schemes, reflecting the diverse industrial, geographical and increasingly ethnic variations of the county. Uniformity could hardly have been pressed by Clegg or the Education Committee, since there were already, by this time, 14 well-established 11–18 comprehensives operating throughout the county. The all-through school (and particularly split-site examples of this genre) was no longer favoured, either by Clegg or Education Committee members, and, of the various schemes put forward by the divisions, only Harrogate favoured the adoption of this traditional model.[18]

During the years 1968 to 1974, when the County Council disappeared as a result of a local government shake-up, the remaining divisions of the West Riding (with the notable exception of Ripon, where the Old Riponians' Grammar School Association was particularly resistant) went comprehensive with little evidence of controversy. Moreover, consistent with the experience of the LEAs surveyed in Chapters 4 and 5 in this book, the return of the Conservative Party to local office in the spring of 1967 failed to spark a selective schools revival. Of the disputes that did occur, most were confined to the small number of divisions, such as Mexborough and Normanton, where selection could be abolished only by amalgamating existing grammar schools (Gosden and Sharp, 1978, pp. 192–3).

EDUCATIONAL PROGRESSIVISM: THE UNDERSTATED COUNTY CONTRIBUTION

The contributions of both counties surveyed in this chapter were important in challenging what Robin Pedley, the original architect of tiered comprehensive schemes, described as 'both of the bogeys which had hitherto seemed to create an 'either/or' situation: selection at 11 and giant comprehensives' (Pedley, 1980, p. 458). The Leicestershire plan 'was an ingenious solution to the problem of making an immediate transition to comprehensive education utilising existing buildings'

(Simon, 1991, p. 207), while the middle-school reorganisation model 'was probably the West Riding's single greatest contribution to national education in the post-war period' (Gosden and Sharp, 1978, p. 189). Though they were not typical of English and Welsh county LEAs, the part played by both in the reappraisal of the term *comprehensive education* serves as a useful antidote to the notion that large, urban authorities exclusively led the drive away from tripartism.

By the early 1970s, these two innovative forms had come to be much more similar than their originators would at first have expected. The Leicestershire system had been transposed into one in which the two tiers served students aged 10–14 and 14–18, while the West Riding schools served students from 9 to 13 and from 13 to 18. The lower tier was called a *high school* in Leicestershire and a *middle school* in the West Riding. But in both systems, having a lower and upper tier made it possible to provide a *comprehensive* school experience for students at both the younger and older age levels.

One characteristic that emerges from studying the reorganisation process in both the West Riding and Leicestershire is that political arguments were less in evidence than debates about what was best for children. Undoubtedly, the absence of significant numbers of denominational or direct-grant schools in both counties limited the potential of preservationist forces. Neither county conformed to the traditional stereotype that demands for comprehensive education were simply associated with the Labour Party. Indeed, it was West Riding *Conservatives* who, in the wake of the 1944 Act, led demands for an alternative to tripartism in that county, and the Leicestershire experiment was also launched and extended as a county-wide plan during a period of solidly Tory control.

In Leicestershire, Stewart Mason, the Director of Education, was the beneficiary of political feudalism. So long as he enjoyed the support of the key county magnates, he was guaranteed support for his administrative plans. Those plans were always skilfully presented in the most moderate language, even to the extent of studiously avoiding all mention of the term *comprehensive*. It was not until after 1971, the year of Mason's retirement, that the cut-and-thrust of political invective entered the arena of educational decision-making in Leicestershire, precipitated by the county's additional responsibilities for administering the city of Leicester's schools.

Leicestershire stood out as an LEA that did not permit extraneous factors to stand in the way of educational matters, even during the politically charged months immediately before and after the publication of Circular 10/65. Although Mason could be uncompromising on occasions, particularly when the early success of the Leicestershire plan seemed threatened by the Ashby governors' objections, there was much to recommend what he termed the authority's 'policy of gradualness',[19] which tended to facilitate the acceptability of the plan. Though the West Riding context was more politicised, conflict within the Labour Party about *how* – not whether – reorganisation should occur was the principal cause of disputes, particularly between the fiercely independent divisional executives and the Chairmen of Education. On occasions, such tensions also affected the relationship between the CEO and the Education Chairman, which was generally less happy than in Leicestershire. But it was by no means as strained as that which existed between, say, John Elliot and his political masters in Manchester (see Chapter 5). Perhaps inevitably, the more complex political structure of the West Riding conspired to create more practical impediments to comprehensive reorganisation, making the uniform application of a county plan impossible. However, in some ways, the absence of uniformity was a strength, rather than a weakness, of the West Riding experience, since the process of policy-making was participatory. In the West Riding, in striking contrast to Leicestershire, policy-making was essentially democratic, as the authority's valedictory report recalled:

> the amount of discussion was time-consuming and often frustrating but it meant that the teachers and the local Committees became thoroughly involved. Teams of teachers, officials and advisers would meet to hammer out a scheme which almost invariably was accepted by the local Committee and the County for submission to the DES.
>
> (West Riding Education Committee, 1974, p. 191)

ALTERNATIVE ROUTES

These two innovative counties provided important models of reorganisation that permitted the introduction of comprehensive schools within the limitations set by school buildings designed for the selective system. Both counties' plans received intense examination and evaluation, and features of both plans were adopted by other LEAs.

Although the plans were similar in their final forms, they were arrived at by very different routes. The Leicestershire plan was originally designed in a way that essentially *avoided* the introduction of comprehensive schooling while the West Riding plan was directed from the outset *towards* a comprehensive system. The two plans were also implemented very differently. In Leicestershire the Director had unparalleled power to reorganise the system as he wished, while in the West Riding the CEO had a much more complicated task involving persuasion and compromise.

The innovative success of both counties owed much to the remarkable dynamism of their CEOs, both of whom were driven not just by a desire to bypass the 11+, but also by a passion for high quality *primary* education, free from the 'backwash' effects of selection. Within the context of this research, it may be concluded that the personal contributions of Stewart Mason and Alec Clegg, as *enablers*, extended beyond their localities. They were the key shapers of a new order in comprehensive education, which stressed flexibility rather than rigidity, and tiered schemes utilising existing small schools in preference to vast all-through comprehensives.

While there had been a little variation in the ways in which LEAs went about responding to the comprehensive school initiative before the introduction of these new schemes, there was much more afterwards. There was so much variation, in fact, that it became unclear just what the limits were to the use of the term *comprehensive*. One of the issues brought to the fore in the comparison of these two cases, though, was the continued use in some LEAs of some form of selection. That was the major point of disagreement between Mason and Clegg during the years in which their plans were being refined. Whatever the *form* of organisation, whatever the age or ages at which transfer from one school to the next occurred, if some students were able to make that transfer and others were not, Clegg felt that the term *comprehensive* was inappropriate.

NOTES

1. WYAS, West Riding Education Committee minutes, 23 Dec. 1958.
2. PRO ED 152/458, Leicestershire 1956–61 file, memorandum from D. Evan Morgan to Miss K.A. Kennedy, 13 Feb. 1958.
3. Interestingly, the Borough Education Officer for Keighley Excepted District, which wished to follow exactly the Leicestershire example, was Frank Pedley, brother of Robin, the architect of this reorganisation model. The three divisional executives seeking to implement two-tier variations on the Leicestershire model were Hemsworth, Castleford and the Don Valley.
4. CHL, School Organisation and Staffing Committee minutes, 16 Jan. 1959.

5. Ibid., 20 Feb. 1959, memorandum by Mason.
6. Ibid.
7. Ibid.
8. Ibid., 20 Nov. 1959.
9. Ibid., 25 March 1960, memorandum by the governors of Ashby Boys' Grammar School.
10. Ibid., 16 Sept. 1960, minutes of a meeting between four Ashby governors and two Ministry of Education officials, 25 July 1960.
11. Ibid., 14 Sept. 1962, memorandum by Mason entitled *The Extension of the Leicestershire Plan.*
12. Ibid.
13. WL, Local Information files, Education, Box 10, County Council of the West Riding of Yorkshire Education Department, *The Organisation of Education in Certain Areas of the West Riding*, 1 Oct. 1963.
14. A term used by Clegg in a letter to a ministry official, dated 30 Dec. 1963, quoted in Gosden and Sharp, 1978, p. 188.
15. CHL, School Organisation and Staffing Committee minutes, 3 May 1963.
16. WYAS, West Riding Education Committee minutes, 27 Oct. 1964. The 5–9, 9–13, 13–18 reorganisation of Hemsworth division was effected in September 1968.
17. CHL, School Organisation and Staffing Committee minutes, 19 Feb. 1965, memorandum by Mason entitled *The Leicestershire Plan and the School Leaving Age.*
18. There were a few variations worthy of note. Keighley initially went ahead with transfer at 14, as an interim step towards establishing 10–13 middle schools, although administrative difficulties in the operation of these arrangements forced a rethink in 1973, when it resolved to switch to the 5–9, 9–13 and 13–18 pattern from September 1977 (see Gosden and Sharp, 1978, 191). Castleford abandoned its preference for a two-tier model in favour of the 5–8, 8–12, 12–18 scheme recommended in the 1967 Plowden Report. Mexborough division's reorganisation, on the other hand, included the establishment of a sixth-form college to serve 11–16 schools.
19. CHL, School Organisation and Staffing Committee minutes, 8 Nov. 1968, memorandum by Mason entitled *Leicestershire Plan – The Next Step: Four Year High Schools.*

8

The Cautious County Approach: West Sussex, Glamorgan and Northumberland

The two counties described in Chapter 7 both played a central role in the history of comprehensive reorganisation. The personal contributions of their CEOs in challenging conventional thinking about non-selective secondary schooling permits the confident assertion that they were atypical examples of county (or, indeed, urban) LEAs during the period under review. However, this does not necessarily assist us in determining what a more *typical* LEA reorganisation experience was, given the large number of English and Welsh LEAs, each with its own procedural and decision-making peculiarities and a unique set of factors which may be described either as *enablers* or *impediments*. Although aspects of the reorganisations undertaken by the three counties surveyed in this chapter may be characterised as forward-looking (and even pioneering, in the case of Crawley New Town, West Sussex), they perhaps approach typicality rather more closely than any of the other seven authorities examined closely in this book.

Meeting the requirements of the 1944 Education Act for separate primary and secondary institutions preoccupied the three counties during the immediate post-war period. From the outset, Labour-controlled Glamorgan typified the Welsh resistance to tripartism by contemplating comprehensive schools in rural areas, but George Tomlinson, the Minister of Education, rejected this aspect of the development plan on the grounds that the schools proposed were too small (Simon 1991, p. 205). Despite this setback, the widely held reservations about the ability to discern technical aptitudes continued to hold the LEA back from a position of total conformity with the national government's favoured approach. *Bipartite* rather than tripartite secondary arrangements were introduced, with technical education courses being taught in grammar and secondary modern schools,[1] a policy which both Northumberland and West Sussex were also to adopt before the end of the 1950s.[2]

Of the three counties, the most important pre-Circular 10/65 comprehensive developments occurred in the unlikely setting of West Sussex, a county which, like Leicestershire, was more representative of the older order than the new, with many county politicians drawn from the traditional gentry élite. The council was, until 1967, Independent-controlled, but with an allegiance in matters of national politics to the Conservative Party. In general, however, the determination of educational policy was left to LEA administrators, who demonstrated an early recognition that bipartism did not address all of the difficulties experienced in what was, undoubtedly, a county of significant socio-economic contrasts. The peculiarities of demography in West Sussex, which led to the partial development of comprehensivisation before 1965, merit further investigation and are discussed below.

DEMOGRAPHIC CHANGE AS AN ENABLER IN WEST SUSSEX

West Sussex may be classified as a predominantly rural, medium-sized LEA, having a population of 322,880 in 1951. The one large town of this period, Worthing, became an excepted district after the 1944 Education Act, but the majority of the county was characterised by villages and small country towns, boasting small grammar schools. However, the county also had a more densely settled and prosperous coastal strip, with a number of seaside resorts which also functioned as retirement towns.

New socioeconomic developments transformed parts of the county in the post-war years. The south-western corner was much affected by suburbanisation, which reinforced its middle-class character and created a demand for additional grammar-school places. There were also very rapid industrial and residential developments centred on particular towns, notably Shoreham (resulting from the establishment of new oil installations), and Crawley and Three Bridges, whose older settlements were dramatically transformed by the formation of a London overspill district at Crawley New Town. Thus, the county authority had to cope with exceptional demographic pressures in some areas, while taking account of other districts with low density and relatively static populations. This was a situation which had not been envisaged when the education development plan for the county had been drawn up after the Second World War.

As early as 1953, the county received an expression of interest in comprehensive education by the Crawley and Three Bridges Labour

Party, purporting to favour a comprehensive school in place of the proposed development of selective schools on the Tilgate campus. This demand was, initially, a side-effect of a more concerted and less political campaign to improve the provision of secondary school places in Crawley New Town. The influx of a young, highly skilled population, with strong educational and social aspirations, together with a relatively small number of old people, quickly produced a very high rate of natural increase which saw the proportion of the population in the age range 5–14 rise from 14.7 per cent in 1952 to a peak of 16.3 per cent in 1959 (Rigby, 1975; Cooke, 1968, p. 431).

The New Town, of which Crawley was one of several national examples, had the function not only of being an overspill area for London, but of developing into a socially mixed and balanced community. Consistent with this idea, the local Development Corporation promoted the idea of the campus site (intended to accommodate other educational and cultural buildings, in addition to secondary schools). This has been described as 'Crawley's contribution to the science and art of new town planning' (*Architects' Journal*, 10 March 1949, p. 229). The development of campuses, which increasingly became features of new town developments was the brainchild of the Development Corporation's planning consultant, Anthony Minoprio, who visualised education as a 'vitalising and continuous process teaching people of all ages in every sphere of life' (Rigby, 1975, pp. 72–5).

At a time when interest in (and practical experience of) multilateral schooling was burgeoning, the campus idea, which was gently encouraged by the Conservative national government of 1951–64, could be seen to offer a kind of insurance policy; the schools were capable of being run separately as two or three discrete institutions, but could be combined at some stage in the future as a single, large comprehensive school. Publicly, at least, this did not colour the thinking of West Sussex County Council, which turned down Labour's 1954 proposal. This decision did not halt agitation for extra secondary-school places, however, not only from local politicians, but also from an alliance of parents, trades council representatives, influential employers and the Chief Executive of the Development Corporation. The view was represented that obsolete and overcrowded schools were inadequate and that the LEA had been negligent and unnecessarily secretive in their planning of educational facilities for the New Town (ibid., pp. 72–115). The co-ordinator of these protests, designed to press the Education Committee to reconsider its decision, was a local general practitioner (and, from 1955, Labour County Councillor) Dr I. Clout.

It was Clout who also became the chief link between the campaign for accelerating the provision of schools and the agitation that developed against 11+ selection (ibid., pp. 129–43).

An atmosphere of greater flexibility prevailed in the second half of the decade, as a result of personnel changes in the Chichester Education Offices of the West Sussex LEA. In 1958, Dr C.W.W. Reid was installed as Director of Education, following the retirement on health grounds of E.T. Davies. The process of developing a practical initiative which embraced the comprehensive spirit had already begun in September 1957, when the Deputy Director, R.M. Parker, proposed a new scheme for the Tilgate campus. After discussions by the Secondary Education sub-committee and the Education Policy sub-committee, it was agreed that instead of separate grammar and modern schools on the Tilgate site, there should be a single bilateral school, to be known as the Thomas Bennett School. Since building was already behind schedule and the chronic shortage of secondary places was worsening by the day, Parker managed to secure further approval in these exceptional circumstances for a temporary school that would take in both modern and grammar school children to work under one head teacher, on the understanding that the bilateral form would be adopted once the building programme was completed.[3]

The school opened in its (supposedly) interim form in September 1958, and in the light of subsequent events the suggestion that the school would be split eventually in two seems to have been a subterfuge. The Deputy Director may have had the idea of a comprehensive school in mind from the start. This is suggested by the appointment of the deputy head of Forest Hill comprehensive, London as headmaster with powers to choose his own staff. While there was some discontent, initially from parents of grammar school-eligible children who had been sent to this unproven school, the appointment of a young and well-qualified staff quickly established a pattern – which it retained – of hard work and lively activities. With Parker as clerk to the governors and a substantial measure of support from the governing body for the comprehensive principle, the school became comprehensive as a *fait accompli* (ibid., pp. 157–80; *Crawley Observer*, 30 July 1965).

This development in Crawley was by no means the prelude to the rapid abandonment of bipartism elsewhere in West Sussex. Nevertheless, an expression of satisfaction with selective procedures in 1957 was accompanied by a decision to rename its modern schools 'county secondary schools', into which, three years later, grammar and technical streams were introduced for the first time.[4] While this new policy, which again emanated from the Deputy Director, was *prima facie* intended to strengthen the bipartite system by making it more acceptable, its implementation was to prove an important enabler, which eased the transition to comprehensive education in a number of unexpected ways.

The newly built Hazelwick secondary modern school in Crawley was quickly upgraded to the status of a bilateral[5] on the grounds that, in spite of its new examination courses and highly qualified staff, it suffered a disadvantage resulting from parents preferring their children to attend either Thomas Bennett School or the Grammar School at Ifield. The status of the latter school's secondary modern neighbour on the Ifield campus also benefited from a collaborative programme of admissions and shared courses (West Sussex County Council, 1964, pp. 54–5), reflecting the LEA's policy (which mirrored the thinking of Conservative Education Minister Sir David Eccles) of upgrading secondary modern schools without eroding the position of the grammar schools (Simon, 1991, pp. 203–4).

Developments in Crawley were followed with interest, and by the beginning of the 1960s, bilateralism was beginning to be seen as a solution to the pressure on grammar-school places in other districts of the county. Bilateral provision at the Kings Manor Girls School at Shoreham seems to have been easily achieved, despite some evidence of protest from parents who preferred Worthing's traditional grammar school,[6] but a proposed scheme for bilateralism in Midhurst was summarily rejected by Eccles, apparently on the grounds that the arrangement would be harmful to Midhurst Grammar School.[7]

The shortage of grammar-school places was most acute on the Worthing–Littlehampton–Bognor Regis coastal belt, and was compounded by the fact that the county's single, anomalous technical school at Worthing did not enjoy a parity of esteem (in the eyes of parents) with grammar schools. However, it is clear that during the years 1961–1965, when local anger concerning the continuing shortage of academic opportunities manifested itself via public meetings and local press correspondence,[8] the LEA was steadily becoming less attracted to the idea of establishing further grammar – or, indeed, bilateral – schools, and more inclined to develop strategies to introduce comprehensive schools in the coastal district.[9] An amendment of the development plan's provision for Bognor Regis was proposed at the beginning of 1964 by Dr Reid so as to substitute a six-form entry 'comprehensive or bilateral' school in place of the two smaller schools originally planned.[10] At Littlehampton, during the following year, the governors of the schools were asked to consider 'ways in which a comprehensive arrangement might work'.[11]

With the rural Petworth–Midhurst area in mind, Reid was also quick to seek to take advantage of Edward Boyle's 1964 Education Act, which permitted a limited number of LEAs to vary the age of transfer. He obtained the support of the Secondary Education sub-committee for a gradual reorganisation, eventually permitting the establishment of a 10–13 intermediate school in either Midhurst or Petworth, with transfer to a 13–18 school at Midhurst.[12] He argued that children would benefit by leaving the small, rural primaries one year earlier, but that a transfer age of under ten would have too drastic an effect upon the village schools and would involve very young children travelling considerable distances. In view of the 'desirability of abolishing completely selection for secondary education in the area', the intermediate school would, Reid claimed, make possible a phased transfer to comprehensive education. The proposal was rejected by the DES, however, on the grounds that the scheme would be inconsistent with the interests of a grammar-school foundation trust at Midhurst.[13]

The West Sussex LEA's quinquennial report for 1959–64, though cautiously worded, illustrated the progressivism of the authority's directorate. In so far as this document offered support for bipartism at all, it was lukewarm, and, with academic and technical streams now operating in all county schools, differentiation between school types was deliberately and skilfully blurred. It was regretted, for example, that fewer than half the grammar-school intake successfully completed a sixth-form course, yet the secondary modern – or, rather, county secondary – schools were praised for having 'set an exhilarating pace' which had led to more than 30 per cent of pupils staying on for a fifth year to sit GCE O-Levels. Experience in the county had demonstrated 'a real awareness that secondary modern schools can be lively, pro-gressive places in their own right' (West Sussex County Council, 1964, pp. 19–20). Significantly, reference was also made to the impact which comprehensive schools were likely to have in the years ahead. Already, it was noted, there were three examples of such schools in the county – Crawley's Thomas Bennett (with 1,811 pupils on the roll) and Hazel-wick (with 1,071) schools, together with Kings Manor School at Shoreham (with 756) – which were successfully conforming to the comprehensive principle. No doubt seeking to assuage the troubled middle-class conscience, the report argued that the comparatively large size of these schools was a strength, rather than a weakness.

Their high calibre of buildings, courses, teaching staffs and internal structures ensured 'that no individual is lost in some impenetrable, unintelligible organisation' (West Sussex County Council, 1964).

Further evidence that the authority saw advantages in comprehensive education before the publication of Circular 10/65 may be found in its handling of the so-called 'Ifield affair' in 1964–65. Although there had been close co-operation, including the development of a common sixth form, between the Sarah Robinson County Secondary and Crawley Grammar schools on Crawley's Ifield campus since the early 1960s, strong parental opposition to amalgamation prevented the development of a truly comprehensive campus school of the kind which Thomas Bennett had become. However, this was precisely the type of arrangement which the chairman of the grammar-school governors (none other than the redoubtable Dr Clout) claimed had always been envisaged. The aspirations of the governors, who voted 8–2 in favour of amalgamation in April 1965,[14] coincided with those of the LEA directorate, which moved to amalgamate the schools 12 months later, overriding the wishes of the grammar school headmaster, Dr D. Henschel (who left to take up another post), and a parental action group (*TES*, 16 March 1965; *The Teacher*, 25 June 1965).

AMBITIONS UNFULFILLED: NORTHUMBERLAND AND GLAMORGAN 1944–65

Northumberland was not affected by rapid urban expansion or New Town developments. However, it is interesting to note that the gradual introduction of secondary school campuses (though with separate selective schools, rather than a Crawley-style comprehensive) was suggested in a Northumberland Development Plan, submitted to the Ministry of Housing and local government as early as 1952 (Northumberland County Council, 1952, p. 5). One such campus at Walbottle, consisting of a grammar and two modern schools was opened in 1959, but the authority's admiration of the model was not matched by success in bidding for ministerial building grants to develop further examples.

The principal priorities for Northumberland, which faced the greatest post-war difficulties of the three counties discussed in this chapter, lay in overcoming its legacy of all-age schools, necessitating the building of more than 100 new schools during the period 1944–64. It was a county of dramatic geographical contrasts, industrialised in

142

the south-east, where coal-mining and shipbuilding activity was based, yet rural and agricultural elsewhere. Some outlying villages remained unconnected to the public utility supplies of water, gas and electricity, and communication links were prone to winter disruption. LEA-administered boarding schools served the most isolated communities, including Holy Island, but even elsewhere it was common, except in the south-east urban pocket, for children to face a long daily journey to school (Northumberland County Council, 1963, p. 10).

Faced with such a challenging set of circumstances, the absence of an early interest in comprehensive education in Northumberland does not seem surprising. By 1963, bipartism appeared to be working effectively, with the Labour-controlled LEA declaring satisfaction that 'it is possible to differentiate with reasonable accuracy between children endowed with a facility for acquiring knowledge by the abstract means of the written or spoken word, and those for whom practice in the crafts is an essential means for the acquisition of knowledge and the expression of ability' (Northumberland County Council, 1963, pp. 25–6).

By contrast, in the early 1960s, Glamorgan's Director of Education, Trevor Jenkins, had become frustrated by the absence of opportunities to bypass 11+ selection, which not only impeded 'experiment and freedom' in the primary classroom, but also 'produces results which emphasise the gulfs in society, when we would wish that the education service might help to minimise the disunities which exist and by its influence help to integrate the community'.[15] Although the development of small comprehensives had been blocked by the ministry in the 1940s, Glamorgan did succeed in establishing purpose-built comprehensives, serving the expanding communities of Treorchy, Porthcawl and Port Talbot by the end of the following decade (Simon, 1991, p. 205). With the 11+ examination continuing to operate, however, the comprehensiveness of these early comprehensives must be doubted, and the majority of school-building work during the period 1944–64 was restricted to minor programmes to provide laboratories and practical rooms in pre-war secondary schools. Nevertheless, the pioneering reorganisation schemes, developed by authorities including Croydon, Leicestershire and the West Riding seemed to offer a more optimistic outlook, even for an LEA such as Glamorgan which had been – and realistically expected to remain – starved of cash. An important battle was won in 1964, when the Ministry of Education accepted the authority's request to abandon selection altogether in the Port Talbot and Glyncorrwg division, in which the largest comprehensive, Sandfields, was already operating. The scheme to be applied to the remainder of the division resembled the Leicestershire plan in so far as it involved an upper and lower secondary tier, but differed by contemplating their linkage to form 11–18 schools, under the leadership of a single head teacher.

Strong interest in going comprehensive (by various methods) had already been expressed by other Glamorgan county divisions, and, in December 1964, Jenkins presented the Education Committee with a radical blueprint for change. The Port Talbot–Glyncorrwg approach should, he maintained, be applied to the remainder of the county, creating split-site comprehensives with more than 1,000 pupils on the roll. The age of transfer between sites could be determined according to the most convenient use of facilities, since 'this aspect of the organisation does not assume the same importance as it would were the lower school to be established as a separate school'.[16] Though he acknowledged the imperfections of this solution, Jenkins recommended that Education Committee members should not balk at the prospect of achieving full comprehensivisation, which would not, as in some other authorities, permit the co-existence of selective and non-selective schools:

> No-one would deny that it would be best to have a single comprehensive school on one site. But it has to be decided whether something less than the ideal is acceptable in the overriding interest of comprehensive arrangements which will not otherwise be practicable in the areas concerned for an indefinite period of years'.[17]

Detailed proposals followed for the reorganisation of secondary education in each of the remaining eight divisional areas, including the Rhondda excepted district. It amounted to a far-reaching plan, involving the amalgamation or redesignation of 31 county grammar schools. Local discussions, involving the Director, the Education Committee and divisional executives, began immediately (*Education*, 124, 11 December 1964, p. 1048). In these circumstances, it might be argued that protests of some sort were inevitable, but sometimes self-interest was more in evidence than ideological objections to comprehensive education. For example, a 1963 proposal by the mid-Glamorgan division (which foreshadowed the Director's recommendations of the following year) attracted criticism from teachers at the Bridgend County Grammar School for Girls on the grounds that, after comprehensivisation, the school, along with the local secondary modern, was envisaged to be a lower-tier institution, feeding the existing boys' grammar school. One complainant feared that, in addition to 'the complete destruction' of her school, which would lose its examination work, senior posts in the upper school would go to male staff already in place at the boys' school. The same correspondent evidently felt much relieved when, a few months later, she reported that her school was now earmarked to become the upper, rather than lower, tier school in the new arrangement.[18]

The divisional political structure of Glamorgan parallels the situation in the West Riding (discussed in Chapter 7), and, like Alec Clegg in the latter county, Glamorgan's Director of Education needed to pay more than lip-service to local sensibilities. Though none of the county divisional executives declared themselves against reorganisation, the Director's proposals were not universally admired. For example, the Aberdare–Mountain Ash and West Glamorgan divisions both expressed early preferences for the Leicestershire plan, which the Director was known to dislike on the grounds that parental aspirations and class factors tended to exert an unwelcome influence upon transfer at 14. In due course, the possibility of West Glamorgan being subject to a possible boundary change caused its divisional executive to favour no action for the present, but the Director had other ideas, including the controversial amalgamation of sites at Gwauncaegurwen and Ystalyfera, estimated to be seven miles apart. The plans of the Director and the Pontypridd–Llantrisant divisional executive were also at variance, with the former preferring mixed-sex schools, and the latter favouring separate facilities for girls and boys.

It was during this period of consultation and negotiation that Circular 10/65 was published. Its appearance served to shift the dynamics of the ongoing debates in numerous LEAs throughout England and Wales, including Glamorgan and West Sussex.

THE IMPACT OF CIRCULAR 10/65 IN GLAMORGAN AND WEST SUSSEX, 1965–74

It was clear, after Labour's October 1964 general election victory, that pressure would be exerted upon LEAs to put forward schemes for comprehensive reorganisation, and the policy became manifest with the appearance of Circular 10/65, nine months later. By that time, the three counties that are scrutinised in this chapter had reached contrasting positions in relation to the question of preferred secondary school structures. Glamorgan was strongly committed to the concept of comprehensive education and was in the midst of a process intended to permit its county-wide application. In West Sussex a watershed position had been reached. With the exception of Crawley, where the development of comprehensive education had originally been justified in terms of special circumstances, there remained an official commitment to bipartism. However, this commitment had been steadily eroded since the late 1950s, as conceptual and practical distinctions between grammar and county secondary schools had been marginalised. Moreover, it is possible to characterise the LEA as being led by a deputy Director who viewed comprehensive education as a means of increasing educational opportunity, and a Director who viewed it as a convenient means of eliminating the perennial shortage of grammar-school places. In contrast, Northumberland had not approached the comprehensive issue, having long been preoccupied with satisfying the terms of the 1944 legislation.

In West Sussex, decisions had been taken to proceed with two-tier comprehensive schools for Littlehampton and the Midhurst–Petworth district just before the publication of Secretary of State Crosland's circular. However, since the precedents had already been set for a piecemeal approach towards reorganisation, taking account of all relevant views, the Secondary Education sub-committee was reluctant to force through a county programme.[19] The first step was to initiate a series of meetings with the Diocesan Schools Committee, governors and staff of aided schools and groups of parents. Reporting on these discussions, the Director pointed out that county teachers had revealed greater enthusiasm for comprehensive education than had existed some years ago, and that the governors had expressed strong feelings of dissatisfaction with the principle of selection. Yet he did not underestimate the likely difficulties of securing full co-operation.[20] Reid's report made clear that divisions of opinion existed in some schools and that strong traditions and sentiment were likely to fuel opposition to changing the status of existing schools in certain districts. In Chichester, the director predicted that a conflict over the comprehensive issue *per se* was not likely, but rather over the question of creating a co-educational school, which was strongly opposed by many women teachers, particularly at the Girls' High School. The situation at Horsham was still more acute because the established grammar schools, Collyer's Boys' and the Girls' High School, were on opposite sides of the town from the Forest Secondary Schools. He speculated that the logical solution of Collyer's becoming a sixth-form college, fed by the other three schools, was unlikely to be acceptable.[21]

At Worthing also, the number and distribution of schools, including the anomalous technical school, made reorganisation difficult, and a strong local Conservative Association, which had already brought pressure to bear on the Secondary Education sub-committee in defence of selective schools,[22] threatened to complicate matters further. Not seeking to precipitate confrontation, the Director put forward a proposal that the LEA's response to Labour's circular should embrace a philosophy of *gradualism*, with proposed structures being decided on an area-by-area basis when local agreement had been reached, rather than the pursuit of uniformity. For the time being, this meant leaving Horsham's and Worthing's problematical buildings out of the scheme to go forward to the DES.[23]

In the period to September 1969, ten schools were either fully established as comprehensives or had begun the transition by admitting one or more all-ability age groups. In some districts, such as Bognor Regis and Steyning, the initiative was taken by governors and staff of existing schools to combine into an all-through comprehensive,[24] the same model adopted by Billingshurst and Lancing. However, progress was slower in districts which had witnessed little or no population increase, or in which buildings continued to prove an impediment to change.

Given the problems involved in securing local support, it is perhaps not surprising that the Director for West Sussex began to press for the introduction of middle schools after the Plowden Report of 1967. His proposals were highly varied, however. The idea of the intermediate or middle school for rural districts had already become part of the authority's thinking, generally on the 10–13 model. However, a 5–9, 9–13 and 13–18 model was put forward in 1969 for several areas, initially including Horsham, while the existing all-through comprehensives of Crawley and Shoreham were thought to be best complemented by a scheme which included the preferred Plowden 8–12 middle school.[25] The sixth-form college model also received fresh consideration, and it provided an acceptable solution to the difficulties posed by sites and grammar-school sentiment in Horsham (although reorganisation was not completed until the mid-1970s) and Worthing, where a four-tier scheme, involving transfer at 8, 12 and 16 was eventually adopted (West Sussex County Council, 1969).

Dr Reid's role, as the energising force which kept the process of reorganisation going, gradually rubbed off on county politicians, who continued the tradition of non-interference in matters which pertained to the education directorate during the full period under review here. It may be considered something of a curiosity that West Sussex, a Conservative stronghold, was, by the end of the 1960s, the guardian of the largest comprehensive in England and Wales (Thomas Bennett School), yet this was a source of county pride, evidenced by politicians' disappointment at Crawley's decision to seek excepted district status in 1968.[26]

The initial difficulties involved in meeting the aspirations of the New Town's parents and political representatives proved to be a useful learning experience which fostered a pragmatic and sensitive policy towards the question of reorganisation elsewhere in the county. Although the last remaining elements of the reorganisation, including Horsham, were not set in place until the mid-1970s, the patchwork pattern of various non-selective structures, tailored to meet local wishes, had been established without significant controversy by the time of Reid's retirement in 1969. In the same year, R. Martin, the chairman of the Education Committee, offered the following apologia, in a foreword to the LEA's quinquennial report:

> So far as comprehensive education is concerned, I believe that the Committee's policy of slow integration has been the right one and has removed from our deliberations any suggestion of political influences. The final removal of the 11+ selection procedure from our schools will, I am sure, be welcomed on all sides while at the same time making sure that our brilliant children are not handicapped in our reorganisation plans.
>
> (West Sussex County Council, 1969)

Paralleling the situation in West Sussex, Glamorgan experienced no sudden change in the wake of Circular 10/65, but the pronouncement did serve to crystallise a process that was already under way, via discussions at the divisional level. The LEA was in a position, at last, to abandon selection altogether in the Port Talbot– Glyncorrwg district from September 1965, a move which had been approved in advance of both the Director's reorganisation plan of December 1964 and Crosland's circular. This paved the way for the establishment of four further comprehensives (to complement the Sandfields school) serving Port Talbot, Kenfig Hill and several surrounding rural communities. It had also been hoped to reorganise the towns of Barry (south-east divisional district) and Maesteg (mid-Glamorgan) at the same time, but the representations of parental pressure groups persuaded the authority to delay for twelve months until new building work was completed (*Western Mail*, 26 May 1965). Thus, by September 1966, there had been significant progress in Glamorgan, with the reorganisation of the Mountain Ash–Aberdare and Garw–Ynysawdre districts, as well as Barry and Maesteg (*Western Mail*, 4 and 12 May 1966)

In general, it may be remarked that Circular 10/65 was well received by the Glamorgan divisional executives. Although it contemplated a greater degree of organisational variety than had been previously recommended by the Director, a majority of divisions continued to favour the all-through model, with tiered arrangements being viewed as only a short-term means to achieving that end. The period of transition to comprehensive education was not without controversy, however, particularly in the Swansea Valley, where a four-year campaign was waged against the participation of the Ystalyfera Grammar School in the proposed comprehensive scheme. A petition was forwarded to Prime Minister Harold Wilson, and another to Shadow Education Minister Edward Boyle,[27] prompting the latter to investigate their grievances. Boyle was assured by a DES Welsh Office official, however, that the preservationists' behaviour was more indicative of grammar-school sentimentality than wider community feelings:

> it is now clear that the only opposition to the Authority's proposal comes from the Ystalyfera Parents' Association and the staff of the Ystalyfera School. As against this, the Welsh parents have signified strong support for the proposal.[28]

The school was eventually redesignated in September 1970, becoming one of only two county bilingual comprehensives, the other being situated at Rhydyfelin, Pontypridd (*Western Mail*, 19 May 1970).

By the time of the 1970 general election, it was estimated that 15,000 of Glamorgan's 50,000 secondary school population were accommodated in 13 comprehensive schools. More significantly, however, a programme was in place for a further 30,000 pupils to be in such schools by 1973, subject to the approval of building plans intended to meet demands stemming from the raising of the school-leaving age during that year (*Western Mail*, 19 May 1970). In September 1970, two further comprehensives were established to serve Penarth in the south-east division of the county, and interim arrangements began to operate for the excepted district of Rhondda, where the impediments of existing buildings and the diminution of population posed particular organisational difficulties for the authority. Reorganisation was extended to Bridgend and Porthcawl in 1971 and, in spite of some evidence of preservationist opposition in the Vale of Glamorgan, a further bilingual school was created by amalgamating the county's only state boarding school, Cowbridge Grammar with Cowbridge Girls' High School (*Western Mail*, 12, 17 and 26 June 1970).

The number of Glamorgan comprehensive schools had risen to 46 by 1974 (accommodating the high proportion of 90.3 per cent of secondary-age children), by which time the NCDS cohort had reached the age of 16. This left just nine modern and five grammar schools operating in remote parts of the county, representing the success of a policy which had been necessarily pragmatic over a period of more than 30 years.

NORTHUMBERLAND'S AWAKENING

In terms of the challenge posed by Circular 10/65, it might be argued that Northumberland is the most interesting of the counties discussed in this chapter, because the county had taken no steps towards comprehensivisation before 1965. The circular's publication coincided with the end of a 20-year period, during which the county's education provision was modernised in line with the 1944 Act, so the prospect of reorganising schools which were in many cases themselves the recent products of an administrative upheaval loomed. Curiously, the question of comprehensive reorganisation was referred to the Further Education and Youth sub-committee, which immediately declared itself not entirely satisfied with any of the six reorganisation models indicated in Labour's circular, but nevertheless made provision for the establishment of an ad hoc committee, representing teacher unions, to consider the matter further.[29] It is interesting to note, however, that this body was not constituted immediately, and the process of considering a response to the circular started within the confines of County Hall.

One matter which the authority quickly sought to resolve concerned the so-called Tyneside Special Review Area, which consisted of the boroughs of Wallsend and Whitley Bay, the urban districts of Gosforth, Longbenton, Newburn, and Seaton Valley, plus the rural district of Castle Ward. Since 1959, when a local government commission was established, a process had been under way which seemed destined to transfer administrative responsibility for this part of the county either to a single, newly created county borough, or to several existing borough councils. Whatever the eventual outcome, it was considered to be a near certainty that around 40 per cent of the county's residential population would be removed at a not far distant date, prompting an Education Committee request to the DES that the Tyneside Special Review Area should be exempted from their planning. When this was refused, the committee resolved to respond to the circular in two stages, giving first priority to that part of the county which they expected to retain, followed by a separate plan for the Review Area.[30]

Once planning was under way, the Director of Education, C.L. Mellowes was quick to impress upon his fellow administrators the advantages which a uniform scheme would offer to children transferring from one district to another, a point which ultimately weighed heavily in the LEA's thinking. Recalling the events of ten years previously, Michael Spicer, Assistant Education Officer for Northumberland, recalled:

> It was decided that the aim should be to find a system which appeared to offer the best opportunities to the individual child in the light of current educational thought and to prepare a plan which could be implemented within a reasonable period of time bearing in mind the practical, including the financial, limitations which existed.[31]

By the early summer of 1966, in remarkably quick time, a proposal had been drafted for a three-tier, 5–9, 9–13, 13–18 comprehensive school scheme for the county (excluding the Review Area), which purported to make the best possible use of existing buildings, keeping necessary alterations and additions to a minimum. With the raising of the school-leaving age to 16, scheduled at that time for 1971–72, it was expected that the required building could be funded from the scheduled major and minor works programmes.

Only at this point, it should be noted, was the teachers' consultative committee formally established. There was confusion about the function of this body, however, which was to prove the object of some resentment. It is clear that the teachers believed that they were a *working party*, with a brief to put forward policy recommendations, yet not only were they confronted with a district-by-district scheme which had been devised by the Director, they were also expected to work within a tight time schedule to permit the presentation of a finalised plan to the Education Committee in July, and the full County Council the following month.[32] In view of the radical nature of the plan, which would affect the organisation of every existing county school, the teachers obtained the Chairman of Education's permission to consult more widely with colleagues. But the revised deadlines took no account of the schools' summer vacation, being extended only to October and November, respectively.

The Director, meanwhile, was authorised to commence discussions with school governors and head teachers,[33] as a result of which he reported in October that 'there appeared to be general acceptance of the draft proposals'. Concern had, however, been expressed about the likely length of some children's daily journeys, and the possible damage to village life, resulting from the diminution of rural primary schools.[34]

Schools of uneven size were part of the price to be paid for the uniformity of the Director's plan, and the situation was further complicated by the fact that, by the mid-1960s, some of the parts of the county were expanding rapidly, while the anticipated school population of others was static or declining. Planning documents revealed that the anticipated numbers on the roll at middle schools would vary dramatically between 165 and 600 pupils, with upper schools accommodating between 500 and 1,650.[35]

However, in a perceptive move to head off expected criticism, the Finance and General Purposes sub-committee recommended that no child under the age of 13 should be expected to make a journey of more than 30 minutes or travel more than five miles.[36] Alderman Mrs Mitchell, the Chairman of Education, offered the further assurance that boarding facilities would be available to middle- as well as upper-school children.[37] These moves anticipated the main weaknesses of the scheme, as identified by the teachers' consultative committee, but they could not prevent a 'stormy meeting' of the Education Committee in October (*Newcastle Evening Chronicle*, 10 October 1966).

Still angered by the belief that their terms of reference had been altered, the teachers' report focused upon what they saw as the LEA's twin obsessions with haste and uniformity:

> it had been understood that the ad hoc Committee was to be a working party and not an advisory body. Clarification of its terms of reference would appear essential before study of the Tyneside area of the county begins. The Committee challenges the assumption that one scheme of reorganisation is desirable in such a diverse county as Northumberland ... The Committee was agreed that in some instances, alternative schemes examined were both educationally sound and more practicable in considerations of buildings, staffing and transport.[38]

Alderman Mitchell's somewhat ambiguous prediction that 'a plan as comprehensive as this is bound to meet opposition and even more complete inability to comprehend' (*Newcastle Evening Chronicle*, 10 October 1966), and the narrowness of the 46–41 vote at the full Council meeting in November show that the LEA's plans were seen as contentious. According to Lord Ridley (elder brother of Nicholas, later a government minister) the plan had been 'bulldozed through' (ibid., 3 November 1966), but press reports of teacher opposition were greatly exaggerated, according to the local NUT,[39] and there was no hesitation in forwarding the scheme to the DES, immediately after the meeting.

While an official reply was awaited, the task of developing recommendations for the Tyneside Special Review Area was begun. Special difficulties were faced there, not just because of likely boundary changes, but also because Wallsend was an excepted district, necessitating extra negotiations. It was also deemed important that the Tyneside proposals should not be inconsistent with those of neighbouring Newcastle LEA, where the future pattern of secondary schooling remained unknown. Within that city, Northumberland was financially responsible for purchasing approximately 1,000 annual places in direct-grant schools, but it was decided to defer consideration of this arrangement until the outcome of the review was announced.[40]

In view of their recent strongly worded protest about expecting to be more than an advisory body, it is remarkable that the teachers' consultative committee was again confronted with an LEA-devised draft set of proposals, backing the application of the county scheme for Tyneside also, when they assembled for the first time in early December 1966. Moreover, they were again asked to work to a tight timetable. Although the suitability of buildings in the Longbenton area was in some doubt, the teachers were, on this occasion, happy with the three-tier arrangement. A proviso was added, however, that the authority should satisfy itself that the 9–13 middle school arrangement was preferable to the 8–12 Plowden-style school before proceeding. As for the existing direct-grant arrangements, the committee recommended that no further places should be purchased after a date to be decided by the Education Committee.[41]

Evidence tends to point to the conclusion that, regardless of the teachers' findings, County Hall's mind was already made up. Certainly, there is no suggestion that the application of Plowden middle schools was seriously investigated, and this second plan was forwarded to the DES early in the spring of 1967. No official news was heard about the acceptability of the county's proposals until the beginning of the following year, but during the intervening period there was some correspondence between C.L. Mellowes, Northumberland's Director of Education, and officers of HMI. It is clear that although a three-tier reorganisation was generally viewed favourably, the disparate size of anticipated schools caused concern. The Director acknowledged that certain schools might otherwise be considered unrealistically small, but argued that 'geography (and geology) has in one way or another been the ruling factor', citing the instance of Allendale, an existing secondary modern and proposed 9–13 school for just 175 pupils as a case in point. A number of children already travelled eight miles to this school, but alternative reorganisation schemes would involve pupils making a twice-daily journey of over ten miles over roads subject to frequent winter closure.[42] Perhaps fearing for the fate of what were, in effect, *his* reorganisation proposals, Mellowes offered the assurance that the size of school buildings would not be allowed to influence the quality of education provided within them, and that staff would be well-prepared by the time the scheme was launched:

> it is our intention to glean all the information we can from other authorities – some of us have visited various comprehensive schools already – and we hope that you and your colleagues will continue to be as helpful to us as you have been in the past. We have a very intensive programme of in-service training for the change to comprehensive organisation, embracing all the aspects of it we can foresee already planned and are making a start in September of this year. The programme will cover all three tiers.[43]

However, quite apart from doubts as to whether the county's plans would be acceptable to the Secretary of State, a measure of political uncertainty had been created by the results of the May 1967 local elections which had rendered Northumberland a hung council, with local Independents – Conservatives in all but name – holding the balance. Although a full-scale revision of the reorganisation proposals was not proposed, there was some political support for a revision of the plan's application to certain rural areas. Though rumoured to be a preservationist, the new Education Chairman, Lionel Taylor adopted a cautious stance, knowing that a decision from the DES was soon expected.

News arrived early in January that the Secretary of State accepted both parts of the plan, having concluded that 'the authority has selected the form of organisation best suited to the characteristic circumstances of the county'.[44] However, the LEA was asked to reconsider the variable sizes of middle schools, by this stage anticipated to range between 140 and 900 places, so that it could 'develop schools within a range which, in its view, strikes a right balance between the needs of the younger and older pupils'.[45] While this issue, most relevant to rural areas, was being further contemplated, the Education Committee decided to proceed with the reorganisation of nine of the 19 county districts.[46] The local evening newspaper presented this decision as a sensational climbdown ('County Tories drop educational bombshell', *Newcastle Evening Chronicle*, 22 February 1968), but it is clear that the doubts of county Independents existed principally at the practical, rather than the ideological level. As far as urban districts of Northumberland were concerned, few apparently doubted that the three-tier solution was entirely sound. Indeed, the same meeting resolved to accept the Finance and General Purposes Committee's recommendation that the plan should be introduced 'as a matter of urgency in areas of rapidly growing population'.[47] Wallsend (in the Review Area) and Seaton Delaval were earmarked for reorganisation from September 1969, with Killingworth, West Denton (also both on Tyneside) and Cramlington districts following, 12 months later.[48] This can hardly be construed as the policy of a Conservative administration opposed to comprehensivisation.

Perhaps mindful of previous criticism regarding the inadequacies of teacher participation, three working parties (representative of the three organisational tiers) were then formed. Each working party consisted of LEA officers and former members of the teachers' consultative committee. Mellowes acted as liaison with local head teachers and governors.

The three-tier system was introduced to Seaton Delaval and Wallsend on schedule in September 1969. The reorganisation of Cramlington, a rapidly expanding urban district, was also moved forward by 12 months to join them. By the launch date of the initial phase, which involved the redesignation of 53 schools accommodating 13,000 children, the Education Committee had devised a provisional schedule for the remaining urban districts of the county to reorganise gradually during the period to 1975. However, following the Conservatives' 1970 general election victory and the publication of Margaret Thatcher's Circular 10/70, the County Council rejected the five-year plan, urging the Education Committee to give further consideration to the Secretary of State's actions.[49] It was clear that Northumberland Tories were divided over the issue, but Councillor Lionel Taylor, the recently retired Chairman of the Education Committee, who had been expected by some (including the anti-comprehensive local evening newspaper) to advocate the retention of some grammar schools, was conspicuously silent (*Newcastle Evening Chronicle*, 30 September 1970). Not only did the Education Committee reaffirm their backing for the reorganisation schedule at their next meeting, they also indicated support for rural, as well as urban, districts to be included in the scheme. It was reported to the County Council in November 1970 that they had considered 'but rejected as impracticable' the possibility of retaining at least one selective school for the county.[50]

In each subsequent year, with the exception of 1971, the three-tier scheme was extended to at least one further district of the county, and by 1976, 73 per cent of county secondary pupils attended reorganised schools (including denominational ones, which had adopted the county pattern). In 1976 the 11+ examination was held for the last time in Alnwick and Amble, the last remaining selective areas of Northumberland, which then phased in comprehensive education during the period 1977–80.[51]

REFLECTIONS ON THREE COUNTY REORGANISATIONS

Each of the three counties discussed in this chapter experienced a gradual transition to comprehensive education, yet contrasts emerge in the timing and type of reorganisation. Political and parental preservationist activity was not an especially prominent feature of the reorganisations, reflecting, to a degree, the relative independence from external forces which the three Directors of Education enjoyed. Each of them appears to have been strongly supportive towards comprehensive education, though differing circumstances gave rise to varying motivational forces.

The clearest indications of ideological support for comprehensives may be attributed to Trevor Jenkins of Glamorgan, who had determined, some months before the appearance of Circular 10/65, that the county's early commitment to non-selective schooling had to become more manifest, despite the continuing impediment of inauspicious buildings. He appears to have started a process which Crosland's circular merely continued, by encouraging divisional executives to consider comprehensive solutions. The characteristic Welsh dissatisfaction with the 11+ seems to have been as apparent in Glamorgan as in other parts of that country, and may be seen as an important enabler which galvanised the relationship between the director and local politicians.

The comprehensive philosophy of Dr C.W.W. Reid and C.L. Mellowes (in West Sussex and Northumberland, respectively) was more guarded, yet just as influential. Reid's support for abandoning selection may be seen in terms of a conversion over time, and, in part, a consequence of working closely over a long period with an enthusiastically pro-comprehensive Deputy Director, R.M. Parker. Regardless of whether Crawley's bilateralism evolved into comprehensivisation by accident or design, the experience of the New Town demonstrated to the Director that educational concerns about the fairness of 11+ procedures could be addressed at the same time as the administrative problem of meeting grammar-school demand. Reid's actions reveal a firm yet low-key commitment to comprehensive education in advance of 1965, and the potential for resistance to Labour's circular was minimised by the fact that West Sussex already had several schools which were, in effect, functioning as comprehensives by that time.

No such practical experience had been gained in Northumberland where, from the outset, Mellowes personally directed developments. It was at his insistence that, unlike West Sussex and Glamorgan, Northumberland developed a uniform plan, and he defended the scheme resolutely. Like Reid, Mellowes helped to create a situation such that, by the late 1960s, a majority of local Conservative politicians could be counted among the supporters of comprehensive schools. The reorganisation of Northumberland (at a time when the political climate was becoming less favourable to comprehensive education) and parts of West Sussex was undoubtedly eased by the tiered nature of schemes, whereby changes affecting existing grammar schools could be justified in terms of reorientation, without necessitating amalgamation or closure. This enabling factor did not exist in Glamorgan, where the options for change were more restricted, and where, in any case, preservationist tendencies were less in evidence.

NOTES

1. A small number of specialist technical schools were established in Glamorgan, however.
2. West Sussex LEA cancelled plans to build two technical schools and closed one small technical school which had received an adverse report from HMI (WSRO Secondary Education sub-committee minutes, 26 March 1957). However, efforts

to persuade the excepted district of Worthing to disestablish a technical school failed after encountering determined middle-class resistance (ibid., 3 March 1959; Policy sub-committee minutes, 13 March 1959, including a memorandum by the Director entitled *Secondary Education in the Coastal Belt of the County and the Excepted District of Worthing*).

3. WSRO, Secondary Education sub-committee agenda file, attached memoranda, 10 Sept. 1957; Policy sub-committee minutes, 15 Oct. 1957.
4. The development of this policy can be traced through the following memoranda accompanying Secondary Education sub-committee minutes: *Extended Courses in Secondary Schools*, 8 Jan. 1957; *The Needs of Secondary Schools*, 15 Feb. 1957 and *Review of Policy*, 26 April 1957.
5. WSRO, Secondary Education sub-committee minutes, 13 Dec. 1960 and 14 Feb. 1961.
6. Ibid., 18 July 1961.
7. Ibid., 10 April 1962.
8. WPL, file of newspaper cuttings concerning the establishment of comprehensive education in the county.
9. WSRO, Secondary Education sub-committee minutes, 9 June 1964. The Director of Education argued that although the West Sussex development plan included provision for the establishment of a further grammar school for Littlehampton, the provision of secondary education had to take account of the requirements of the coastal belt as a whole, and Worthing, in particular.
10. Ibid., 14 Jan. 1964.
11. Ibid., 14 Sept. 1965.
12. Ibid., 12 May 1964 (with attached memorandum entitled *Report from the Director of Education on the Midhurst–Petworth area*) and 9 June 1964.
13. Ibid., 13 Oct. 1964.
14. Ibid., 13 April 1965.
15. WUMRC, AAM records, MSS 59/3/1/5, 'Comprehensive Reorganisation: Glamorgan, 1963-67' file, Glamorgan Education Director's Report, 2 Dec. 1964.
16. Ibid.
17. Ibid.
18. Ibid., letters from Mary Jones to Miss S.D. Wood, AAM Secretary, 4 Nov. 1963 and 4 March 1964.
19. WSRO, Secondary Education sub-committee minutes, 12 Oct. 1965.
20. Ibid., 8 March 1966 with attached memorandum by the Director on The Reorganisation of Secondary Education.
21. Ibid.
22. Ibid., 12 Oct. 1965.
23. Ibid., Policy sub-committee minutes, 14 June 1966.
24. Ibid., Secondary Education sub-committee minutes, 11 Jan. and 11 June 1966; Policy sub-committee minutes, 21 March 1967.
25. Ibid., Policy sub-committee minutes, 18 June 1968, including memoranda concerning Horsham and Crawley by the Director.
26. Ibid., 17 Dec. 1968.
27. ULBL, BP, MS 660/25987, Ystalyfera Grammar School Parents' Association resolution, 18 Sept. 1968.
28. Ibid., MS 660/25992, Elwyn Davies to Boyle, 8 Oct. 1968.
29. NRO, Further Education and Youth sub-committee minutes, 29 Sept. 1965.
30. CHM, SP, Northumberland County Council Education Committee, *Reorganisation of Secondary Education: The Tyneside Special Review Order*, 1967, p. 1.

31. Ibid., draft article for *County News*, 26 Feb. 1976.
32. Ibid., Mellowes to Education Committee members, 22 June 1966.
33. NRO, Education Committee minutes, 28 June 1966.
34. Ibid., 10 Oct. 1966.
35. CHM, SP, Mellowes to Education Committee members, 22 June 1966.
36. NRO, Finance and General Purposes sub-committee minutes, 21 Sept. 1966.
37. NRO, Education Committee minutes, 10 Oct. 1966.
38. Ibid., appendix entitled 'Memorandum submitted by teacher members of the Ad Hoc Committee for Secondary Reorganisation', 13 Sept. 1966.
39. CHM, SP, 'Ad Hoc Committee' file, minutes of a meeting attended by the teachers' committee, the Director and the Chairman of the Education Committee, 23 Jan. 1967.
40. Ibid., Northumberland County Council Education Committee, *Reorganisation of Secondary Education: the Tyneside Special Review Order*, 1967, p. 2.
41. Ibid., undated paper by Spicer, entitled 'Consultations on the Proposals for Reorganisation'.
42. Ibid., Mellowes to HMI H. Boyer, 15 June 1967.
43. Ibid.
44. NRO, Finance and General Purposes sub-committee minutes, 7 Feb. 1968, appendix, H. Stevens, DES official to Mellowes, 11 Jan. 1968.
45. Ibid.
46. NRO, Education Committee minutes, 22 Feb. 1968.
47. NRO, Finance and General Purposes Committee minutes, 7 Feb. 1968.
48. NRO, Education Committee minutes, 22 Feb. 1968.
49. NRO, County Council minutes, 6 Aug. 1970.
50. Ibid., 5 Nov. 1970, memorandum from Education Committee.
51. CHM, SP, draft article for *County News*, 26 Feb. 1976.

9

Summary of the LEA
Case Studies

The importance of the actions of individual LEAs in carrying through comprehensive reorganisation in England and Wales has been well recognised (Fearn, 1983), but the dynamics of the process have been relatively little studied. What lay behind the actions that LEAs took in preparing and implementing comprehensive schemes? What were the implications of having a pluralist system of LEAs for the way that comprehensive schooling was brought into being and the form it assumed?

The preceding historical reconstructions have shown that it is not easy to provide general explanations to account for the timing and form of reorganisation adopted in LEA plans or the progress of the movement to comprehensive schooling. In each case, it has been apparent that a distinctive combination or mix of elements was involved. This does not rule out the possibility of studying some of these elements in a more systematic way and for the country as a whole, as will be undertaken in the following chapters. But the main concern in providing local examples of the change to comprehensive schooling is to identify and compare the way in which the different elements in the local mix interacted.

The preceding studies describe in selective cases the interactions among local socioeconomic circumstances, political control and ideological commitment, the activities of pressure groups, and the attitudes and powers of the local educational adminstrators, especially the CEO. Our aim in presenting them is to deepen understanding of how these different elements operated at the local level to facilitate or impede the process of educational change. This concluding section to the local studies summarises and discusses a number of the major factors that have been observed in these ten case studies.

THE ROLE OF LOCAL CIRCUMSTANCES

An initial point to come out of the case studies is that comprehensive reorganisation was instituted in a variety of different circumstances, not all of them propitious. Local authorities had different starting points, different resources, and different sets of problems with which to contend. At first sight, it seems reasonable to assume that authorities with large working-class populations were more likely to be committed to the idea of comprehensive education than authorities in rural or suburbanised areas. But this was not always or necessarily the case. Indeed, some authorities in predominantly rural districts were among the earliest to introduce the change to a comprehensive system. On the other hand, the circumstances of county authorities with rural districts were different from those of urbanised counties or cities, and this has to be taken into account as an element affecting change in some counties.

It seems clear, for example, that county authorities responsible for mainly rural districts or for mining districts with relatively stagnant populations, were held back from making major changes in the organisation of secondary education by meagre resources and a back-log of problems. To some extent, all authorities had to contend with resource problems in the 1950s, but these were particularly acute in such counties as Northumberland and Glamorgan, as the previous chapter has emphasised.

In the case of Labour-controlled Glamorgan, ambitions for comprehensive reorganisation prior to 1965 were frustrated by resource problems and building grant disapproval. In contrast, at the time of the issue of Circular 10/65, Northumberland had only just succeeded in putting into place the mechanisms demanded by the 1944 Act. Its post-war heritage of all-age and one-teacher schools was undoubtedly a constraining factor in putting comprehensive reorganisation on the agenda, and it was the only authority among the case studies not to have approached the comprehensive issue by 1965. West Sussex was another authority that had to contend with the special difficulties of rural areas. Both of these counties had the problem of providing schools of a viable size, without imposing unduly long travelling distances on village children. West Sussex also illustrates the point that a predominantly rural authority, as it was in the period before 1944, tended to inherit old-fashioned attitudes and a tiny administrative staff initially unable to cope with new population pressures.

On the other hand, as Leicestershire shows, even a rural authority could develop a tradition of strong bureaucratic direction going back to the pre-war period. In Leicestershire, an enterprising and strong-minded CEO anticipated an argument that was to be subsequently used in other counties in claiming that a non-selective system was

161

particularly appropriate for rural districts and a way of overcoming resource problems to provide greater opportunities for the children of that county.

In contrast, cities and counties with growing urbanised districts had site availability and resource advantages which were undoubtedly important in facilitating the development of comprehensive schooling, especially in the pre-1965 period. After 1944, the rapid growth of council housing estates in green field sites on the edges of the city and the formation of New Towns, such as Crawley in West Sussex, put enormous pressures on secondary education provision but, at the same time, it created opportunities and a rationale for the building of new, purpose-built comprehensives. The relationships between comprehensive reorganisation, new town development and suburban housing expansion is well-illustrated in the West Sussex and Bristol examples. This is a theme which deserves to be further developed. But in the context of this project, it is sufficient to point out that such a development of new school building was consistent with the post-war expansion of housing.

Purpose-built schools were rarities in the 1970s, not only because of the slowdown in urban expansion but also because of the escalating costs of building materials and the impact of niggardly building grants which were forcing all LEAs to reorganise within the framework of existing buildings. The failure of central government to make special provision for building grants after 1965 has been noted several times in the preceding accounts as a hindrance to the progress of reorganisation among authorities that were quite different in their social composition and style of planning.

The resource advantages were not all on the side of the cities and growing urban districts, although clearly these did play an important role in the early stages of comprehensive reorganisation. Not only Northumberland and Glamorgan, with their legacy of small schools in districts with stagnant populations, but also industrialised counties such as the West Riding of Yorkshire were strikingly affected in their progress towards comprehensive reorganisation by the constraints of buildings and site availability. Moreover, the older cities had to contend with the special problems of population transfer and of the difficulties posed by a heavily built-up central core.

The London study illustrates particularly well the special problems of bringing about change in a metropolitan city of great complexity and size. The planning of the London education service was bound to be a mammoth task, complicated throughout by the need continually to upgrade the development plan in the face of massive demographic movements, with the transfer of population to outer suburban districts. However, the problem of site availability in the central areas was less acute than it might have been in London because of extensive war damage.

The problem of the older provincial cities was highlighted by the Birmingham CEO, Sir Lionel Russell, who pointed out, in one of his several ill-fated reports, that a widespread system of city comprehensive schools would appear to be impractical, not merely because of the need to use existing school buildings as far as possible, but in order to comply with ministerial regulations of providing a ten acre site for an eleven-form entry school. It was not only that such sites were not available in the central areas of the older cities, but that these areas, as in Bristol, were the location of the city's older and most prestigious grammar schools.

A heritage of relatively small schools was everywhere an impediment to change, but this posed special difficulties for authorities set on developing all-through comprehensive schools. In the case of several other authorities, not only London and Bristol, but also Glamorgan and West Sussex, reorganisation almost invariably involved amalgamations, frequently entailing the use of split sites, or closures – all of which could and frequently did engender local protest. The difference seems to be that in the cities, localised protests could be more readily orchestrated into a concerted preservationist campaign, as the examples of London and Bristol dramatically show.

Moreover, in the larger cities with extensive socially differentiated built-up areas, such as Manchester, Bristol and London in our studies, the problems of zoning and the issue of neighbourhood schools were controversial matters around which anti-comprehensive groups might focus their opposition. London's educational planning had not only to contend with the problems of socially segregated districts of working-class estates, as in other large cities, but also with the interrelations between territorial and ethnic segregation, as manifested in the formation of white and black schools. This situation lay behind the decision of the ILEA to designate catchment areas.

THE ROLE OF LOCAL POLITICS

The role of politics as an element in change is more problematic in these studies than might initially have been anticipated. As would be expected, there was much greater political activity and concern about the issue of comprehensive reorganisation in the cities and the counties with mining, industrialised and urbanised districts than in counties with extensive rural districts, whose councils were mostly Conservative or Independent in political complexion. But it was far from axiomatic that comprehensive reorganisation was dependent on control of the council by Labour. Indeed, it is not at all clear whether the existence of a strongly politically motivated council necessarily facilitated the pace of reorganisation, and it may actually have retarded it in some instances. In the country as a whole, the strength and commitment of local Labour groups was undoubtedly of importance in accounting for the early formulation of schemes and the *break-out* of LEAs away from selection. Among our case-study authorities, the London Labour Party provides an outstanding example of a local organisation that was more radical and forward-looking than the party as a whole in the immediate post-war years. In Manchester, too, we have noted the influence of a strong tradition of Labour support for comprehensive schooling, as in Glamorgan among the counties. In addition, the accounts of these districts highlight the way that political commitment kept up the pressure for change over a long period. Not all local Labour groups were pioneers of the comprehensive idea or whole-heartedly in favour of moving to a comprehensive system, however. In Northumberland, we found that Labour councillors had, by and large,. settled for a bilateral system before 1965. In Leeds, comprehensive reorganisation was much less politically driven than in Manchester or Bristol, but even in the latter two cities we found some local Labour leaders reluctant to institute changes to a bipartite system which they had helped to create and maintain over many years. Civic pride in the grammar school made senior Labour councillors ambivalent towards the egalitarian arguments for a comprehensive system, hence the foot-dragging and internal divisions that have been noted.

Perhaps more attention should be paid to the activities of Labour groups and pro-comprehensive organisations *outside* the councils as factors in the local political situation which prodded local councillors, whether Labour or Conservative, into some sort of activity. Although earlier discussions have tended to play down the role of pressure groups nationally, our studies have revealed them to be of importance in some authorities. In particular, the account of reorganisation in the industrial area of Yorkshire points to the role of local trades councils in seeking to persuade LEAs of the merits of comprehensive schools, and this was also true of the mining and industrial districts of

Northumberland. In West Sussex, Labour agitated for educational provision and comprehensive schooling in the New Town of Crawley.

We have also noticed that local Labour groups showed greater resolution in their commitment to comprehensive schooling in the 1960s than the 1970s. This may reflect changes at branch level in Labour politics or the influence of trades councils, as an older generation of leaders was supplemented by new people – an aspect of the local political scene that deserves to be investigated more closely than we have been able to do. Given this firmer support for the comprehensive idea at the local level, the election of a Labour government nationally was a catalyst for change, not only for the many authorities which had not yet prepared plans, but also for those which had been seeking to implement plans for some years. This was not simply on account of Circular 10/65 but also because in Labour-controlled authorities there was for the first time, a conjunction between the educational ambitions of local and central politicians. In most of the authorities studied, Circular 10/65 functioned to firm up proposals or concentrate minds, thereby assisting a process of change that was already in being.

At the same time, it should be emphasised that one of the most striking features of the politics of comprehensive reorganisation at the local level was the key importance of particular councillors and figures within the local Labour Party. What emerges most clearly from three of these studies is that so much seems to have depended on the vision, energy and influence of a handful of Labour councillors – for example, Bob Cant in Stoke-on-Trent, Lady [Shena] Simon in Manchester and the Rev. Frederick Vyvyan-Jones in Bristol. Moreover, the significance of the role of particular councillors supportive of comprehensive education is even clearer when these councillors emerged, as they sometimes did, from Conservative ranks. The example of Patrick Crotty, the Conservative Education Chairman in Leeds, who demonstrated a degree of interest in comprehensive education untypical of his party colleagues, was a case in point. Similarly, in Leicestershire, the progress of comprehensive reorganisation was undoubtedly assisted by the support of the chairman of the Education Committee in the 1960s, a Leicester businessman who provides an example of a Conservative opponent of selection.

Comprehensive reorganisation was never a straightforwardly *political* issue. Conservative authorities engaged in comprehensive experiments between 1951 and 1964, and although the issue became more politicised thereafter, it was still the case that Circular 10/65 was not by any means condemned by all Conservative authorities. It is clear from the replies to the Circular that many Conservative authorities shared Edward Boyle's admiration for tiered comprehensive schemes, and even after the sweeping Conservative successes in the 1967 municipal elections, few of the big city administrations sought to reverse the trend away from selection. Although a decentralised system of local democracies made the progress of comprehensive reorganisation vulnerable to changes in party politics, in our case-study areas this was not as great an impediment as might be thought. Between 1967 and 1970, Bristol, Manchester and London, among the study areas, all provide examples of how newly elected Conservative administrations held fast to educational policies which were more benign than their political campaign manifestos had suggested.

At that time, what many Labour and Conservative local authorities were more concerned about was the threat to their autonomy implicit in Edward Short's Bill to compel compliance with Circular 10/65. Many commentators sympathetic to comprehensive schooling now regard that as a lost opportunity, arguing that, had the Bill gone through, it would have made for a more rapid, complete and effective change. But that is arguable, given the sensitivities of the local authorities at the time, and a compulsory measure might have been disruptive.

Moreover, it is worth repeating that the existence of Conservative control did not necessarily slow down the process of change once it had been instituted. Even the opponents of comprehensive schools, such as Kathleen Ollerenshaw, Manchester's Conservative Chair of Education, were not prepared to turn back the clock. Indeed, there is evidence in the papers of Edward Boyle that, despite well-organised and fiercely fought campaigns to save grammar schools on the part of many local Conservative groups, a number of Conservative authorities had become attached to the idea of tiered comprehensive schemes (Crook, 1993). As we have argued in the case of Leeds, the Conservative support for a tiered system in that city was the key to achieving reorganisation in a way that was more acceptable to the various groups within the city.

In existing historical accounts, much attention has been paid to the role of the big city, Labour-dominated councils in the push towards comprehensive education. Our review has been concerned to stress rather more the role of the county authorities. Moreover, in trying to assess how important a strong Labour group was in facilitating comprehensive reorganisation, it is necessary to take into account the way in which cities became the scene of the greatest controversies and conflicts over the comprehensive schools issue during the 1960s, and how this impeded progress by generating a co-ordinated opposition movement. The city-wide plans of Labour-dominated councils, sometimes secretly conceived, seemed to generate the greatest controversy and anger. This was partly because the ancient grammar school foundations of the principal cities tended to spawn the strongest and most vociferous of the anti-comprehensive lobbies, and many of these groups had an influence in the local scene out of proportion to their size.

The experience of the City of Bristol well illustrates the problems which organised opposition could create for educational planners, although in that case the existence of so many prestigious foundations acted in the end to mollify opposition to the takeover of the municipal grammar schools. The older foundations, supported by the wealthiest elements in the city, were able to opt out of the comprehensive scheme. Nevertheless, in Bristol, as in Manchester and London, a sustained campaign of opposition to comprehensive schemes was mounted locally, in which the local press played a prominent part. In these places the editors of the city evening newspapers were themselves frequently the products of local grammar schools, and took it on themselves to defend what they saw as a threat to prestigious city institutions. What all this means is that plans for comprehensive reorganisation could still be frustrated by community opposition, despite the degree of political and ideological commitment they drew on; big cities were not always the focus for rapid change.

THE ADMINISTRATIVE PROCESS

The case studies raise a number of questions about the role of local administrators in the timing and implementation of change and the manner in which the transition to comprehensive schooling was achieved. Did CEOs initiate schemes? What was their role in effecting a transition to a new system? Was success more likely to come from pushing through a uniform scheme, whatever the nature of the opposition to it, or was a slower, area-by-area, tiered scheme more likely to be successful? And how important was consultation in facilitating the process of change? These are some of the issues raised by considering the administrative process of change at the local level.

The first point to be made is that, in several of the authorities studied, the crucial element in the dynamic of change was an educational official. Much seems to have depended upon the accident of appointing an education officer impressed by the need for fundamental changes in the organisation of secondary education. The attitude of the CEO and (as the examples of West Sussex and Northumberland show) the Deputy Director could make all the difference to the pace of change, whatever the political complexion of a local authority. In Labour-controlled authorities, the importance of having a conjunction between political ideology and administrative support is well illustrated in a negative way by Manchester, where education officers unsympathetic to comprehensive reorganisation were able to contrive ways of slowing down and modifying the pace and nature of change, even in an authority which experienced long periods of Labour control. However, the examples of London, Bristol, Stoke-on-Trent and Glamorgan all illustrate the different roles that the CEO could play when this conjunction of views existed, devising plans, sustaining momentum, and handling complicated negotiations.

In a city or county with a climate hostile towards the changes being proposed, the momentum of change was heavily dependent on the skill and ability of the CEO. But there were, nevertheless, distinct limits as to what a CEO could achieve, whatever the quality of his working relationships. In the study of Stoke-on-Trent's reorganisation scheme, we make the point that, however good the relationships between CEO and Education chairmen were, and whatever the merits of the scheme they sought to implement, the scheme was doomed if the wider political climate in the city had been hostile.

In authorities controlled by the Conservatives (or Independents), the role of the CEO seems to have been enhanced in circumstances where the Council was not strongly politicised. The freedom from political constraints which Stewart Mason enjoyed in Leicestershire and which allowed him to pursue his own idiosyncratic ambitions for secondary reorganisation was perhaps exceptional, as was his despotic control over the authority. But other Independent councils also gave their CEOs considerable freedom, as in West Sussex, where the County Chairman boasted of the Council's non-ideological approach towards comprehensive reorganisation. In that county, the Independent council was concerned primarily with encouraging the CEO to allow a variety of schemes to be devised, in order to meet local circumstances, rather than insisting on any one scheme (or none at all).

The examples of the West Riding and Glamorgan illustrate the importance of differing administrative styles and arrangements among the County authorities. Sir Alec Clegg in the West Riding, another able and innovative education officer committed to comprehensive reform, did not enjoy the same degree of power as Stewart Mason to implement change. This was less a matter of political considerations than of the county's complex administrative structure. As we have seen, Clegg could only act with the support of the divisional executives of the various county districts districts which had their own unique preferences and prejudices. In the county of Glamorgan too, the CEO had to carry divisional executives with him, some of whom had their own ideas about the *type* of reorganisation most appropriate to their district. The West Riding and Glamorgan were not the only counties in which socioeconomic diversity made a more flexible approach necessary – Northumberland and West Sussex are other examples we have studied – but the West Riding in particular had an exceptional degree of administrative decentralisation which inevitably inhibited the move to comprehensive reorganisation on a county-wide basis. However, there were other elements in that county's situation which ensured that a scheme did eventually go through.

STRATEGIES OF CHANGE

Finally, consideration needs to be given to *how* a scheme was implemented. There are two main issues here. One concerns the role of consultation as a strategy of implementation, and the other concerns the flexibility of a local authority in relation to the type of scheme that was favoured.

On the first of these matters, it is hard to think of a local government process since the Second World War which has involved such an extent of public consultation and participation as comprehensive reorganisation. There is no evidence to support the views of some of the opponents of comprehensive schemes that they were impractical arrangements devised by insensitive and all-powerful local bureaucrats. It is true, nevertheless, that significant variations occurred in the *extent* of consultation and types of procedures followed in the various LEAs.

Authorities in which consultation was ignored or assumed a low profile included Leeds, whose Education Department seems to have been untypically secretive, with politicians, rather than educationists, retaining a monopoly of the decision-making powers. The Leicestershire Plan was implemented by County Hall officials and, although initially designated an experiment, was never evaluated with reference to parental or teacher opinions. In other study areas there were allegations that the Education Department had not properly consulted teachers and parents or had done so only at a superficial level. The most vociferous complaints in that regard among our study authorities came from Northumberland teachers, although a teachers' consultative committee had been established in that county. In contrast, in West Sussex, teachers, as well as school heads and governors, seem to have been directly involved in determining the future of their schools. Elsewhere, the pattern of establishing teacher working parties was fairly general, and while the degree of parental consultation varied enormously, parental representations – usually concerned with such matters as zoning rather than ideological objections – were treated seriously.

How important was consultation then to the process of change? It was only after the unhappy experience of the mid-1960s plans for neighbourhood comprehensive schools in Bristol (and also Liverpool) that consultation became a major issue, but it is arguable whether this added much to the difficulties of reorganisation. Bristol had such a tangle of vested interests that opposition and controversy was bound to occur whether significant consultation was attempted or not. One has to bear in mind the possibility that an elaborate consultation procedure could be devised in order to slow down the process of change. As we have argued in the case of Manchester, it was sometimes necessary to adopt a heavy-handed approach and push a scheme through if it was not to go on being stalled.

On the other hand, some education officers initiated public discussions partly because of a belief in the democratic rights of parents and teachers to be kept informed about changes which were frequently seen as momentous, but also because they were convinced that consultation would point the way forward by alleviating anxieties. The larger the authority, the more difficult and time-consuming the task of testing public opinion would be. None of the case-study authorities was in the position of Nuneaton, an excepted district of Warwickshire, which was small enough for parents to be asked to fill in a questionnaire (*TES*, 27 September 1963). In London, by contrast, an elaborate programme of public meetings was instituted in 1966–67: in all, 42 public meetings were attended by 19,000 parents. The fact that most of these were attended by the Deputy CEO, together with Education Committee members, suggests that the authority wished to pay more than lip-service to community feelings. Yet, for all that, the consultation procedure did not lead to modifications of London's inflexible comprehensive scheme.

The long evolution of comprehensive education in London was exceptional, yet in most of the authorities studied the process of reorganisation was generally a protracted one, stretching over several years. It is very difficult to judge whether the type of scheme favoured by these authorities was a factor in this. All we can do is point to the situation that developed in London, Bristol, and Leeds to an extent, where an early ideological commitment to the all-through comprehensive school was maintained for a long period, despite logistical or political impediments to achieving uniformity. In the examples of London and Bristol, certainly, there seem to be grounds for arguing that an ideological commitment to a particular form of comprehensive education reduced the momentum of change. This was certainly the belief of Peter Newsam, the penultimate ILEA CEO. Newsam favoured smaller schools in a two-tier comprehensive system, but by the time he was in a position to be influential, the conditions affecting London education had changed so radically that a uniform pattern of all-through comprehensives had become impractical. What is perhaps most surprising about the London story is that all-through comprehensive schools had continued to be formed over a period of years, despite the power and strength of the preservationist lobby in the metropolis.

Two further points need to be made about the way comprehensive reorganisation was planned. The first is that some of the authorities in our study areas had started out with ambitious plans for city-wide systems of 11–18 comprehensives, but found it expedient or necessary to compromise eventually. Various kinds of compromise may be observed in the introduction of *interim schemes*, some of which allowed grammar schools to coexist with so-called comprehensive schemes. Other compromise moves that seemed to mollify opposition, as in the case of Bristol, involved accepting the continuance of direct-grant schools, and even supporting these with local authority-funded places. In some cases an authority compromised by giving up earlier plans for all-through comprehensives in favour of tiered schemes.

Second, there can be no doubt that in the country generally, and in several of our study areas in particular, the adoption of a tiered scheme or the modification of an all-through scheme with a compromise arrangement was frequently a catalyst for change. As we have seen, before 1965, several authorities moved very cautiously towards comprehensive reorganisation, some of them merely engaging in occasional experiments, others favouring bilateral arrangements on campus sites as a kind of halfway stage. The subsequent adoption of a middle-school scheme was important both in helping to facilitate comprehensive reorganisation on the part of Conservative-dominated councils and in resolving impasse situations for some Labour councils. The middle-school pattern allowed LEAs to remove selection without becoming embroiled in disputes about controversial amalgamations. The idea of sixth-form colleges was also important in the 1970s, helping to resolve difficult situations that had arisen over the future of old-established grammar schools in some of the cities, an idea which enjoyed Conservative as well as Labour support. Yet the adoption of a tiered scheme did not necessarily expedite change.

Much depended again on the strategies employed. Stoke-on-Trent embarked upon six years of planning, on the grounds that the choice of a comprehensive scheme had to be based on thorough research and consultation. The authority's desire to avoid a messy arrangement also led them to resist pressure for an interim scheme. Although some of our studies show how authorities struggled to push through a scheme in its original or amended form, other authorities deliberately adopted a policy of *gradualness*. Gradualness was the line taken by Leicester-shire and West Sussex, for example, both counties favouring an area-by-area approach, which in the former county took 12 years to complete. In both cases, the authority's contention was that such a timespan was justified, since reorganisation would eventually be more successful as a result of relatively little disruption or discord. Similarly, in Northumberland, the decision to go for a uniform three-tier scheme throughout the county – a scheme that seemed to enjoy the support of politicians of both parties – was phased in gradually over a period of more than 20 years.

Thus, an explanation for the drawn-out character of comprehensive reorganisation in England and Wales has to take account of a range of factors: the early start that was made by some authorities at a time when no general consensus existed in favour of comprehensive educa-tion, the strategy adopted by some authorities of bringing in piecemeal or area-by-area reorganisation, and the way in which reorganisation was affected by political changes, local pressure groups and other bodies, such as diocesan boards. In some of the cities, and also in counties such as West Sussex, the type of reorganisation scheme eventually adopted very much reflected the outcome of negotiations over a period with groups which included teachers' unions, parents' organisations and former pupils' associations all seeking to exert influence on the policy outcome.

FLEXIBILITY AND VARIATION OF FORM

Because local authorities had scope for policy-making on their own account and not merely as an instrument of central government, the process of comprehensive reorganisation was characterised by a flexibility of approach to the idea of the comprehensive school that would not otherwise have existed. While social and educational idealism was not entirely absent, in many authorities the schemes adopted had more to do with what was practicable and acceptable to local communities than the early socialist visions of what a comprehensive school system should be. At the same time, this flexibility of approach and the willingness of authorities to accommodate pressures and introduce compromise arrangements enabled a considerable degree of reorganisation to be achieved. More importantly, perhaps, it fostered a consensus in favour of reorganisation and against the principle of 11+ selection, which even the Conservative Secretary of State Margaret Thatcher in the 1970s could not reverse.

The chief advantage of the decentralised system of local government in England and Wales, then, was in providing scope for local authority initiative in bringing schemes forward and finessing them through. But, as we have seen, those schemes were highly varied, and many did not seem to live up to the original definition of what a comprehensive school should be. Although a great deal of comprehensive reorganisation occurred, it is difficult to speak in terms of a comprehensive *system* emerging in England and Wales.

Our case studies have suggested that certain comprehensive forms emerged more commonly in the counties than in the cities, or in working-class rather than middle-class areas, or in LEAs controlled by the Conservatives rather than by Labour. They have also suggested that particular reorganisation models were more easily accepted by those who wanted to *protect* the established grammar schools.

The varied nature of English and Welsh comprehensive schools and the possible association between their form and the settings within which they emerged, lead to two kinds of further questions. First, are the impressions gained from our case studies indicative of more general patterns found throughout England and Wales? Second, if some of the organisational forms were more palatable to more Conservative areas, does that mean that adopting those kinds of comprehensives actually required a less complete change in the system? That is, did some kinds of comprehensives continue some of the features of the selective system more than others? We turn to those questions in the next two chapters.

10

Sources of Variation in LEA Action

In this and the next two chapters we return to a broad view of the process of reorganisation of secondary education during the 1960s and 1970s. The earlier chapters have described the historical context of the movement towards comprehensive schools and have shown, through detailed case studies, how varied the local conditions and actions were. Although this was a national movement, it is clear that the LEAs differed widely both in their rate of change and in the kinds of decisions they made about establishing comprehensive schools. By the mid-1970s, some LEAs had shifted completely to comprehensive secondary schools, while others had yet to establish their first one. We explore possible reasons for that variation in the rate of reorganisation in this chapter.

As we have also seen, the comprehensives that were established were not all the same. In some cases, especially in the early years, wholly new schools were built, designed as comprehensives. In most cases, however, existing schools were changed from being grammar or secondary modern schools to being comprehensives. Some LEAs introduced middle schools and other tiered forms of organisation, and many comprehensives did not include a sixth form. In this chapter we seek to increase our understanding of the reasons for this variety by systematically analysing the characteristics of the LEAs that responded to the reorganisation movement in these different ways. Were all of the newly established schools equally comprehensive, or did some of them retain some of the features of the selective system? Did the same forces that served to accelerate or resist comprehensive reorganisation also lead to particular kinds of reorganisation when it did occur?

While these changes in the organisation of the schools were taking place, the educational process continued unabated. Students flowed into, through and out of the state-supported secondary schools; teachers continued to teach, and the evaluation of student performance proceeded as before. But did the shift to comprehensive schools make a difference? Did it affect the distributions of students into different kinds of schools? Did it alter the way the schools functioned? Did it affect students' academic achievements? These questions guide the investigations reported in Chapters 11 and 12.

The analysis in these three chapters is based on data from and about a cohort of English and Welsh students who were passing through the secondary school system during the period of rapid change. The cohort was the one used as the basis for the National Child Development Study (NCDS). The NCDS began as a study of all the babies born in England, Scotland and Wales during the first week of March 1958. Follow-up data were collected from the members of the cohort, their parents and the schools they attended when they were 7, 11, and 16 years old. Information about the school examinations they passed was collected from the schools when they were 20 years old, and extensive interviews were conducted with the cohort members when they were 23 years old.[1] Consistent with the rest of the analyses presented in this volume, only the English and Welsh members of the cohort are included in the present analysis. Most of the analysis is based on data collected when they were 16 years old and still in secondary school. However, data from earlier periods are used to control for their varied backgrounds, and data from the later collection points are used to describe their achievements.

This cohort was part of the first to be affected by the then newly established minimum school-leaving age of 16, so they were all still in school for the 1974 data collection. Those who entered secondary school at age 11 did so in 1969, and those who stayed in secondary school until they were 18 left in 1976. Thus, the members of this cohort were in secondary school during the period of most rapid change in the system. Many of them entered secondary schools that had already become comprehensives, and others were in secondary school when their schools changed status.

Since the change from selective to comprehensive schools was not complete, even by 1976, members of this cohort attended all types of schools – grammar, secondary modern, comprehensive and independent (private) schools. The primary focus of our analysis in this chapter and the next is on the characteristics of the comprehensives that the LEAs introduced and the experiences of students who attended already established comprehensives. However, it is also informative to make comparisons between comprehensive schools and the state-supported selective schools. That is the focus of Chapter 12.

In this chapter, we turn first to an analysis of the differences in the LEA responses to the comprehensive schools movement. We examine the great variation in both the *amount* of change and the *kinds* of comprehensives that were established. It will become apparent that the breadth and depth of coverage in this chapter is very different from that in the chapters about the individual LEAs. Although we have some valuable information available about the LEAs, their schools and their pupils, the amount and kind of information is more limited and of a rather different kind from that used in our analyses of the ten LEAs. For instance, we have no information for the full set of LEAs about the local leaders, the role of the press, or the degree of public involvement in the change process.

However, the fact that we have information here about all of the LEAs is also an important difference. The ten LEAs we studied in depth were not a random sample of LEAs; they were chosen because of their special characteristics, as discussed earlier. They tended to be more active participants in the transition to comprehensive schools, and they include LEAs that were unusual in the kinds of educational systems they established. For instance, Stoke-on-Trent adopted arrangements that were essentially unique. In addition, we have not included among our ten focal LEAs any that failed to establish any comprehensives by 1974, but those LEAs are included in the quantitative data. We will return to the implications of these differences at the end of this chapter, but it would be well to keep them in mind as we present these broadly based analyses.

DISTRIBUTIONS OF SCHOOLS AND STUDENTS

As a preliminary indication of the diversity of LEA responses to the comprehensive school movement, we examined the 1974 distribution among the LEAs of school[2] types and of the pupils in those different kinds of schools. It is abundantly clear not only that there was a great deal of variation among the individual LEAs, but also that the overall rate of change was very uneven in the several regions of the country.

Table 10.1 reports, by region, the distribution of the types of schools[3] attended by the NCDS cohort and the proportions of the NCDS students attending those schools when they were 16 years old in 1974. Those two sets of proportions do not fully agree because the comprehensive schools tended to be rather large while the independent schools tended to be quite small. Although, overall, there were more comprehensive schools than any other type, and more students were attending comprehensives than any other type in 1974, there were

176

many grammar, secondary modern and independent schools, and sizeable minorities of the NCDS cohort were attending each of these other types of schools.[4]

The distribution of schools and students in the four school types varied greatly in the ten regions. In particular, comprehensive education was much more fully established by 1974 in Wales and in the East and West Ridings than it was in the north-western and the southern regions or in London and the South East. The proportion of schools that were comprehensive in Wales was more than twice that in the southern region, and the difference in the proportions of students at comprehensives was almost as great.

Why should there have been so much regional variation in the adoption of comprehensive schooling? The conventional wisdom suggests that the greater the control by the Labour Party, the more rapidly the change to comprehensive education should have taken place, and some of the case-study LEAs (especially those in large cities) are consistent with that expectation. However, we have also seen in the earlier chapters that there were some striking exceptions. Some Conservative LEAs (such as Leicestershire) reorganised quite early and rapidly. The overall pattern might still have been for Labour LEAs to change most often, however, so it is wise to examine the validity of that conventional wisdom more systematically here using the NCDS data.

POLITICAL CONTROL AND
THE PACE OF COMPREHENSIVISATION

Our analysis focuses on the nature of LEA political control during the period from 1964 to 1973: the critical period of change from selective to comprehensive schools that could be reflected in the NCDS data. There were many patterns of political control in the LEAs during that period, so that any analysis of the association between political control and the change to comprehensives must use some simplifying classifications. As Chapter 2 reported, there was a general political shift at the local level to the Conservative Party beginning in about 1967–68, so we have divided the years covered into an early and a late period, using 1967–68 as the dividing point (thus, the two periods are from 1964 to 1967–68 and from 1967–68 to 1973). We have also simplified the classification of political control by combining the few cases of control by independents with control by the Conservative Party because most of the political positions of the independents were closer to those of the Conservatives than to those of Labour. The term *Conservative* is used for the combined category.

Many LEAs had clear Labour or clear Conservative control during either or both periods, but there were also some mixed cases. The mixed cases were of two types. In some LEAs, no party was in control during one or both of these periods while, in others, control shifted back and forth. Both of these patterns would reduce the likelihood of party-based actions, so they are classified together and referred to as 'mixed'. Finally, a few of the LEAs had such atypical political control histories that they could not be classified into any of these categories and are simply referred to as 'other'. There are six resulting categories of political control in the LEAs during the two periods: Labour–Labour, Labour–Mixed, Labour–Conservative, Mixed–Conservative, Conservative–Conservative and Other. The other possible combinations (for example Conservative–Labour) were not found owing to the strong swing towards Conservative control in 1967–68.

Table 10.2 reports the number of LEAs in each political control category and the relationship between LEA political control during those years and several characteristics of the LEAs' schools. The proportions of the LEAs' state-supported schools that were comprehensives in 1974,[5] shown in the first column of Table 10.2, are generally in accord with the conventional wisdom. The average proportions were by far the largest in those 11 LEAs that were continuously controlled by Labour. Those controlled by the Conservatives during both periods had next to the lowest proportion of comprehensives, only the Mixed–Conservative category having a lower proportion.

Not shown in Table 10.2 is the distribution of LEAs that had yet to establish a single comprehensive school by 1974. There were 19 such LEAs. Nine of them (47.4 per cent) were LEAs controlled in both periods by the Conservatives. Six (31.6 per cent) were LEAs with mixed control in the early period but Conservative control in the later period. The other four were LEAs controlled by Labour in the early period but with mixed control in the later period. All of the LEAs with the other three types of control (Labour–Labour, Labour–Conservative, and Other) had established at least one comprehensive school by 1974.

Additional insight can be gained from the other data in Table 10.2. We have distinguished there between comprehensives founded before 1970 and those founded in the period 1970–74. That division has particular relevance for the later analysis of the experiences of the

NCDS cohort members, as we explain in Chapter 11, but it is also a meaningful division here. If local political control affected the founding of comprehensive schools, presumably it took at least a year or two for the schools to be established, since plans had to be developed and then approved by the DES. A change of control in 1967–68 could not be expected to have had an effect before 1969 or 1970. So, the division of founding dates parallels our division of periods of political control with about a two-year time lag. It is also important to remember that 1970 was the year in which Margaret Thatcher issued Circular 10/70, effectively invalidating Circular 10/65, which had called for comprehensive school planning.

In most categories of LEAs about two-thirds of the comprehensive schools existing in 1974 were actually founded in 1970 or later, but there were two striking exceptions. LEAs that shifted from Labour control to Conservative control established the majority of their comprehensives in the earlier period, suggesting that the Conservatives cut back sharply on the comprehensivisation begun by Labour. The other exceptional category is made up of LEAs that shifted from mixed control to Conservative control. Ironically, the great majority of the comprehensive schools in those LEAs were founded in 1970 or later. It is important to note, though, that this category also had the smallest proportion of comprehensives by 1974, which is consistent with the idea that Conservative LEAs were not leaders in the comprehensive school movement. It is also informative to note the distributions of independent schools among the LEAs. While children living in a particular LEA would not necessarily have attended independent schools in their own local area, the distribution of those schools was also consistent with reasonable assumptions about the relationship between school types and political control. Independent schools tended to be used most often by the middle class, and the middle class more often supported the Conservatives, rather than the Labour Party. Consistent with those associations, we find here that the smallest proportions of independent schools in 1974 were in those LEAs that had been controlled by Labour during both periods, while the largest proportions were in those LEAs that were controlled by the Conservatives in the more recent period.

Yet, control by the Conservatives was far from uniformly associated with rejection of comprehensivisation, and not all LEAs controlled by Labour favoured comprehensives. Many within the Labour Party were hesitant to abolish the selective system because they saw it as a relatively democratic mechanism for working-class children to succeed at school. There were also some clear exceptions to Conservative resistance to comprehensive schools, especially in the less densely populated areas. Although Table 10.1 shows that the fullest apparent commitment to comprehensive education was found in Wales, seven of the 16 Welsh LEAs were controlled by the Conservatives throughout both periods.

It is also important to remember that, although there was a strong general political shift towards Conservative control in the later period analysed here, about two-thirds of all comprehensive schools were founded in that period. It was primarily in the 1960s that Labour was at the forefront of the comprehensive movement. It became a more general movement in the early 1970s, and many comprehensive schools were founded in LEAs controlled by the Conservatives. So, political control was not the only factor influencing the varied actions of the LEAs.

MULTIPLE SOURCES OF THE CHANGE TO COMPREHENSIVE SCHOOLS

It would not be surprising, of course, if political control did not completely explain the introduction of comprehensive schools. It is apparent from the information presented in the earlier chapters that a combination of factors affected the kinds of response the LEAs made to the growing pressure to introduce comprehensive schools. The earlier chapters have suggested that several kinds of community characteristics were associated with the pattern of shift to comprehensive schooling. In some cases it appears that the more rural and poorer LEAs introduced comprehensives earlier, and the high proportion of comprehensive schools in Wales strengthens that impression. We have also seen that much of the resistance to the change to comprehensives was generated in middle-class neighbourhoods with well-established grammar schools. At the same time, it was apparent that there were costs associated with comprehensivisation, and some less well-funded LEAs evidently moved more slowly than they might otherwise have done for that reason.

Some of these community characteristics may have been correlated with political control in the LEAs, but they may have had an independent effect as well, so it may be informative to consider their effects along with those of political control. We can gain some indication of the possible multiple sources of change through the data in Table 10.3. There we report the results of a set of linear regression analyses, using the LEA as the unit of analysis, in which the proportion of the LEAs' secondary schools that were comprehensive schools in 1974 is used as the dependent variable.[6]

In the first analysis, we consider the effects of several community characteristics. The first four of these are based on 1971 census data. To reflect the nature of the community and its economy, we include measures of the proportion of the labour force in agriculture and in mining or manufacturing. To reflect the socioeconomic level of the community, we include the proportion of the labour force in non-manual occupations and the proportion of the dwellings that were owner-occupied. Finally, as a rough indicator of the resources available to education, we include the average pupil–teacher ratio in the schools in each LEA in 1973. The results of the first analysis lend little support to the reasoning that led us to include these five variables in the analysis. The only variable significantly associated with the proportion of students in comprehensives is the average pupil–teacher ratio in the LEAs' schools. The negative coefficient indicates that there is a tendency for LEAs with low pupil–teacher ratios to have high proportions of their students in comprehensive schools. We considered the possibility that intercorrelations among these variables might have led to their cancelling each other's direct effects. This was not the case, however. None of the variables is individually associated with the proportion of schools that were comprehensives. Moreover, the full set of measures of community characteristics explains only 4.9 per cent of the variance in comprehensive school enrolment. We can only conclude that these community characteristics are not very important sources in explaining the degree of comprehensivisation up to 1974.

Dummy variables are added in the second analysis that represent the pattern of political control in the LEA. Those LEAs in which there was consistent Conservative control are used as the reference category. Thus, the coefficients for each of the other types of political control indicate how LEAs with that type of control differed from LEAs consistently controlled by the Conservatives. As the previous discussion suggested, this analysis shows that LEAs controlled by Labour had a strong tendency to establish comprehensive schools. LEAs with all three political control patterns involving Labour control in the early period had significantly higher proportions of schools that were comprehensive in 1974 than did those consistently controlled by the Conservatives. The strongest effect is found for LEAs that were continuously controlled by Labour in both periods. There is also a sharp increase in the R^2, the combined community characteristics and political control variables explaining 12 per cent of the variance in the proportions of comprehensive schools.

The proportion of the LEAs' comprehensives that were founded before 1970 is added in the third analysis. The inclusion of that particular variable has the effect of focusing the analysis on those factors that affected shifts to comprehensive schools in the 1970s. Its inclusion weakens all of the positive effects of the three dummy variables indicating control by Labour. The dummy variables indicating control by Labour in the early period but loss of control in the later period are no longer statistically significant. The reduction is especially sharp for those LEAs that shifted from Labour to Conservative control. This is the category of LEA in which a majority of comprehensive schools existing in 1974 had been established before 1970 (see Table 10.2). Overall, what we see here is that because the change to comprehensive schools was more widespread in the 1970s, political control does not help nearly as much to explain the establishment of comprehensives in the 1970s as it did in the 1960s.

Clearly, political control was an important factor influencing the change to comprehensive schools, especially before 1970. There is little evidence of the influence of the other factors we have considered, although there is a suggestion that LEAs with greater educational resources (reflected in a low pupil–teacher ratio) moved more rapidly towards comprehensive schooling. It is apparent, however, that neither community characteristics nor political control were as important in explaining the increases in comprehensive school enrolments in the 1970s as they were in the 1960s.

These results support the conventional wisdom regarding the importance of political party control, especially during the early period. But they do not support some other expectations, especially the expected relevance of socioeconomic level and urban–rural differences. This may well be the result of some of the cross-cutting influences referred to in our earlier chapters. Although ideological issues appeared to be dominant in decisions about comprehensive schools in urban areas (Chapters 4 and 5), it was often more a matter of economics (Chapter 8) or educational philosophy (Chapter 7) in the more sparsely populated areas. In addition, the middle class was of two minds regarding comprehensive schools. While middle-class support for the well-established grammar schools was apparent in many areas, others saw comprehensive education as a means to escape the restrictive limits on grammar-school access via the much-disliked 11+ examination. For many, comprehensives evidently did seem to promise a 'grammar school education for all'.

It may be important here to remember that our analysis has used the LEA as the unit of analysis. That is, all LEAs are given equal weight in the computations. When we consider that some of these LEAs were huge (for example London, the West Riding) and others were very small (for example Eastbourne, Worcester), it may be that the kind of analysis we have conducted does not provide the clearest picture of the general factors involved in adopting comprehensive education.

Finally, our analyses may also reflect the fact that widely varied kinds of schools are subsumed under the heading 'comprehensive'. We need to remember that Circular 10/65 allowed for several kinds of comprehensive schools, and we have already seen that the dynamics of local decision-making often led LEAs to accept one of these more easily than the others. As the next section indicates, we can learn a great deal about the differences among LEAs by investigating which of the available alternatives the LEAs chose to adopt.

TYPES OF COMPREHENSIVES

The comprehensive schools in existence in 1974, when the NCDS secondary school data were collected, varied in several ways that need to be taken into account if we are to understand the *process* of change. Some of them had been in existence for a decade or more, while others had only recently been established. Moreover, they had originated in different ways, and had different internal structures. We examine those kinds of variation here, and find that the *kinds* of comprehensives established by LEAs were even more clearly influenced by community characteristics and political control than was the overall rate of comprehensivisation.

Comprehensives came into existence in four different ways. Some were newly established schools in new buildings; we will refer to them as 'purpose-built' schools. However, most comprehensives were established in buildings that had formerly housed grammar schools or secondary modern schools. In some of those cases, though, a single school was formed by amalgamating two or more schools.[7] Some of the analysis in Chapter 11 is concerned with whether these different origins affected the ways in which the comprehensives functioned, and, in particular, whether there was a tendency for those that had been grammar or secondary modern schools to continue some of the features of the selective system. But our concern at this point is to attempt to identify any factors that might have influenced the LEAs to establish comprehensives in one, rather than another, of these ways. The comprehensive schools also differed in the way they were organised. Schools were asked for the ages of their youngest and oldest students in 1974. Most were 'all-through' schools, recruiting pupils at the age of 11 and retaining some until they were as old as 18 or 19. As the previous chapters have shown, however, this was not universally true. Some comprehensives reported that their youngest pupils were 12, 13, or even 14 years old, and some reported that their oldest students were only 16 or 17 years old.

A number of changes were occurring during the years covered by our analysis. In addition to the tiered Leicestershire plan, middle schools were being introduced in a number of LEAs, and this meant that pupils entered secondary school at ages *other* than 11. Also, some LEAs introduced sixth-form colleges for those who planned to study for A-Levels, and other LEAs offered a sixth form in only *some* of their comprehensive schools. That made it possible for some comprehensives to have only compulsory-age pupils, the others transferring either to another secondary school or to a sixth-form college if they wished to study for A-Levels.

We do not have adequate information to classify all schools according to the specific kinds of programmes offered, but we will assume that those schools with no pupils older than 16 or 17 did not offer sixth-form courses, and in the rest of the discussion we refer to such schools as not having a sixth form. Students from such schools who wanted to carry on to the sixth form had either to attend a sixth-form college or to transfer to another school to study for the A-Level examinations.

Table 10.4 reports the distribution of comprehensive schools according to their type of origin (purpose-built, etc.), their age structure,[8] and the period in which they were founded. Several important features of the pattern of transition to comprehensive schools are reflected in that table. First, as already noted in Table 10.2, most of the comprehensives (63 per cent) in existence in 1974 were founded between 1970 and 1974. This was after most of the NCDS students had entered secondary school. Second, most of the purpose-built comprehensives were established before 1970, and the great majority of the comprehensives founded in the 1970–74 period were based on existing grammar or secondary modern schools or combinations of two or more selective schools. Third, as reported in the total rows, comprehensives founded in the two periods were about equally likely to have late entry ages (12 or older), but comprehensives founded in the 1970–74 period were much less likely than those founded earlier to have a sixth form. This was at least in part because sixth-form colleges were a relatively late innovation.

Finally, and of great importance for our analysis in Chapter 11, the different age structures were unequally distributed across the comprehensives having the four types of origins. Comprehensives that had been grammar schools were much more likely than any other type to have their students entering at age 13 or later, and the former secondary modern schools were least likely to do so.[9] The difference was somewhat greater for schools founded before 1970, but it can be seen for schools founded in both periods. The former secondary modern schools were also much less likely than any of the other three types to have sixth forms.[10] Again, this difference was especially great for schools founded before 1970, but it can be seen for schools founded in both periods. While we do not have full information about their experiences between ages 11 and 16, these data clearly suggest that a significant minority of the NCDS students had attended some kind of middle school and had entered secondary school relatively late. Also, it is apparent that many of them attended comprehensive schools without sixth forms.

There was an association between the schools' intake ages and their maintenance of a sixth form, as shown in Table 10.5. Almost all of the schools with the oldest intake ages enrolled sixth-form students, while a large minority of the schools with younger intake ages had no sixth-form students. This was true for schools founded in both periods, but schools with age 11 intake founded in 1970–74 were much less likely than similar schools, founded earlier, to have a sixth form. There was a general increase in the number of sixth-form colleges during the later period, but we will see that this only partially explains the sharp increase in comprehensives without sixth forms in the later period. It also became increasingly common in the later period for LEAs to establish some comprehensives with and some without sixth forms and to require students at the latter to transfer to some other school if they were to stay on for the sixth form. Schools with age 12 intake were the least common, but they were also quite unusual because they were very unlikely to have a sixth form in either period. The Plowden Report (DES, 1967) had recommended an age 12 intake, and the great majority of such schools in Table 10.5 were founded after the publication of the Plowden Report. The idea of sixth-form colleges was gaining ground at about the same time, and some LEAs (for example Stoke-on-Trent and Southampton) eventually adopted uniform systems featuring age 12–16 secondary schools and sixth-form colleges, although reorganisation had not always been fully accomplished by 1974. In other LEAs, however, there remained a mix of this combination with the more usual types of 11–18 comprehensives (for example, Warwickshire and Buckinghamshire). The combination of age 12 intake and sixth-form colleges never became a dominant pattern, but it did grow in popularity, especially in non-metropolitan LEAs. The clearest patterns in Tables 10.4 and 10.5, though, are for some schools with late intake ages to have been especially likely to enrol sixth-form students and for many other schools with early intake ages to have had no sixth-form students. Former grammar schools most often fit the first pattern, and former secondary modern schools the second. The linkage between late intake age and the offering of sixth-form courses was strong for schools founded in both periods, but the linkage between early intake and the lack of a sixth form was much stronger in the 1970–74 period than earlier.

These data demonstrate the great variety of kinds of schools subsumed under the label comprehensive. They also raise many questions. Why did some LEAs build new comprehensive schools and others transform their selective schools? Why were there such different age structures? That many of the schools with late intake and a sixth form were former grammar schools is perhaps understandable. If LEAs adopted a tiered system, they could be expected to use their former grammar schools for the upper forms because those schools had the staff and facilities needed to offer sixth-form courses. Yet, it remains unclear whether there were some general characteristics of LEAs that led them to adopt a tiered system with late intake ages. Similarly, were there particular kinds of LEAs that introduced comprehensives without sixth forms? We turn to these questions next.

SOURCES OF VARIATION IN ORIGIN AND STRUCTURE

We begin our analysis by seeing whether schools with the four kinds of origin (purpose-built, amalgamated, secondary modern, grammar) and the different organisational structures (regular or late entry, with or without a sixth form) were more likely to have been established in some kinds of LEAs than in others. Whereas the analysis presented in Table 10.3 used the LEA as the unit of analysis, we have chosen here to use the school as such, and a word of explanation concerning that decision is in order.

We noted earlier that the LEAs varied greatly in overall size (that is by the number of secondary schools they administered). It is also apparent that the LEAs varied greatly in the proportions of their secondary schools that were comprehensives. Finally, it was apparent from our preliminary analyses that few of the LEAs with comprehensives had only one single type. It was impossible to typify most LEAs according to the kind of comprehensive they had chosen to establish – Stoke-on-Trent was a rare exception with its uniform adoption of age 12–16 comprehensives followed by a sixth-form college. It is thus wiser to conduct these analyses at the school level, rather than at the LEA level, since each school can be classified according to type.

The analyses tell us whether schools of particular types were more likely to have been located in certain kinds of LEAs rather than whether certain kinds of LEAs were more likely to establish particular types of schools. Since some LEAs had many more comprehensives than others, this factor naturally gives greater weight in our computations to large LEAs, and their characteristics affect the analyses more than the characteristics of LEAs with few comprehensive schools. The analyses thus tell us about the social contexts within which the various types of comprehensives were more frequently founded.

We turn first to an analysis of factors associated with the kinds of comprehensive schools that were founded. Table 10.6 reports a series of multinomial logistic regression analyses in which the independent variables are the same LEA measures used in Table 10.3 to explain the degree to which the LEAs had shifted to comprehensive education by 1974. Here we use the category of purpose-built schools as the reference category, and thus the coefficients represent the contrasts between the characteristics of LEAs that founded each of the other three types with the characteristics of LEAs that founded purpose-built comprehensives. As before, we present the results using three increasingly elaborate analyses. The first uses as explanatory variables the four community characteristics (percentage of labour force in agriculture, percentage of labour force in mining or manufacturing, percentage in non-manual occupations, and percentage of dwellings owner-occupied) and the average pupil–teacher ratio. The second analysis adds the dummy variables indicating the types of political control, and the third adds the proportion of comprehensive schools founded before 1970. One very striking aspect about all three analyses reported in Table 10.6 is the fact that all of the coefficients for pupil–teacher ratio are significantly negative. This means that all types of comprehensives represented in the table (former grammar, former secondary modern, and amalgamated) were more often located in LEAs that had relatively low pupil–teacher ratios compared with the LEAs where purpose-built schools (the reference category) were most often located. Or, put more simply, purpose-built schools were more often established in LEAs with relatively high pupil–teacher ratios. This suggests that purpose-built comprehensives appeared most often in LEAs with relatively limited educational resources. This tended to be true in both periods.

Almost as striking is the fact that all but two of the political control coefficients in the second and third analyses have positive signs. Not all of those coefficients are statistically significant (though many of them are), but the consistency of their signs suggests that all three of these types of comprehensives were more often established in LEAs with Labour control. This, in turn, suggests that purpose-built comprehensive schools (the dependent reference category) were most often established in LEAs consistently under the control of the Conservative Party (which is the independent reference category). The sharpest contrast is between the amalgamated type (associated with Labour control) and the purpose-built type (associated with Conservative control).

Although several of the community characteristics coefficients are statistically significant in the first analysis, only those associated with the establishment of comprehensive schools in what had been secondary modern schools remain significant throughout the three analyses. LEAs with relatively high proportions of their labour forces in agriculture and in mining or manufacturing were more likely to transform secondary modern schools into comprehensives than they were to establish purpose-built comprehensives. Although that tendency appears to have been stronger in the early period, when most purpose-built comprehensives were established, it is found in both periods.

There are definitely differences among the LEAs that established the four kinds of comprehensives, but the clearest differences involve the contrast between LEAs with purpose-built comprehensives and those with comprehensives that had formerly been selective schools (especially the amalgamated type). The consistencies in Table 10.6 indicate that LEAs with fewer educational resources (high pupil–teacher ratios) and Conservative Party political control were most likely to establish purpose-built comprehensives rather than transform selective schools into comprehensives.

Among the three types of comprehensives based on transformed selective schools, the clearest effect of community characteristics is found for former secondary modern schools. The LEAs with high proportions of their labour forces in agriculture, mining and manufacturing were most likely to transform secondary modern schools. It is also noteworthy that, although the coefficient for 'per cent before 1970' is significantly positive for the other two types of comprehensives, it is much weaker (though positive) for those that had been secondary modern schools. This indicates that the former grammar and amalgamated types were more often established in the 1970s, but the former secondary modern type of comprehensives were established at about an equal rate in the two periods. Overall, however, low educational resources and control by Labour were generally associated with transforming selective schools into comprehensives across both periods, and areas more heavily devoted to agriculture, mining and manufacturing more often transformed secondary moderns into comprehensives.

These results are at least consistent with some of the impressions gained from our case studies and our general overview of the change process presented in Chapter 2. Purpose-built comprehensives were less likely to be established in the 1970s (see Table 10.4) in part because national government funding was less available. Also, especially in the 1960s, the DES had been somewhat more sympathetic to comprehensive reorganisation in the counties than in large urban authorities, for economic reasons. In addition, although those areas were often controlled by the Conservatives, they had fewer grammar schools, so the economic incentives were not as likely to be counterbalanced by 'old school' sentiments.

Further insight into the process of change can be gained by distinguishing between the kinds of LEAs that decided to establish comprehensives with late intake ages or no sixth form. Since those characteristics are associated with the schools' former statuses, however, we can expect some similarities between those analyses and the ones in Table 10.6. Tables 10.7 and 10.8 report the results of analyses dealing with those structural characteristics. The analyses in Table 10.7 of the locations of schools with late intake ages differentiate between intake at age 12 and intake at age 13+. Schools with age 11 (or younger) intake are the reference category. If one scans the results in Table 10.7, two things immediately stand out. First, there is a consistent, highly significant negative effect of the pupil–teacher ratio on the establishment of both types of late-entry school. That is, late-entry schools were consistently more often established in LEAs with greater educational resources (that is low pupil–teacher ratios). Second, both types of late-entry schools were more commonly established in the 1970s than earlier (as indicated by the significant negative coefficients for 'per cent before 1970'). These two results might have been expected, since late entry depended on relaxing mandatory age 11 intake, and given the previously reported findings suggesting that late intake grew in popularity in the more affluent areas. However, although those two results make the two types of late intake comprehensives look very similar, there are other factors that clearly distinguish between them, and those results deserve careful attention. Neither community characteristics nor political control differentiate at all clearly between LEAs that established comprehensives with age 11 (the reference category) as against age 13+ intake, but there is a much greater difference between the locations of age 11 and age 12 intake comprehensives. The settings of age 12 intake schools were thus strikingly different from those of schools with intakes at both age 11 and age 13+.

LEAs with age 12 intake comprehensives were distinctive by generally being controlled by the Conservatives (clearly not controlled by Labour), and they tended to have low proportions of the labour force in agriculture, low proportions in non-manual occupations, and high proportions of owner-occupied dwellings. Since those LEAs also had low pupil–teacher ratios, these appear to have been solid conservative working-class communities that invested significant resources in education. About the only thing that distinguishes LEAs that established comprehensives with age 13+ intake rather than age 11 intake was their much higher level of educational resources.

Table 10.8 presents the analysis of the LEA characteristics associated with establishing schools without sixth forms. There is a consistent set of results across the three columns in the table, and they parallel some of the results in Table 10.7. We see throughout that comprehensives without sixth forms were more often established in LEAs with low proportions of their labour forces in agriculture or in mining and manufacturing, but they were also LEAs with low proportions in non-manual occupations and high pupil–teacher ratios. In addition, they tended to be LEAs controlled by the Conservatives; and, of course, the last column in Table 10.8 shows that comprehensives without sixth forms were more commonly established in the 1970s.

The late entry and sixth form analyses in Tables 10.7 and 10.8 provide some interesting parallels and contrasts. The higher the proportion of non-agricultural but manual workers, the more likely was an LEA to establish comprehensives with age 12 entry and without sixth forms. LEAs with Conservative control were also more likely than those with Labour control to establish comprehensives with age 12 entry and without sixth forms. There is much less parallel between the characteristics of LEAs with age 13+ intake and those either with or without sixth forms. Neither the socioeconomic nor the political control factors are as significantly linked with age 13+ intake as they are with both age 12 intake and having comprehensives without sixth forms.

In an effort to further clarify these results, we conducted an additional set of multinomial logistic regression analyses. In these analyses, the dependent categories are combinations of age of intake and whether the school had a sixth form. The reference category is schools with age 11 intake and a sixth form, which is both the most common type of comprehensive school (48 per cent) and what might be considered to be the 'typical' form of comprehensive school organisation. The analysis thus considers what factors differentiated LEAs that more frequently established several kinds of 'atypical' comprehensives from those that established all-through comprehensives with students aged 11 to 18.

The kinds of atypical forms of organisation used in this analysis are: (a) age 11 intake and no sixth form; (b) age 12 intake and no sixth form; (c) age 12 intake and a sixth form; and (d) age 13+ intake and a sixth form. (Only seven schools had age 13+ intake and no sixth form [see Table 10.5], so there were too few of them to include as a separate category.) For simplicity, the categories are referred to in terms of the predominant ages of their youngest pupils and whether there was a sixth form. Thus, the reference category is referred to as 11–Sixth, and the four dependent categories are referred to as 11–No Sixth, 12–No Sixth, 12–Sixth and 13–Sixth. The coefficients for each of those dependent categories indicate differences between that category and schools with age 11 intake and a sixth form. The results of these analyses are reported in Table 10.9.

As before, the results are presented in three increasingly elaborate analyses. Also, as before, there are some consistencies across these analyses. Strikingly, there are statistically significant coefficients with the same signs that appear in all three analyses for either three or all four kinds of atypical organisation. That means that most of these

191

forms of organisation more frequently appeared in LEAs with characteristics that differed significantly from those where the usual all-through (ages 11–18) organisation was more common.

With the exception of the 12–Sixth category in the second analysis, there is a consistent association between all of these atypical forms and low proportions in agriculture, mining and manufacturing and low proportions in non-manual occupations. Although including the measures of political control weakens these associations with the 12–Sixth form in the second analysis, the third analysis suggests that even the 12–Sixth form appeared most often in those kinds of LEAs in the 1970s. In most of the analyses, also, most of these forms were found in LEAs with high levels of owner-occupied dwellings. It is also true, of course, that all four atypical forms were much more common in the 1970s than in the 1960s, as shown by the significant negative coefficients for the 'per cent before 1970' dummy variable in the third analysis.

These similarities are important, but before commenting on them it is equally important to recognise some differences in the results for these four atypical forms. Particularly striking is the variation in the effects of the average pupil–teacher ratio. That coefficient is consistently significantly positive for the 11–No Sixth organisation, consistently significantly negative in the 13–Sixth organisation and non-significantly negative for the other two organisational forms. This indicates that the 11–No Sixth form was more often found in LEAs with low levels of educational resources (high pupil–teacher ratios) and the 13–Sixth form was more often found in LEAs with high levels of educational resources.[11]

The political control coefficients also differ for the four organisational forms. There is a clear tendency for LEAs under Labour control not to establish 11–No Sixth comprehensives, but this seems to have been a much more common form in LEAs controlled by the Conservatives. Although most of the political control coefficients for the other three forms also suggest they were more common under Conservative control (that is, most of the coefficients are negative), that was less true for the 12–Sixth and 12–No Sixth forms than the 11–No Sixth or 13–Sixth forms of organisation. Three of the coefficients are positive for the 12–No Sixth type and the Labour-Mixed co-efficient is actually significantly positive for the 12–Sixth type in the third analysis. Overall, though, political control was not a very clear factor except for the 11–No Sixth form which was rarely used by LEAs controlled by Labour.

Here we see some similarity among those LEAs with each of the atypical forms of organisation in that the four atypical forms were more often adopted in solid non-agricultural, conservative, working-class communities. Beyond that degree of similarity, however, there were some striking differences. In particular, the 11–No Sixth form was different from the others in having been more common in LEAs with low levels of educational resources (that is high pupil–teacher ratios) while the 13–Sixth form was more common in LEAs with high levels of educational resources.[12]

We did not observe much association between community characteristics and the degree to which LEAs had adopted comprehensive schools by 1974, although there was a strong association between political control by Labour and establishing comprehensive schools, especially in the early period. In contrast, Tables 10.6, 10.7, 10.8 and 10.9 indicate that the *types* of comprehensives established varied greatly both by community characteristics and political control. LEAs with higher levels of educational resources were more likely to transform selective schools into comprehensives, and their comprehensives were more likely to have older intake ages and sixth forms. LEAs with low proportions in agriculture and yet high proportions in manual occupations were more likely to adopt all of the atypical organisational forms, and most of those forms were more common in LEAs under Conservative control.

It is thus apparent that the comprehensive school movement was both a very general one and a highly diversified one. It was so general that, although the Labour Party provided the early impetus, even political party was a weak source of explanation of comprehensivisation in the 1970s. But not all comprehensive schools were alike. It oversimplifies the change process to classify all comprehensive schools together, and we learn much more about the process by taking the diversification of types of comprehensives into account. Educational resources and the socioeconomic characteristics of the labour force influenced the organisational form of the comprehensives as well as the new schools' previous status (if any).

VARIATIONS WITHIN LEAs

The analyses presented in Tables 10.6 to 10.9 have used the school as the unit of analysis and have summarised the characteristics of LEAs that had established comprehensives of various kinds. While that kind of analysis is very informative, we must be careful not to misinterpret it. If each LEA had established only one of the kinds of comprehensives differentiated here, it would be reasonable to say that LEAs of type X introduced schools of type A while LEAs of type Y introduced schools of type B. However, very few of the LEAs had established only one of the types of comprehensives differentiated in these analyses. For instance, many LEAs had *both* purpose-built comprehensives and those based on former selective schools. These analyses reflect the overall weighted associations between the characteristics of LEAs and the types of comprehensives, not any simple one-to-one association between the two.

It is especially important to recognise the variations *within* LEAs when we consider the distribution of comprehensives without a sixth form, a type of school that becomes very important in the analysis in Chapter 11. Although Table 10.5 indicates that only 19.2 per cent of the comprehensives established before 1970 and only 36.8 per cent of those established between 1970 and 1974 had no sixth form, a majority (55 per cent) of the LEAs that had established any comprehensives by 1974 had some with *and* some without sixth forms. So, we need to keep in mind that the 457 comprehensives without sixth forms (out of the 1,507 comprehensives classified in Table 10.5) were widely scattered among the LEAs. The analyses in Tables 10.8 and 10.9 tell us about the kinds of LEAs in which they were *more commonly* established, but they were not found *only* in LEAs with those specific characteristics.

Establishing comprehensive schools without a sixth form did not mean that students in those LEAs could not study beyond the age of 16, of course. Sixth-form courses could be provided in a sixth-form college, a further education college, or in another secondary school to which students could transfer. Although our data are not wholly adequate to identify the particular pattern used in each LEA, it appears that these alternatives were not necessarily mutually exclusive. Our data indicate that NCDS students in at least 20 LEAs had attended sixth-form or other colleges, but practically all of those LEAs also had comprehensive schools with sixth forms in 1974. In fact, all of the comprehensives in three of those 20 LEAs had sixth forms, suggesting that in at least some LEAs students could choose between staying at a comprehensive school with a sixth form or attending a college after the age of 16.

This variation means that the analyses in this chapter are fundamentally different from those in the earlier chapters dealing with the ten LEAs we examined intensively. In the case-study chapters, it is possible to examine each characteristic of that particular LEA and assess its importance in affecting the specific actions taken in that LEA during the period under study. Although we have specific information of the type used in this chapter on all of the LEAs, including the ten discussed in detail earlier, our purpose here is to see if it is possible to make *general* statements about the kinds of LEAs that were more likely to take particular kinds of actions during this period.

The pictures of the period obtained by these two methods do not always agree perfectly, but they complement each other and thereby provide a more informative indication of the processes involved. In this chapter's final section, therefore, we will both summarise the analyses just presented and refer back to the ten specific LEAs. Those ten are sometimes appropriate examples of what we have found and sometimes they are exceptions to the general pattern.

OVERVIEW OF LEA RESPONSES TO THE COMPREHENSIVE SCHOOL MOVEMENT

There was considerable variation among LEAs in both the rapidity and the extent of comprehensive reorganisation. By 1974, all of the state-supported secondary schools were comprehensives in 42 LEAs, but 19 LEAs had not yet established a single comprehensive. Only one of our ten focal LEAs (Leicestershire) had *wholly* changed to comprehensives by 1974, although Bristol and Stoke-on-Trent had come close. Yet, our ten LEAs were generally among those in the forefront of the comprehensive movement. Eight of them were above the median in the proportion of their state-supported secondary schools that were comprehensives, and the lowest level of comprehensivisation (37.5 per cent in Northumberland) was greater than more than one-third of the LEAs. Also, of course, none of our focal LEAs was among those 19 that had failed to establish a single comprehensive.

Overall, those LEAs controlled by Labour tended to change from the selective to the comprehensive form earlier than others, and those LEAs that had been controlled by Labour were, by far, the most fully comprehensive by 1974. Although two of our ten focal LEAs clearly fit that pattern (Glamorgan and Stoke-on-Trent), Leicestershire was fully comprehensive in 1974 and West Sussex's schools were 85 per cent comprehensive despite being under Conservative control throughout. In general, though, our ten focal LEAs were more heavily committed to Labour than were most LEAs, especially before 1967–68 when eight of them were controlled by Labour. And that, of course, is consistent with their greater than average changeover to comprehensive secondary education. We have not found in this chapter as clear an association as we had initially expected between the social characteristics of the LEAs and the degree of comprehensive reorganisation. The accounts of the ten focal LEAs suggest some of the reasons for that. The dynamics of decision-making and the factors influencing moves towards change varied widely, and they seemed to be rather different in the large urban LEAs (for example, London or Manchester) than in the more sparsely populated areas (for example, Leicestershire or Northumberland). The overall analysis in this chapter could not fully reflect the varied components of the decision-making dynamics.

The majority (63 per cent) of the comprehensives in existence in 1974 had been established in the 1970s, a fact of great significance for our analysis in the next two chapters. Our ten focal LEAs varied greatly in the dates they established their comprehensive schools. All of the NCDS comprehensives in existence in 1974 in Manchester had been established before 1970. In contrast, all of the comprehensives in existence in 1974 in Northumberland had been established in the 1970s. Thus, any analysis that is limited to comprehensives established before 1970 (like, for instance, much of the analysis in Chapters 11 and 12) will include all of the comprehensives in Manchester but none of those in Northumberland.

The comprehensives founded during this period were highly varied, both in their former status and in their internal organisation. More than half of the purpose-built comprehensives were established before 1970 (29 per cent of all comprehensives established before 1970 were purpose-built), largely as a result of the greater availability of building funds at that time. Between 1970 and 1974, the great majority (87.2 per cent) of newly established comprehensives were former grammar or secondary modern schools or combinations of the two. Our analysis has provided only limited information about these patterns. It suggests, however, that LEAs under Labour control and with greater educational resources were more likely to transform selective schools into comprehensives. This was clearest in both time periods for comprehensives that were formed by amalgamation. This finding may reflect a tendency of the DES to allocate building funds more often to needy LEAs under Conservative control.

A basic question that guided much of our analysis was whether there may have been a continuation of some of the philosophy of selective education even in LEAs that had established comprehensive schools. Most comprehensives were all-through schools with students ranging in age from 11 to 18 or 19, but there were two kinds of atypical arrangements. Some of the comprehensives admitted their pupils later than the conventional age 11, and some did not include a sixth form. Both of those organisational forms were clearly useful solutions to the problem of fitting a comprehensive school into an existing selective school building, and our case studies have shown how building sizes affected LEA decisions. Yet, the distribution of these organisational forms also suggests a possible linkage to some of the principles at the core of the selective system of secondary education.

Establishing a secondary school without a sixth form continued the selective system pattern found in most secondary modern schools, and that seemed to violate the very idea of what a comprehensive school should be. We also thought that perhaps schools with late entry ages had selective intakes, admitting only those with high academic promise. That impression was strengthened by the fact that practically all comprehensives with age 13+ intake had sixth forms while one third of those with age 11 intake did not. Also strengthening the impression of continuity from the selective system was the fact that 79 per cent of former grammar schools had sixth forms, while only 46 per cent of former secondary modern schools did.

Comprehensives without sixth forms would naturally be found in LEAs that had introduced sixth-form colleges, such as Stoke-on-Trent. However, the great majority of LEAs, even many with sixth-form colleges, had comprehensives both with and without sixth forms. Such distinctions within an LEA clearly paralleled features of the selective school system. Eight of our ten focal LEAs had comprehensives both with and without sixth forms, the only exceptions being Bristol, where all comprehensives had sixth forms, and Stoke-on-Trent, where none had sixth forms.

We sought to identify factors associated with the establishment of comprehensives with late entry ages and without sixth forms. Both of these organisational forms and their combinations were more common in Conservative-controlled LEAs with non-agricultural manual labour forces, although the strength of those associations varied. There were also clear differences among the kinds of atypical comprehensives. In particular, the 11–No Sixth organisation form was more common in LEAs with low educational resources (high pupil–teacher ratios) while the 13–Sixth organisational form was more common in LEAs with high levels of educational resources.

Both Leicestershire and Stoke-on-Trent were special cases in these respects, the first having adopted a uniform system of late entry and the second having adopted a uniform system of late (age 12) entry to schools without sixth forms. None of the other focal LEAs was a clear example of any of the general patterns we have observed, although Leeds had many of the characteristics of the 13–Sixth pattern indicated in Table 10.9. About two-thirds of Leeds' comprehensives had late intake ages and only about one-fifth were without sixth forms. The city had a low proportion in agricultural occupations, about an average proportion non-manual, and a very low pupil–teacher ratio. Labour was in control during the early period, but the Conservatives were in control from 1968 to 1972 when four-fifths of the comprehensives in existence in 1974 were established.

The Leeds example is a relatively rare case of a reasonable match between one of our ten focal LEAs and the general patterns we have observed. The LEA characteristics we have studied are not highly correlated with each other, and thus the ten focal LEAs cannot adequately represent the full set of 150 LEAs included in the overall analysis. There is too much variation along these dimensions. That same variation also often served to weaken the overall associations found in our analyses.[13]

The two most general impressions gained from these analyses, though, are: (1) LEAs controlled by Labour adopted comprehensive education earlier and more fully than those controlled by the Conservatives, but (2) the two atypical forms of organisation of comprehensive schools (late intake and no sixth form) were more often utilised in non-agricultural working-class LEAs under Conservative Party control. Those two atypical forms of organisation appear to have reflected features of the selective system and to have been linked to the previous status of the comprehensive schools established.

We recognise that both of these atypical forms of organisation addressed the problem of fitting comprehensive school student bodies into school buildings that had previously housed grammar or secondary modern school student bodies. But these findings also raise further questions. Why were the atypical forms more often located in heavily working-class LEAs? Is it significant that those LEAs tended to be under Conservative control? Do the atypical forms actually perpetuate some of the features of the selective system, or are these associations with socioeconomic status and political control simply the result of administrative decisions unrelated to selectivity?

One way to seek answers to these questions is to examine the patterns of attendance and the academic achievements of pupils at the schools with the atypical organisational forms. If these atypical forms of organisation represented a continuation of features of the selective system, they would have enrolled pupils with different socioeconomic origins and prior academic achievements, and those pupils would have performed at different levels from comparable pupils attending other kinds of comprehensive schools. We pursue these possibilities in our analyses in the following chapter.

TABLE 10.1

1974 PERCENTAGE DISTRIBUTIONS OF SCHOOLS AND STUDENTS
BY SCHOOL TYPE, BY REGION

| | *School Type* | | | | |
Region	*Comprehensive* (%)	*Grammar* (%)	*Secondary Modern* (%)	*Independent* (%)	*Total* (No)
North Western	37.8	15.6	34.3	12.3	505
Northern	49.6	10.2	34.6	5.6	266
East and West Riding	65.2	9.2	17.6	8.1	273
North Midlands	39.5	18.3	36.9	5.3	301
Eastern	46.2	12.4	29.6	11.8	355
London and South Eastern	39.5	19.6	30.3	10.6	653
Southern	32.5	17.3	35.7	14.1	277
South Western	40.6	12.2	31.1	16.1	286
Midlands	42.5	17.3	33.9	6.3	398
Wales	71.8	7.3	13.6	5.0	201
Total	42.2	14.9	30.7	9.8	3,514

| | *Students* | | | | |
Region	*Comprehensive* (%)	*Grammar* (%)	*Secondary Modern* (%)	*Independent* (%)	*Total* (No)
North Western	46.0	14.5	30.1	9.4	1,199
Northern	60.4	10.4	25.9	3.3	692
East and West Riding	78.0	6.5	11.2	4.3	797
North Midlands	54.3	13.4	29.0	3.3	766
Eastern	57.7	9.7	24.3	8.4	849
London and South Eastern	47.3	18.6	26.9	7.1	1,462
Southern	43.5	15.7	31.7	9.0	630
South Western	51.7	10.2	25.9	12.2	664
Midlands	52.2	15.2	28.0	4.6	929
Wales	82.6	5.9	9.3	2.2	592
Total	55.7	12.8	24.9	6.6	8,580

TABLE 10.2

1974 DISTRIBUTION OF SECONDARY SCHOOLS BY
LEA POLITICAL CONTROL

LEA Control 1964–1973	% Comp. by 1974	% Comp. Before 1970	% Comp. 1970–74	% Independent	Number of LEAs
Labour–Labour	81.3	34.8	65.2	2.3	11
Labour–Mixed	65.5	38.1	62.9	8.6	29
Labour–Conserv.	68.5	55.5	45.5	11.9	19
Mixed–Conserv.	41.1	15.0	85.0	10.8	26
Conserv.–Conserv.	48.5	32.9	67.2	10.7	47
Other	60.0	32.9	67.1	7.2	15
Total	56.8	36.8	63.2	9.8	147

Note: The first column (% Comp. by 1974) reports the percentage of the state-supported schools in LEAs with the indicated type of political control that were comprehensive in 1974. The second and third columns (% Comp. before 1970, and % Comp. 1970–74) report the percentages of those comprehensives that were established before 1970 and in 1970–74. The fourth column (% Independent) is the percentage of all secondary schools in the LEA that were private. Wholly adequate political control data were unavailable for three LEAs, so only 147 are included in this table.

TABLE 10.3

FACTORS AFFECTING THE PROPORTION OF LEA STATE-SUPPORTED
SCHOOLS THAT WERE COMPREHENSIVE IN 1974

Independent Variables	Analysis		
	(1)	(2)	(3)
% Agriculture	0.004	0.012	0.003
% Mining or Manufacture	0.002	−0.001	−0.003
% Non-manual	−0.003	0.003	−0.003
% Owner-occupier	−0.006	−0.001	−0.001
% Average pupil–teacher ratio	−0.045†	−0.055†	−0.040†
Political Control			
Labour–Labour		0.419*	0.282†
Labour–Mixed		0.229†	0.202
Labour–Conservative		0.321*	0.148
Mixed–Conservative		0.010	0.072
Other		0.191	0.077
% Comprehensive before 1970			0.229*
Intercept	1.675*	1.395*	1.414*
R^2	0.049	0.120	0.135

† $p < 0.05$, * $p < 0.01$, ** $p < 0.001$.

TABLE 10.4

1974 DISTRIBUTION OF COMPREHENSIVE SCHOOLS BY PRIOR
STATUS, INTAKE AGE, PRESENCE OF A SIXTH FORM, AND
PERIOD FOUNDED (BEFORE 1970, 1970–74)

Prior Status and Period Founded	*Age of Youngest*					
	11	*12*	*13+*	*No Sixth*	*Sixth*	*Total*
Purpose-built						
Founded before 1970	139	8	16	15	148	163
Founded 1970–74	85	13	24	48	74	122
Amalgamated						
Founded before 1970	156	10	6	20	152	172
Founded 1970–74	227	29	15	68	230	298
Secondary Modern						
Founded before 1970	100	11	6	59	58	117
Founded 1970–74	289	24	15	184	144	328
Grammar						
Founded before 1970	64	2	39	13	92	105
Founded 1970–74	126	22	54	50	152	202
Total						
Founded before 1970	459	31	67	107	450	557
Founded 1970–74	727	88	135	350	600	950

TABLE 10.5

PERCENTAGE OF COMPREHENSIVE SCHOOLS HAVING A
SIXTH FORM, BY INTAKE AGE AND PERIOD FOUNDED

	Founded before 1970			*Founded 1970–74*		
Intake Age	*% No 6th*	*% 6th*	*N*	*% No 6th*	*% 6th*	*N*
11	20.3	79.7	459	42.2	57.8	727
12	45.2	54.8	31	40.9	59.1	88
13+	0.0	100.0	67	5.2	94.8	135
Total N	107.0	450.0	557	350.0	600.0	950
Total %	19.2	80.8	100	36.8	63.2	100

201

TABLE 10.6
MULTINOMIAL LOGISTIC REGRESSION ANALYSIS OF
CHARACTERISTICS OF LEAs THAT ESTABLISHED COMPREHENSIVE
SCHOOLS WITH DIFFERENT PRIOR STATUSES

		Prior Status	
Characteristic	*Amalgamated*	*Grammar*	*Secondary Modern*
Analysis 1			
% Agriculture	–0.001	0.050	0.070†
% Mining or manufacture	0.000	0.022*	0.032**
% Non-manual workers	–0.016	0.063	0.033
% Dwellings owner-occupier	–0.017*	–0.005	–0.005
Average pupil–teacher ratio	–0.212**	–0.402**	–0.127†
Constant	3.421*	3.355†	–1.497
Analysis 2			
% Agriculture	0.049	0.069†	0.090*
% Mining or manufacture	–0.000	0.018	0.027*
% Non-manual workers	0.018	0.041	0.036
% Dwellings owner-occupier	0.003	0.001	–0.002
Average pupil–teacher ratio	–0.238**	–0.427**	–0.148*
Political Control			
Labour–Labour	1.191**	0.725†	0.525†
Labour–Mixed	0.961**	0.348	0.154
Labour–Conservative	0.519*	0.373	0.599**
Mixed–Conservative	–0.025	0.216	–0.056†
Other	0.682*	0.466	0.520†
Constant	1.404	3.217†	–1.437
Analysis 3			
% Agriculture	0.047	0.059	0.085*
% Mining or manufacture	–0.001	0.014	0.021†
% Non-manual workers	0.009	0.027	0.019
% Dwellings owner-occupier	0.007	0.005	–0.000
Average pupil–teacher ratio	–0.188*	–0.383**	–0.114†
Political Control			
Labour–Labour	1.203**	0.706†	0.494
Labour–Mixed	0.857**	0.236	0.152
Labour–Conservative	0.315	0.191	0.535*
Mixed–Conservative	0.253	0.468†	0.224
Other	0.650*	0.422	0.491†
% Comprehensive before 1970	0.825**	0.751**	0.301
Constant	0.409	2.644	–1.462

† $p < 0.05$, * $p < 0.01$, ** $p < 0.001$.

TABLE 10.7

MULTINOMIAL LOGISTIC REGRESSION ANALYSIS OF
CHARACTERISTICS OF LEAs THAT ESTABLISHED COMPREHENSIVE
SCHOOLS WITH LATE INTAKE AGES

Characteristic	*(1)*		*(2)*		*(3)*	
	Intake at 12	*Intake at 13+*	*Intake at 12*	*Intake at 13+*	*Intake at 12*	*Intake at 13+*
% Agriculture	−0.173**	−0.021	−0.206**	−0.017	−0.268**	−0.047
% Mining or manufacture	−0.015	−0.013	−0.000	−0.007	−0.018	−0.020
% Non-manual workers	−0.059*	−0.025	−0.040	−0.011	−0.072*	0.040
% Dwellings owner-occupier	0.024**	0.016†	0.020†	0.016	0.019†	−0.015
Average pupil–teacher ratio	−0.461**	−0.804**	−0.440**	−0.808**	−0.954**	−0.822**
Political Control						
Labour–Labour			−0.494	−0.151	−0.702†	−0.324
Labour–Mixed			−0.447†	−0.077	−0.362	0.039
Labour–Conservative			−0.844**	−0.206	−0.743**	−0.100
Mixed–Conservative			−0.736**	−0.430†	−0.757**	−0.361
Other			−0.776*	0.145	−0.849*	0.103
% Comprehensive before 1970					−0.954**	−0.759**
Constant	7.399**	12.356**	6.661**	11.905**	8.768**	13.853**

† p<0.05, * p<0.01, ** p<0.001.

TABLE 10.8

LOGISTIC REGRESSION OF CHARACTERISTICS OF LEAs THAT
ESTABLISHED COMPREHENSIVE SCHOOLS WITHOUT SIXTH FORMS

Characteristic	*(1)*	*(2)*	*(3)*
% Agriculture	−0.116**	−0.167**	−0.182**
% Mining or manufacture	−0.033*	−0.043**	−0.049**
% Non-manual workers	−0.140**	−0.193**	−0.206**
% Dwellings owner-occupier	0.011	−0.000	−0.001
Average pupil–teacher ratio	0.229**	0.235**	0.247**
Political Control			
Labour–Labour		−0.811*	−0.934**
Labour–Mixed		−0.600*	−0.522†
Labour–Conservative		0.019	0.158
Mixed–Conservative		0.332	0.295
Other		−0.230	−0.227
% Comprehensive before 1970			−0.710**
Constant	0.014	2.595	3.138†

† p<0.05, * p<0.01, ** p<0.001.

TABLE 10.9

MULTINOMIAL LOGISTIC REGRESSION ANALYSIS OF
CHARACTERISTICS OF LEAs THAT ESTABLISHED COMPREHENSIVE
SCHOOLS WITH COMBINATIONS OF EARLY OR LATE INTAKE AND
WITH AND WITHOUT SIXTH FORMS

	Organisational Structure			
Characteristic	*11* *No 6th*	*12* *No 6th*	*12* *Has 6th*	*13+* *Has 6th*
Analysis 1				
% Agriculture	−0.804 *	−0.804**	−0.161†	−0.122†
% Mining or manufacture	−0.027 †	−0.174**	−0.051†	−0.038*
% Non-manual workers	−0.129 **	−0.467**	−0.097†	−0.078*
% Dwellings owner-occupier	0.016 †	0.052*	0.020	0.039**
Average pupil–teacher ratio	0.131 †	−0.187	−0.264	−0.889**
Constant	1.057	19.054**	6.333†	16.282**
Analysis 2				
% Agriculture	−0.170 **	−0.773**	−0.1671	−0.161*
% Mining or manufacture	−0.032 *	−0.172**	−0.045	−0.036†
% Non-manual workers	−0.197 **	−0.454**	−0.064	−0.090*
% Dwellings owner-occupier	0.004	0.043†	0.047*	−0.032*
Average pupil–teacher ratio	0.127 †	−0.235	−0.239	−0.886**
Political Control				
Labour–Labour	−0.1450**	0.134	−1.228	−0.912†
Labour–Mixed	−0.768 **	−0.198	0.800	−0.544
Labour–Conservative	−0.183	0.256	−1.053†	−0.446
Mixed–Conservative	−0.183	0.428	−0.472	−0.464
Other	−0.248	−7.367	−0.572	−0.248
Constant	4.574 *	19.766**	3.444	17.283**
Analysis 3				
% Agriculture	−0.194 **	−0.812**	−0.198†	−0.190**
% Mining or manufacture	−0.048 **	−0.187**	−0.060†	−0.051*
% Non-manual workers	−0.216 **	−0.472**	−0.093	−0.117*
% Dwellings owner-occupier	0.004	0.046†	0.042*	0.031*
Average pupil–teacher ratio	0.147 †	−0.226	−0.276	−0.899**
Political Control				
Labour–Labour	−1.669 **	−0.044	−1.521	−1.117†
Labour–Mixed	−0.664 *	0.029	1.110†	−0.293
Labour–Conservative	0.007	0.598	−0.503	−0.095
Mixed–Conservative	0.107	0.335	−0.601	−0.525
Other	−0.299	−7.346	−0.593	−0.172
% Comprehensive before 1970	−1.124 **	−1.400†	−2.552**	−1.647**
Constant	5.565 **	21.068**	6.498	19.414**

† $p<0.05$, * $p<0.01$, ** $p<0.001$.

NOTES

1. The NCDS was an extension of the 'Perinatal Mortality Survey', a study of 'virtually every baby born in England, Scotland and Wales during the week of 3 to 9 March [1958]' (Davie, *et al.*, 1972, p. 10) that collected extensive data at their birth. The true NCDS began with a follow-up at age seven and continued with follow-up data collections at ages 11, 16, 20 and 23. There were 17,733 babies in the original cohort. Attrition through death, emigration, refusal and the research team's inability to locate members of the cohort was significant, but lower than in most panel studies. Of those thought to be alive and still living in Great Britain, 86.7 per cent were included in the age 16 sweep and 77.1 per cent in the age 23 sweep. Extensive information was collected from parents, teachers and medical personnel, as well as from the individuals themselves. Details of the study are reported in Davie, *et al.*, 1972; Fogelman, 1976, 1983 and Kerckhoff, 1990, 1993.
2. School-level data are not directly provided in the data set, and individual schools are not identified. Rather, each individual student's file reports characteristics of the school he or she attended. In order to conduct analyses using the school as the unit of analysis, it was necessary to distil school level data from the data on individuals. This was done by grouping all individuals together who had the same values on the school variables and assigning a school identifier to them. There were some problem cases, possibly owing to coding errors, but they were resolved without making extreme assumptions.
3. Only the four major categories are reported in Table 10.1. A few students attended 'technical' schools, but for ease of analysis, they are combined with the grammar school students. A fifth, residual, 'other' category was also used to code the NCDS cases, but it accounted for very few cases, and varied kinds of schools were subsumed under this heading, so they (and the students who attended them) are dropped from the analysis.
4. Unfortunately, missing information in the NCDS data set made it impossible to classify all schools and all students according to school type. About one-fifth of the students are thus unavailable for this and later analyses. This does not distort the distribution of school types or students, however. A comparison between the data in Table 10.1 and official statistics produce the following percentages at the three LEA-supported school types (not including independent schools). In each case, the official percentage is presented first and that derived from Table 10.1 second: Comprehensive schools, 51.0:49.4; Secondary modern schools, 33.9:34.1; Grammar schools, 15.1:16.5; Comprehensive school students, 62.8:59.6; Secondary modern school students, 25.7:26.7; Grammar school students, 12.1:13.7. These data suggest that our samples slightly over-represent grammar schools and their students and slightly under-represent comprehensive schools and their students, but the differences are well within acceptable sampling error ranges.
5. It must be remembered that the NCDS data set is based on a sample of English and Welsh students, those born in the first week of March in 1958. It is highly likely that some schools did not have any students born in that week, and thus we have no data for those schools. Also, given the attrition from the NCDS sample and the amount of missing data about school type, there was a real danger that our analyses would be distorted. As discussed in note 4, this was not true of the basic distributions of schools and students. Further analysis also shows that our data by LEA on the percentage of the students attending comprehensive schools in 1974 correlate 0.90 with the percentages reported in official government statistics. This

suggests that losses from the NCDS data set were essentially random with respect to school type.

6. A parallel analysis was also conducted in which the proportion of students in LEA-supported schools who were in comprehensive schools was the dependent variable. The results were very similar to those reported in Table 10.3.

7. A few unusual comprehensive schools could not be classified in any of these four types, so they are deleted from the analyses presented here.

8. Four schools reported students younger than age 11. They are combined in Table 10.4 with the age 11 intake schools, and the students attending them are treated likewise.

9. Late entry age was not a particularly common feature of grammar schools. Only 3.9 per cent of the NCDS cohort attending grammar schools in 1974 were at schools that entered students at ages 13 or 14, compared with 13.4 per cent of those at comprehensive schools and 30.3 per cent of those at comprehensives that had formerly been grammar schools. So, this excess of late-entry schools among those that had formerly been grammar schools cannot be attributed to a carry-over from their former status. Rather, it is part of the process of change to a comprehensive system in some LEAs, a process that served to continue the élite status of the former grammar schools.

10. Most secondary modern schools had historically not offered sixth-form courses, and that is reflected in the NCDS data. Only 17.3 per cent of the NCDS cohort attending secondary modern schools in 1974 were at schools with a sixth form. This is in contrast to 74.1 per cent of those attending comprehensive schools and all but six of those attending grammar schools. Thus, the lack of a sixth form in most of the comprehensives that had previously been secondary modern schools could be viewed as a carry-over from their earlier status.

11. It is important to remember here that the pupil–teacher ratios are for the *entire LEA*, not for the individual schools or school types. At the individual school level we would expect a lower pupil–teacher ratio in schools with sixth forms because sixth-form courses usually have smaller classes. Thus, on average, the 13–Sixth schools would have lower pupil–teacher ratios than the 11–No Sixth schools. Since these ratios refer to all of the schools in the LEA, and since very few LEAs had only one of these types of organisation, however, the results point to overall differences in setting, not differences between school types.

12. Not all of the results in Table 10.9 appear to be wholly consistent with those in Tables 10.7 and 10.8, but that is due to the different ways of defining the categories being compared. In particular, in Table 10.7 the reference category is all age 11 intake schools, while in Table 10.9 the reference category is only those age 11 intake schools that had sixth forms. It is clear from the results reported in the first column of Table 10.9 that age 11 intake schools without sixth forms were most often located in very different kinds of LEAs than were age 11 intake schools with sixth forms. We also see in the third and fourth columns of Table 9 that LEAs that established age 13+ intake comprehensives with sixth forms had superior educational resources (lower pupil–teacher ratios) compared with LEAs which established age 12 comprehensives with sixth forms. So, the analyses in Tables 10.7 and 10.8, using only one dimension of organisation, necessarily give a somewhat different picture from those in Table 10.9.

13. There is one clear example from our ten focal LEAs of how variations among LEAs served to weaken the overall associations we have observed. Stoke-on-Trent had adopted an organisational form which involved students entering comprehensive schools at age 12, but none of their comprehensives had sixth forms,

because they had also adopted sixth-form colleges. So, their schools would be classified in the 12–No Sixth category in Table 10.9. One of the reasons for the lack of a significant association between political control and the 12–No Sixth category in Table 10.9 is the fact that Stoke-on-Trent was consistently controlled by Labour. Several LEAs controlled by the Conservatives had some schools with the same organisational form, but students in no-sixth form schools had to transfer to other comprehensives if they were to study for A-Level examinations. In Stoke-on-Trent the 12–No Sixth form was essentially a 'liberal' innovation, while in other LEAs with less commitment to sixth-form colleges it was much less so.

11

Schools and Students in a Changing System

In this chapter we examine the nature of the newly established comprehensive schools and their student bodies. The process of change from the selective to the comprehensive form of organisation occurred over an extended period and involved progressively more of the students who were enrolled in state-supported secondary schools. As we have seen, the change went more smoothly and was more complete in some places than others. As a result, different comprehensive schools and students become relevant to our analysis, depending on the point in time when the data for the analysis were collected.

To some extent, the comprehensive schools movement took place 'from the bottom up'. The early changeover occurred disproportionally in working-class areas. The fact that existing school buildings in the selective system were used to house most of the new comprehensives also affected the pattern of change because much of the resistance to the movement involved efforts to retain established grammar schools. Thus, the earlier changes from selective to comprehensive school status more often involved secondary modern than grammar schools. The ratio of students at secondary modern schools to those at grammar schools dropped rapidly during the period of change studied here. While the ratio was about two to one in 1974, it had been about three to one in 1967 (*Regional Statistics*, Vols. 3 and 10). The success many LEAs experienced in 'saving' their grammar schools meant that there was a degree of 'creaming' of high-ability students from the comprehensives.

Our data about the comprehensive schools and their students come from a study of a single birth cohort. Since it was a 1958 birth cohort, these children generally entered secondary school in 1969 when they were 11 years old. This was in the early period of the change process. It is thus possible that the results of the analyses we can conduct with these data may be somewhat different from what we would obtain from a later cohort, but we cannot tell with confidence. We must acknowledge, however, that pupils in comprehensive schools during this part of the changeover process were undoubtedly somewhat different from those who experienced the change later on.

It is also true that the change from a selective to a comprehensive form of education cannot be accomplished instantly. At least for some period of time, vestiges of the old system would be likely to remain. That would seem especially likely for comprehensive schools that had had a clear previous identity as either a grammar or a secondary modern school. The staff, the students and members of the local communities would tend to view such schools in terms of their past. Even if a school's name were changed, it would be likely to retain some of its old identity, and we should not be surprised if it continued to 'look like' the kind of school it used to be. The more recent its change of status, the more continuity could be expected.

What kinds of continuity might we expect to see? Since the selective system made clear distinctions according to both the 'quality' of the student intake and the kinds of programmes offered, can we expect to find those kinds of differences between former grammar schools and former secondary modern schools that, by 1974, had become comprehensives? Would the ability levels and earlier academic performances of students at the two kinds of comprehensives be distinct? Would the kinds of courses offered and the levels of achievement of students at those two kinds of comprehensives differ in some of the same ways in which the schools and students differed in the selective system? These are some of the questions we investigate in this chapter.

Other features of the newly established schools may also have reflected a continuation of the basic philosophy that supported the selective system. Some LEAs used a tiered system that led to pupils entering secondary school at older ages – 12, 13 or even 14. Many established comprehensives without sixth forms. In fact, most LEAs established two kinds of comprehensives, some with and some without sixth forms. The analysis in this chapter considers whether these newly introduced ways of organising secondary education reflected some of the same kinds of student separation found in the selective system. To the extent that they did, we also investigate whether these structural variations affected student achievements in the same way as had occurred in the selective system.

PARALLELS BETWEEN SELECTIVE SCHOOLS AND KINDS OF COMPREHENSIVES

There has already been some suggestion of continuity between the former status of the comprehensives and their characteristics after changing status. Table 10.4 showed clearly that former secondary modern schools were least likely to have sixth forms. To see if there were other indications of continuity, we reviewed a number of school characteristics that differentiated grammar, secondary modern, and comprehensive schools, and we then examined the kinds of comprehensives to see if there was any evidence of continuity in school characteristics from the selective to the comprehensive systems. Table 11.1 indicates some of the ways in which comprehensives, overall, differed from both of the selective school types and some of the ways in which the two selective types differed from each other. (Comparable statistics for the independent schools are also reported, although they are of less direct relevance to our present interests, other than to show their similarity to the grammar schools.) Comprehensives were clearly much larger than either grammar or secondary modern schools. This, of course, was the source of a major problem faced by LEAs planning comprehensive reorganisation. The proportion of pupils from non-manual families was also much higher in grammar schools than in either of the other school types, although it was slightly higher in the comprehensives than in the secondary modern schools.

As expected, however, the most striking differences among the three types of state-supported schools were in their academic programmes. Grammar school students were, by far, most often studying for O-Level examinations at age 16 and least often studying for the CSE examinations; secondary modern school students were the reverse of that; and comprehensive school students were in between. The same was true for the proportions staying on past the minimum leaving age. Staying on was most common in the grammar schools, least common in the secondary modern schools, and somewhere between the two for comprehensive schools.

In all of these respects, although the comprehensive school students were, on average, somewhere between students at the other two school types, they were in effect more like those at secondary modern schools than like those at grammar schools. This kind of pattern might be expected because a much smaller and more select segment of secondary school students attended grammar schools and thus the mix of students attending comprehensives would be more like those at a secondary modern than a grammar school. Yet, the similarities are greater than a simple mixing of the characteristics of the students from the two selective school types could explain. There were approximately twice as many students attending secondary modern as grammar schools in 1974, but we could not derive the statistics for the comprehensive school students in Table 11.1 from a weighted average of the grammar school and secondary modern school statistics. It was not just the characteristics of the students that produced these differences, it was the nature of the schools and their curricula. As we have seen, early transformations from selective to comprehensive schools more often involved secondary modern than grammar schools.

The same measures as in Table 11.1 are reported in Table 11.2 for comprehensive schools classified by their prior status and the period in which they were founded. There is some evidence of similarities between the two selective school types (shown in Table 11.1) and the comprehensives that were formed from those two types (shown in Table 11.2), although the similarities are much greater for comprehensives founded in 1970–74 than for those founded earlier. All of the academic measures for students at schools founded in 1970–74 strongly favour those at the former grammar schools, and the students at the former secondary modern schools fall short of those at all of the other types of comprehensives on all measures except the proportions staying on past the minimum leaving age.

There are also some notable though smaller differences by former status even among comprehensives founded before 1970. In particular, both boys and girls attending former secondary modern schools were less frequently studying for O-Level examinations than were those at any other type of comprehensive school. This is consistent with the idea that there was some continuity in the way comprehensives functioned before and after their change of status, since Table 11.1 shows low percentages of students at secondary modern schools studying for O-Level examinations.

The distributions of students by family background are also noteworthy. In Table 11.1, there is little difference between comprehensive and secondary modern schools in the percentages of students from non-manual homes, although both percentages are much lower than those of students at grammar schools. In Table 11.2, students at former grammar schools are more likely to come from non-manual homes than are those at any other kind of comprehensive. It is also true, however, that students at comprehensives founded in the 1970s more often came from non-manual families than did those at comprehensives founded in the 1960s. This is another indication of the gradual shift of the comprehensive schools movement from largely a working-class movement to a more general one.

TAKING TIME INTO ACCOUNT

The strikingly different results for the two periods have important implications for the rest of the analysis in this chapter, and they must be understood before proceeding. If we are to interpret appropriately the characteristics of the schools that the NCDS cohort members were attending in 1974, and attempt to measure the ways in which those schools affected their students, we need to take careful account of two processes. The 1974 NCDS data come from a single point in time at which there was an intersection between the flow of the life course of the NCDS cohort and the historical process of change of the secondary-school system from largely selective to largely comprehensive. Both cohort maturation and system change contributed to the characteristics of the 1974 data.

Those NCDS cohort members who entered secondary school at the most common age of 11 did so in 1969. While a great deal of system change had occurred by then, we have seen that most of the comprehensive schools attended by cohort members were founded after 1969. In most cases, then, those changes occurred *after* the NCDS students had entered secondary school. Since our information on the students and their schools was collected in 1974, we need to distinguish between students who attended comprehensives that had had that status at the time they entered and those who attended schools that had become comprehensives while they were there.

It is very difficult to sort the NCDS cohort members on that basis with complete confidence. The period of transition in any school might have been extended, and the recorded date of change may not have been the exact time the students experienced it. Also, some of the changes could have taken place in more than one way. For example, students attending in 1974 an age 13 intake school that is recorded as having been founded as a comprehensive in 1970 might have followed either of at least two very different pathways. They might have attended a middle school and then entered this newly founded comprehensive school in 1971 at age 13, or they might have entered the same school at age 11 before it became a comprehensive and experienced its transformation in 1970. We do not have sufficient information about the schools or the individuals to make such refined distinctions.

As a result, our analysis uses the same simple two-period differentiation made earlier. Comprehensives that were founded before 1970 are distinguished from those founded in or after 1970. The analysis has already shown that there were important differences between the schools founded in those two periods. There is every reason to expect that the students who attended those two sets of schools would also differ in important ways, even if they attended schools with the same prior status and internal organisation. The essential assumption involved in making this temporal distinction is that the vast majority of NCDS students who, in 1974, were attending comprehensives founded before 1970 spent all of their secondary school years at a comprehensive school. Only those few who transferred from a school in the selective system to a comprehensive school would violate this assumption. In contrast, those enrolled in comprehensives that had changed from either grammar or secondary modern schools in 1970 or later probably began their secondary schooling in grammar or secondary modern schools. The range of their academic and social characteristics would tend to look more like those of grammar school and secondary modern school students than like those of comprehensive school students. The data in the bottom panel of Table 11.2 are consistent with that reasoning. A basic question guiding much of our analysis is whether the prior status of a comprehensive school affected its characteristics *after* it became a comprehensive, and whether schools with different prior statuses affected their students in ways that were congruent with their prior statuses. We would obtain a distorted impression if we included in such analyses students who began their secondary education in the selective system of grammar and secondary modern schools. In the analyses to be presented, therefore, the data are restricted to comprehensive schools founded before 1970 and to the students who attended those schools.

SCHOOL STRUCTURE AND SELECTIVITY

The comprehensive schools attended by the NCDS students had varied origins and internal structures, and those variations suggest the possibility that they served different purposes in the overall educational system. We have seen in Table 11.2 that fewer students at former secondary modern schools were studying for O-levels than at any other type of comprehensive. This was even true for schools founded before 1970, schools whose students had entered a comprehensive school, not a secondary modern school. The former status of the comprehensives thus seems to have been systematically associated with the way they functioned in 1974.

Were there similar differences among the schools according to their internal structures? Did late intake schools and schools without sixth forms operate differently? Did they serve different kinds of students? Did they produce different kinds of outcomes? Late intake schools may have been intended for those who were expected to take A-Levels. We have already seen that such schools almost always had a sixth form while schools with age 11 intake often did not. Similarly, schools with no sixth form may have been intended for those who were not expected to take A-Levels. The fact that former grammar schools were most likely to have late intakes and former secondary modern schools were least likely to have a sixth form strengthens the impression that the structural variations among the comprehensive schools mirrored in some way the characteristics of the two kinds of selective schools.

Our first analysis thus considers whether schools with different origins and different structural features served different kinds of students. We examine both the socioeconomic backgrounds of the students and their academic achievements before entering secondary school. The measure of socioeconomic background is the percentage of the school's students whose father's occupation was professional, managerial or other non-manual. We refer to this measure as the per cent non-manual. The academic achievement measures are the school's students' average scores on a general ability test and achievement tests in reading and mathematics.[1] All three of these tests were taken when the cohort members were 11 years old, before their entry into secondary school. The analysis thus serves to determine if the various kinds of comprehensive schools served students with different social and academic characteristics.

Table 11.3 reports these measures for students attending the four kinds of comprehensive schools founded before 1970 (purpose-built, amalgamated, ex-grammar and ex-secondary modern), separated according to whether they were at a school with an 11, 12 or a 13+ intake age. There are no consistent differences in the academic characteristics reported in Table 11.3 between students admitted to secondary school at these three ages. Since late intake schools were most commonly those that had been grammar schools, we might have expected their students to have had higher test scores. But only three of the twelve comparisons between age 11 and age 13+ intake schools' students' scores are of that type. And those admitted at age 12 had relatively high ability and test scores in purpose-built and former secondary modern schools but relatively low scores in amalgamated schools. If we compare the age of intake categories within school types, therefore, there are scattered differences in both directions, but there is no consistent pattern.[2]

There are some socioeconomic differences, however, according to the original status of the schools. Among age 11 intake schools (the only place where there are enough students in both types of schools to make a comparison), students at former grammar schools were more likely than those at former secondary modern schools to have come from non-manual families.[3]

The data in Table 11.3 lead to two observations. First, a school's intake age was not systematically related to the academic level of the admitted students. There is little evidence that intake age was used as a selectivity mechanism. Second, the prior academic achievements of students attending comprehensives that had been established before their entry varied somewhat depending on the prior status of the school, but there was much greater variation in students' social backgrounds. Students at former grammar schools came from non-manual families more often than those at former secondary modern schools.

Table 11.4 parallels Table 11.3, but it divides students according to whether or not their comprehensive school had a sixth form. It appears that schools with a sixth form enrolled students with somewhat higher age 11 test scores than did those without a sixth form. Of the 12 comparisons between the scores of students entering schools with and without a sixth form, 11 favour those entering schools with a sixth form (the exception is the average mathematics score of students entering purpose-built schools). Most of the differences are quite small with the largest, however, being for amalgamated schools, so it is not clear how much weight to give these differences. It is particularly striking that there is almost no difference between the test scores of students attending former grammar and former secondary modern schools founded before 1970, whether they had a sixth form or not.

The differences in family background are again much greater. In three of the four school types, more students in schools with a sixth form came from non-manual families than did those in schools without a sixth form. Former grammar schools are the exception, but former grammar schools had more students from non-manual families than any of the other school types, whether or not they had a sixth form. The social background differences associated with a sixth form were especially large in former secondary modern schools. This is an important contrast, because nearly half of the former secondary modern schools had no sixth form.

There is thus evidence of selectivity, but it does not seem to have involved selectivity according to the schools' different intake ages. Even the presence or absence of a sixth form seemed to have only a limited association with selectivity of intake according to academic achievements. What is more apparent is a clear set of linkages among social class, the former status of the school (grammar or secondary modern), and the presence of a sixth form. Former grammar schools were much more likely than former secondary modern schools to have sixth forms, and both former grammar schools and schools with sixth forms enrolled larger proportions of students from non-manual families. It is important to recall that Chapter 10 also showed an association between the social class composition of the LEA population and the presence of comprehensive schools without sixth forms. There it was found that the lower the proportion of non-manual families, the more likely the LEA was to establish comprehensive schools without sixth forms. Here we see that students from manual families were more likely to attend comprehensives without sixth forms. One purpose of the further analysis to be presented below is to attempt to clarify the relationship between those two findings.

SCHOOL STRUCTURE AND PROCESS

The LEAs may have been selective in the assignment of students to the various kinds of comprehensives, but a potentially more important question is whether these comprehensives offered different educational programmes. Did they provide their students with different opportunities to learn, and did those different opportunities influence student achievements? That former secondary modern schools had fewer students studying for O-Levels and that those schools less often had a sixth form certainly suggest that former status was associated with programmatic differences.

To gain a preliminary indication of such differences, we first examine the average academic achievements of students who attended the four kinds of comprehensive schools. Tables 11.5 and 11.6 report average scores on three secondary-school academic achievement measures. Tables 11.3 and 11.4 show inputs by school type and year founded, Tables 11.5 and 11.6 report outputs. The measures in those tables are the scores on reading and mathematics tests administered at age 16 and an index of the level of secondary-school examinations

(CSEs, O-Levels and A-Levels) passed by age 18.[4] In most respects, the patterns are very similar in the two pairs of tables. There is no consistent difference in Table 11.5 between the average performances at schools with age 11 and later intakes. If anything, the 13+ intake schools' students had lower achievements than those at age 11 intake schools, which is the opposite of what we would expect from the association between late intake and having been a grammar school.[5] There are again more consistent differences among schools classified according to whether they had a sixth form, reported in Table 11.6. In nine of the 12 comparisons between outcomes for students at schools with and without a sixth form, those who had attended schools with a sixth form had superior achievements (the two clear exceptions are reading scores at former grammar schools and mathematics scores at purpose-built schools; there is no difference in mathematics scores of students at former grammar schools). The differences between the reading and mathematics test scores tend to be relatively small, however. By far the largest and most consistent differences are in the levels of secondary-school examinations passed. This is a very significant outcome.

The reading and mathematics tests were administered at age 16 before entry into the sixth form. That there was little difference by the presence or absence of a sixth form at that point indicates that the schools not only had students with similar achievements on entry (as shown in Table 11.4) but that there continued to be only minor differences through to the age of 16. The big differences apparently resulted from what happened *after* the age of 16, which suggests that the presence or absence of a sixth form was the reason for the difference. The advantage of going to a school with a sixth form was that it made it easier for a student to study for A-Level examinations.[6] More generally, schools with sixth forms undoubtedly had a stronger overall academic orientation. It is clear that students in schools with a sixth form passed consistently higher average school examinations than did those in schools without a sixth form.

Differences by the schools' former statuses were rather small and inconsistent, although they were greater for examinations passed than for the age 16 achievement test scores. Yet, it is important to remember that Table 11.6 controls for the presence of a sixth form and that former grammar schools were much more likely than former secondary modern schools to have had a sixth form. Important differences in academic achievement by students according to the former status of their schools actually resulted from the uneven distribution of sixth-form programmes among the kinds of schools. It is instructive to compare the achievements of students at former secondary modern and former grammar schools with age 11 intake, as reported in Table 11.5. Controlling, as that table does, for intake age but not for the presence of a sixth form, it shows essentially no difference in the average test scores at age 16, but, on average, students at former grammar schools passed higher-level secondary-school examinations. Students at schools with a sixth form did better in school examinations than students at schools without a sixth form, and this was true of both former grammar schools and former secondary modern schools, as Table 11.6 shows. But the real advantage of attending one of the former grammar schools was that they were much more likely than former secondary modern schools to have had a sixth form.

Although it is clear that the major difference between the achievements of the students at comprehensives with and without sixth forms was in the levels of secondary-school examinations passed, it is also apparent that it was not simply the structural features of the schools that brought about this difference. Information was available about the kinds of courses the students took at secondary school in 1974 up to age 16, before entry into the sixth form. The pattern of courses taken varied in meaningful ways even at that early point in their educational careers, suggesting that the schools offered different *kinds* of courses. There was a greater problem of missing data with the information about courses taken than with most measures, so these data may not be as representative as the others. Also, because of the very great gender differences in the kinds of courses taken, it is necessary to examine gender-specific patterns, thereby reducing the frequencies in all categories. The data do show some clear differences between the comprehensive schools according to whether they had a sixth form, however.

Only 26.1 per cent of the boys at comprehensives without sixth forms had taken any language courses by age 16, but 34.9 per cent of those at comprehensives with sixth forms had done so. In contrast, 45.2 per cent of the boys at comprehensives without a sixth form had taken two or more technical courses, but only 35.1 per cent of those at comprehensives with sixth forms had done so. The differences for girls were in the same direction though generally smaller, but one stands out. Whereas only 16.3 per cent of the girls at comprehensives with a sixth form had taken two or more domestic courses, 30.6 per cent of those at comprehensives without a sixth form had done so. Because former secondary modern schools were less likely than former grammar schools to have a sixth form, there are similar differences when those two types of comprehensives are compared.

Since these are differences between the kinds of courses the students took by the age of 16, it was not the presence or absence of a sixth form, as such, that was responsible for them. It is apparent that the patterns of courses taken were the result of the different kinds of students attending these two types of comprehensives, or of the schools' different curricular offerings, or of both. It is also apparent that the courses taken must have contributed to the contrast in the levels of examinations passed by age 18. Some differentiation was occurring even before the sixth form.

A consistent pattern emerges from these data. Being a former grammar school, being in an LEA with a non-manual population, and offering sixth-form courses were consistently linked together. The most important advantage of attending a former grammar school was evidently the greater availability of sixth-form courses, and that advantage seems to have led to greater success in passing secondary-school examinations. The most tangible disadvantage for those who attended a comprehensive without a sixth form was the lower likelihood of passing any A-Level examinations. The lack of A-Level passes, in turn, effectively closed access to higher education. We thus find the sharpest evidence of the disadvantage of having attended a comprehensive school without a sixth form at the highest academic achievement level. Only 1.6 per cent of the students in the NCDS cohort whose comprehensive school had no sixth form had obtained a university degree by age 23 compared with 7.3 per cent of those whose comprehensive school had a sixth form.

In summary, then, the analyses presented here indicate that the change to comprehensive schools in England and Wales involved continuation of some of the features of the selective system. Even after they were transformed into comprehensives, former grammar schools and former secondary modern schools continued to differ from each other in important ways. In particular, former grammar schools were more often attended by students from non-manual backgrounds, and they were more likely to offer sixth-form courses.

Whatever a school's former status, however, the presence of a sixth form affected the level of academic credentials that its students obtained. This was true at the end of secondary school when those who had attended a comprehensive school with a sixth form had passed higher level examinations. It continued to be true at age 23 when those who had attended a comprehensive school with a sixth form were four and a half times more likely to have obtained a university degree.

MIXED SCHOOL TYPES WITHIN LEAs

We noted earlier that many LEAs did not simply make a choice between having or not having a sixth form in their comprehensive schools but established schools of both types. Of the 131 LEAs that had established any comprehensives by 1974, the majority (72 or 55.0 per cent) had established some with and some without sixth forms. Nearly one-third of the LEAs (43 or 32.8 per cent) had only comprehensives with sixth forms and about one-eighth (16 or 12.2 per cent) had only those without sixth forms. That means that, of those LEAs that had any comprehensives without sixth forms, the great majority (72 out of 88 or 81.8 per cent) had some with and some without sixth forms. Overall, four out of five (79.5 per cent) comprehensive schools were in LEAs that had both types. As we have seen, students who attended a comprehensive school without a sixth form seem to have been disadvantaged and obtained lower academic credentials. Thus, those LEAs with both types of comprehensives can be viewed as having had a two-track system. Some students in those LEAs had more opportunities than others. An important question to ask, therefore, is whether there were any differences in the kinds of students who attended these two kinds of schools. Is there any evidence of selective access, of discrimination?

To determine if there was selective access, we limited our analysis to students in those LEAs that had founded comprehensives both with and without sixth forms before 1970, and we examined the social and academic characteristics of the NCDS students at those two kinds of comprehensives. The results are reported in Table 11.7. The top panel of the table reports the characteristics of the students as they entered; the bottom panel reports their secondary-school academic achievements.

The top panel of Table 11.7 shows a consistent pattern of differences between the two groups of students when they entered secondary school. Those in schools without sixth forms came less often from non-manual families, and they had consistently lower scores on the age 11 ability, reading and mathematics tests. As would be expected, these measures of social and academic background are intercorrelated, and any analysis using them in combination reflects that fact. We conducted a logistic regression analysis using non-manual family background, ability and gender as predictors of attendance at a school without a sixth form. Gender made no difference, but both non-manual family background and ability were negatively associated with attending a comprehensive school without a sixth form. However, those two coefficients were significant at only the 0.071 and 0.085 levels, respectively.

We noted earlier that comprehensives without sixth forms were found more often in LEAs with smaller proportions of non-manual families but with Conservative Party control. We see here that if such LEAs had comprehensive schools both with and without sixth forms, the latter drew their students disproportionately from manual families, and those students had lower test scores in junior school before entering the comprehensives. Despite the preponderance of manual families in those LEAs, the two-track comprehensive system seemed to work to the disadvantage of students from manual families. Although overall the great majority of the comprehensives had sixth forms, those that did not tended disproportionately to enrol students from manual families with relatively low ability and prior academic achievement.

The bottom panel of Table 11.7 reports the average academic achievements of students at comprehensives with and without sixth forms in LEAs having both types. As indicated by the earlier analysis, those from schools with sixth forms had higher levels of achievement. What is striking here, however, is the fact that students from schools with sixth forms have significantly higher levels of performance on all three measures. This is an even sharper difference than suggested for the whole set of comprehensive schools (shown in Table 11.6). The effect of having a sixth form is much clearer in LEAs having both types of comprehensives.

We have argued that the lack of a sixth form put students at a disadvantage, and the data presented thus far are consistent with that view. Yet, since the students who attended the two types of comprehensives also differed on entry, it is not clear whether having a sixth form made a significant difference once we control for the different kinds of students who attended comprehensives with and without sixth forms. To determine what difference it made, we regressed the same academic achievement measures reported in Table 11.7 on family social status, ability, gender and whether the school had a sixth form. The results are reported in Table 11.8.

All three of the coefficients for the dummy variable identifying students at schools without a sixth form are negative, although only two are statistically significant. When we controlled for the effects of family background, gender and ability, students who attended comprehensives without a sixth form scored significantly lower on the reading test administered at age 16, and they passed significantly lower-level school examinations. Although their average age 16 mathematics test scores were lower than those of students who attended a school with a sixth form, the difference is not statistically significant. There is thus clear evidence of the negative impact of attending a comprehensive without a sixth form, although the effect varies in size and statistical significance.

Two further questions can be raised about these results, however. First, since these comprehensive schools had been in existence for varied periods of time, and since we have noted that the proportion of comprehensives without sixth forms increased during the 1960s and 1970s, are these results affected in part by the length of time the schools had been comprehensives? Second, we have argued earlier that the clearest indication of the negative effect of attending a comprehensive school without a sixth form was the lower level of examinations passed by students in such a school. We have seen here, however, that those at comprehensives without sixth forms also scored lower on the age 16 reading test. Does this weaken our argument, then, because the loss had already occurred before students could have entered the sixth form?

To assess the importance of these questions, we conducted additional analyses, building on those reported in Table 11.8. They are reported in Table 11.9. In the first set of analyses, reported in the first three columns of Table 11.9, we added to the measures used in the analyses reported in Table 11.8 the date of founding of the comprehensive schools attended by these students. That variable was coded in one-year increments from 1965 or before to 1969. The date of founding is not significantly associated with any of the three achievement measures, and its inclusion does not appreciably alter any of the previous results. We still observe a significant negative effect of attending a comprehensive without a sixth form on both the reading test score and the level of examinations passed.

To assess the specific effect of attending a comprehensive school on the level of examinations passed, controlling for achievement by age 16, we included the age 16 reading and mathematics scores in the analysis of examination levels. This focuses the analysis directly on the period after age 16 and on any loss in examinations that could be directly associated with the lack of a sixth form. The results of that analysis are reported in the fourth column of Table 11.9. As would be expected, there are very strong effects of the age 16 test scores on the level of examinations passed, although those effects are balanced by a sharp decrease in the direct effect of the age 11 ability measure. Also, as expected, there is a sharp increase in the explained variance in examinations.

There are other important changes in the effects shown in the last two columns of Table 11.9, however. Whereas gender had no significant effect in column three, females have a strong tendency to obtain higher examination passes, once we control for the age 16 test scores. And whereas socioeconomic status has a very strong effect in column three, that effect is weakened (though not removed) once we control for test performance at age 16. These changes reflect the general tendency for females to obtain higher academic credentials (with males gaining more credentials through apprenticeships and further education) and the strong effects of socioeconomic status before the sixth form.

From our perspective, however, the most striking feature of the comparison between columns three and four in Table 11.9 is the relative stability of the effect of being at a comprehensive school without a sixth form. Despite the great changes in other effects and the great increase in the variance explained, the absence of a sixth form still has a highly significant negative effect on the level of examinations passed. The size of the coefficient is reduced slightly, but it is still quite large. This serves to demonstrate the specific effect of the organisation of the school on student achievements. Even controlled for levels of achievement up to age 16, students at a comprehensive school without a sixth form fell behind. It appears that some degree of selectivity continued in many of the LEAs even after the adoption of comprehensive schools. A large proportion of LEAs maintained two *kinds* of comprehensives, some with and some without a sixth form. Which schools had a sixth form depended in part on the schools' previous status in the selective system. Former secondary modern schools were much less likely than former grammar schools to have a sixth form.

Also similar to the pattern under the selective system, students from manual families and with lower prior academic achievements were more likely to attend the schools without sixth forms. Finally, as in the selective system, controlled for their social and academic backgrounds, students who attended comprehensives without sixth forms had lower academic achievements, even when their family background and their own prior academic achievements were comparable with those attending comprehensives with sixth forms. Neither the selectivity nor the achievement differences were as great as under the selective system, but some clear remnants of that system remained. Lower-status and lower-ability students were placed in disadvantaged educational settings, and being in those disadvantaged settings did reduce their academic achievements.

SUMMARY

There was a great deal of variation in the nature of the comprehensive schools established before 1970. The schools varied in size, in their prior status (if any) and in their internal organisation. There is evidence of linkages between the prior status of the schools and their form and function as comprehensives. In particular, former grammar schools were most likely to have late intake ages, and former secondary modern schools were most likely to lack a sixth form. Since most of the comprehensives without sixth forms were in LEAs that also established comprehensives with sixth forms, there is some continuing suggestion of a dual system paralleling the former selective school system.

There were no systematic differences in either the background characteristics or the academic achievements of students at the comprehensives with age 11, 12 or 13+ intakes. Although former grammar schools were most likely to have a 13+ intake age, their incoming students were not systematically different from those with other intake ages. It may be that the only reason for the association between the schools' former status and the age of intake was that many LEAs with late intake ages used their former secondary modern schools as lower-level schools – middle schools or (as in Leicestershire) 'high schools' – thus converting their grammar schools into late intake comprehensives. Our data are not adequate to determine if that was the case. Whatever the reason, however, intake age was apparently not used as a selection device, and it was not associated with secondary school performance levels.

In contrast, the absence of a sixth form in the comprehensive schools was associated with both intake characteristics and secondary school performance levels. The difference in secondary school performance was found in those LEAs that supported both types of comprehensives, those with and those without sixth forms, and it was found even after controlling for the socioeconomic status and ability levels of the students. The achievement deficit for students at comprehensives without sixth forms was most apparent in the level of secondary-school examinations they passed, and it is clear that the deficit largely occurred after the age of 16. It appears, therefore, that even though all LEAs provided some means for students to study for A-Levels (at least by transfer to another school with a sixth form or attendance at a sixth-form college), the comprehensives without sixth forms provided less adequate academic environments for their students.

Consistently in these analyses we have observed an association between students' socioeconomic characteristics and the kind of comprehensive school they attended. Former grammar schools enrolled a higher proportion of students from non-manual families than did former secondary modern schools. Similarly, schools without sixth forms enrolled a lower proportion of students from non-manual families than did those with sixth forms. Whether this constituted 'discrimination' in any direct sense, we cannot say. But the flow of students through these varied comprehensive schools was such that it served to disadvantage students from manual families.

These results suggest a continuation of some of the features of the selective system, even in LEAs that had established comprehensives. Many LEAs maintained two kinds of comprehensives that provided uneven educational opportunities and produced uneven academic achievements. Students from non-manual families had greater access to the comprehensives with sixth forms, and their academic achievements were superior to those of students who attended comprehensives without sixth forms. Those with disadvantaged backgrounds attended inferior schools. The differences were not as great as those found in the selective system, but they were of the same type.

TABLE 11.1

1974 CHARACTERISTICS OF SECONDARY SCHOOLS BY TYPE

	School Type			
Characteristic	*Comprehensive*	*Grammar*	*Secondary Modern*	*Independent*
Average school size	1,024	625	616	498
% Students from non-manual families	36.6	62.8	31.8	81.4
% Studying for O-Levels				
Boys	11.1	66.8	2.6	73.4
Girls	11.0	61.7	2.9	64.1
% Studying for CSEs				
Boys	36.3	0.8	47.7	2.0
Girls	35.6	0.5	46.9	1.8
% Stayed past minimum leaving age last year				
Boys	56.2	90.7	44.2	86.2
Girls	55.4	87.9	44.4	86.0

TABLE 11.2
1974 CHARACTERISTICS OF COMPREHENSIVE SCHOOLS BY
PRIOR STATUS AND PERIOD FOUNDED

Characteristic	Prior Status			
	Purpose-Built	Amalgamated	Secondary Modern	Grammar
	Founded Before 1970			
Average school size	1,141	1,198	949	954
% Students from non-manual families	30.7	34.6	31.9	39.0
% Studying for O-Levels				
Boys	10.3	11.5	6.9	10.7
Girls	10.4	11.3	7.3	10.9
% Studying for CSEs				
Boys	39.0	34.2	39.1	34.0
Girls	37.4	3.5	37.7	32.4
% Stayed past minimum leaving age last year				
Boys	58.6	57.4	55.5	59.5
Girls	57.2	56.6	53.5	61.4
	Founded 1970–74			
Average school size	1,009	1,176	827	852
% Students from non-manual families	35.2	37.8	35.3	45.5
% Studying for O-Levels				
Boys	10.0	13.5	4.6	21.8
Girls	9.7	13.0	4.9	22.1
% Studying for CSEs				
Boys	38.4	34.2	43.4	23.5
Girls	39.0	33.1	43.5	23.3
% Stayed past minimum leaving age last year				
Boys	47.0	55.4	50.3	68.3
Girls	47.0	54.4	48.6	68.9

TABLE 11.3

SOCIAL AND ACADEMIC BACKGROUND OF STUDENTS AT
COMPREHENSIVE SCHOOLS FOUNDED BEFORE 1970 BY FORMER
STATUS AND BY REGULAR VS LATE INTAKE AGE

Prior Status	Intake Age	% Non-manual	Average Age 11 Ability	Average Age 11 Reading	Average Age 11 Maths	N*
Purpose-built	11	27.1	40.2	15.1	13.9	468
	12	27.3	43.8	16.6	18.1	33
	13+	24.4	38.6	14.1	13.7	82
Amalgamated	11	32.0	40.5	15.6	15.3	500
	12	24.5	38.0	13.2	13.3	49
	13+	34.4	42.5	16.3	16.8	31
Secondary Modern	11	25.2	40.4	15.3	14.6	290
	12	33.3	40.8	16.2	17.3	30
	13+	28.6	32.9	13.1	10.5	14
Grammar	11	35.0	41.1	15.5	15.6	180
	12	00.0	53.4	17.6	20.0	5
	13+	35.4	35.4	15.0	14.6	164

*Frequencies listed are the maximum. Some statistics are based on smaller frequencies owing to missing data.

TABLE 11.4

SOCIAL AND ACADEMIC BACKGROUND OF STUDENTS AT
COMPREHENSIVE SCHOOLS FOUNDED BEFORE 1970 BY FORMER
STATUS AND BY WHETHER THE SCHOOL HAD A SIXTH FORM

Prior Status	Sixth Form	% Non-manual	Average Age 11 Ability	Average Age 11 Reading	Average Age 11 Maths	N*
Purpose-built	No	25.7	40.0	14.7	14.8	40
	Yes	26.8	40.2	15.1	14.0	547
Amalgamated	No	24.1	35.8	13.4	12.6	69
	Yes	33.1	41.0	15.7	15.6	512
Secondary Modern	No	19.6	39.4	15.0	14.5	166
	Yes	30.6	40.6	15.6	14.9	172
Grammar	No	36.7	38.0	15.1	14.7	34
	Yes	35.0	40.1	15.3	15.3	315

*Frequencies listed are the maximum. Some statistics are based on smaller frequencies owing to missing data.

TABLE 11.5

ACADEMIC ACHIEVEMENTS OF STUDENTS AT
COMPREHENSIVE SCHOOLS FOUNDED BEFORE 1970 BY FORMER
STATUS AND BY AGE OF STUDENT INTAKE

		Achievements			
Prior Status	*Intake Age*	*Average Age 16 Reading*	*Average Age 16 Maths*	*Average Age 18 Exams*	*N**
Purpose-built	11	25.1	11.4	2.23	468
	12	27.0	13.1	2.97	33
	13+	23.8	11.2	2.06	82
Amalgamated	11	24.8	11.8	2.44	500
	12	23.7	11.6	1.88	49
	13+	26.9	13.5	2.66	32
Secondary Modern	11	24.7	11.2	2.13	290
	12	26.7	12.9	2.87	30
	13+	22.2	9.4	1.79	14
Grammar	11	24.6	11.5	2.44	180
	12	28.6	12.2	2.40	5
	13+	23.5	11.5	2.27	164

*Frequencies listed are the maximum. Some statistics are based on smaller frequencies owing to missing data.

TABLE 11.6

ACADEMIC ACHIEVEMENTS OF STUDENTS AT
COMPREHENSIVE SCHOOLS FOUNDED BEFORE 1970 BY FORMER
STATUS AND BY WHETHER THE SCHOOL HAD A SIXTH FORM

		Achievements			
Prior Status	*Sixth Form*	*Average Age 16 Reading*	*Average Age 16 Maths*	*Average Age 18 Exams*	*N**
Purpose-built	Yes	25.0	11.5	2.29	547
	No	24.7	11.9	1.78	40
Amalgamated	Yes	25.2	12.0	2.52	512
	No	22.0	10.8	1.55	69
Secondary Modern	Yes	25.4	11.7	2.36	172
	No	24.1	10.9	2.00	166
Grammar	Yes	24.1	11.5	2.42	315
	No	24.7	11.5	1.79	34

*Frequencies are the maximum. Some statistics are computed on smaller frequencies owing to missing data.

TABLE 11.7

AVERAGE SOCIAL AND ACADEMIC CHARACTERISTICS OF
STUDENTS AT COMPREHENSIVE SCHOOLS FOUNDED BEFORE 1970
BY WHETHER THEY HAD SIXTH FORMS IN LEAs HAVING
COMPREHENSIVES WITH AND WITHOUT SIXTH FORMS

Student Characteristics	*Sixth Form Schools*	*Schools without Sixth Forms*	*Significance of Difference*
% Non-manual	31.1	24.0	0.03
Average ability (age 11)	41.1	38.4	0.01
Average reading test score (age 11)	15.5	14.3	0.01
Average maths test score (age 11)	15.1	13.3	0.02
Average reading test score (age 16)	25.2	23.1	0.01
Average maths test score (age 16)	12.0	10.9	0.03
Average examination level (age 18)	2.47	1.77	0.01

TABLE 11.8

EFFECTS OF NOT HAVING A SIXTH FORM ON ACADEMIC
ACHIEVEMENTS, WITH ADDITIONAL CONTROLS

Independent Variables	*Dependent Variables*		
	Age 16 Reading	*Age 16 Maths*	*Age 18 Exams*
Father's occupation	0.259†	0.187	0.163**
Father's education	−0.055	0.348*	0.128*
Mother's education	0.324†	0.184	0.129*
Number of siblings	−0.532**	−0.207†	−0.120**
Gender (female)	−0.471	−1.803**	0.107
Ability	−0.278**	0.255**	0.065**
No Sixth Form	−0.896†	0.026	−0.438*
Intercept	15.677**	3.472**	−0.373
Adjusted R^2	0.512	0.445	0.359

† $p < 0.05$, * $p < 0.01$, ** $p < 0.001$.

TABLE 11.9

EFFECTS OF NOT HAVING A SIXTH FORM ON ACADEMIC
ACHIEVEMENTS, WITH ADDITIONAL CONTROLS

Independent Variables	*Dependent Variables*			
	Age 16 Reading	*Age 16 Maths*	*Age 18 Exams*	*Age 18 Exams*
Father's occupation	0.262†	0.188	0.164**	0.111**
Father's education	–0.053	0.349*	0.129*	0.084†
Mother's education	0.326†	0.185	0.130*	0.055
Number of siblings	–0.535**	–0.207†	–0.121**	–0.046
Gender (female)	–0.473	–1.803**	0.106	0.368**
Ability	–0.278**	0.255**	0.065**	0.007
No Sixth Form	–0.806†	0.049	–0.410*	–0.398*
Year established	–0.075	–0.019	–0.024	–0.018
Age 16 Reading	—	—	—	0.073**
Age 16 Maths	—	—	—	–0.151**
Intercept	20.727**	4.732**	–1.228	–0.699
Adjusted R²	0.511	0.445	0.359	0.516

† $p < 0.05$, * $p < 0.01$, ** $p < 0.001$.

NOTES

1. The age 11 tests were administered in the schools, but they were provided by the NCDS research staff. The first was a 35-item Reading Comprehension Test designed by the National Foundation for Educational Research (NFER) to parallel the Watts-Vernon test of reading comprehension. The second was a 40-item mathematics test, also designed by NFER, which combined both problem and mechanical items. The third was a General Ability Test consisting of verbal and non-verbal parts, each with 40 items. The total score (the sum of the two parts) was used in these analyses.
2. An analysis that parallels that in Table 11.3 based on the schools founded in 1970 or later confirms the expectation that NCDS student characteristics differed sharply at former grammar and former secondary modern schools. NCDS students attending those late-founded former grammar schools had much higher average age 11 scores than those attending late-founded former secondary modern schools (and the average scores of those attending amalgamated and purpose-built schools generally fell in between). The differences in percentages from non-manual families are also very striking. Students at late-founded former grammar schools came from non-manual families much more often than those at late-founded former secondary modern schools. This is what we would expect if the schools' statuses changed while the NCDS students were enrolled and those students had originally entered selective schools. This same pattern is found for schools with all three intake ages. Thus, as expected, if we are to see if there was selectivity in truly comprehensive schools, we must restrict our focus to schools founded before 1970.
3. The amalgamated type of comprehensive was usually based on two schools, one a secondary modern, the other a grammar school. Ideally, we might disaggregate the students at such schools into their two original types, but the available data do not permit that. Thus, our comparative analysis is consistently focused on differences

231

between former grammar schools and former secondary modern schools. It is note-worthy, however, that in all of the analyses we have conducted the amalgamated schools and their students resemble former grammar schools and their students more closely than they resemble former secondary modern schools and students. This may be a function of the tendency to combine two schools of about equal size when forming an amalgamated school. If that were done, the mix of former grammar and former secondary modern school students would be 'richer' than in the overall population where only about one-third of selective school students attended grammar schools.

4. The reading test administered at age 16 was the same one used at age 11. This probably introduced ceiling effects for the more advanced 16-year-olds, a problem which we discuss in Chapter 12. The mathematics test, designed at the University of Manchester, contained 31 problem and mechanical items. The examinations measure ranged from 0 (no exams passed) to 8 (two or more A-Levels), the levels reflecting the number and kind of exams passed – CSEs, O-Levels and A-Levels.

5. As in Table 11.3, the picture is very mixed for students at the age 12 intake schools. Their achievements were quite high at purpose-built and former secondary modern schools but relatively low at amalgamated schools. There were relatively few schools with an age 12 intake and they had varied backgrounds (although few had formerly been grammar schools). There were thus few NCDS students at these schools, and no clear picture of either their backgrounds or achievements emerges from our analyses.

6. The measure of examinations passed used here includes all examinations passed up to 1976, when the cohort was 18 years old, irrespective of where they were taken. The measure thus includes those taken at institutions other than secondary schools (for example, sixth-form colleges or colleges of further education).

12

Selective versus Comprehensive Schools

All of the discussion thus far has dealt with the process of introducing comprehensive schools and the effects of different kinds of comprehensives on student achievement. We have seen that LEAs varied in the degree to which they adopted comprehensive secondary education, and even where comprehensive schools were introduced, they differed in the way they were organised. It has also been apparent that the variety of *kinds* of comprehensives continued to reflect in significant ways some of the features of the selective system. So, even where change occurred, it was not always as complete as it might have at first appeared to be.

Whatever our interpretation of these findings regarding variations among comprehensives, however, the political, ideological and educational debates that have raged on about comprehensive schools have seldom focused on either the origins or the structural variations of the schools. Rather, they have focused on the general concept of comprehensive education, on whether comprehensives are 'as good as' the schools under the selective system of secondary education. A frequently heard argument in favour of selective schools involves the claim that separating students into higher and lower academic streams provides maximally appropriate educational experiences for both groups. Yet, it is also claimed by those who favour comprehensive schools that mixing the more and less talented students works to the advantage of both groups. The NCDS data provide an opportunity to examine the merits of these conflicting positions. That is the purpose of this chapter.

INEVITABLE COMPLICATIONS

The logic of comparing the effectiveness of selective and comprehensive forms of secondary education appears to be rather straightforward. What we need is to observe a set of selective schools and a set of comprehensive schools so as to compare their effects on their students.

Assuming two roughly comparable sets of students attending the two kinds of schools, we need only compare their academic performances after they have experienced the educational programmes of the two kinds of schools. Unfortunately, that is not as easy as it may at first appear to be.

The very nature of the historical process that is reviewed in this volume makes any conceivable analysis subject to a number of undesirable limitations. The process of change from selective schools to comprehensives was an ongoing one. Any feasible analysis must consist of comparing schools that had changed status with those that had not. We know that those that had changed status were not randomly distributed throughout England and Wales, and we know that the distribution was different for those that changed status earlier and those that changed later. In fact, a higher proportion of early comprehensives were purpose-built and thus did not actually 'change status'. We also know that one of the forces restraining the process of change was the strong commitment many communities had to their grammar schools. There was a widespread tendency to retain the 'better' grammar schools, even in those LEAs in which comprehensives were established.

There were only ten LEAs that had fully changed to comprehensives before 1970, and only 42 had fully changed by 1974. And, by this time, 19 LEAs had yet to establish a single comprehensive school. So, even in 1974, most of the comprehensives were in LEAs that also had selective schools. That means that in most LEAs there must have been some mechanism to determine which students went to selective and which went to comprehensive schools. However that was done, it is unlikely that wholly comparable sets of students attended the two kinds of schools. Given the widespread attempt to preserve grammar schools in most LEAs, it is likely that enrolments in comprehensive schools included a smaller proportion of the high ability students than would be found in a fully comprehensive system. Any comparison between comprehensive and selective school students is thus almost certain to put comprehensive school students at a disadvantage.

It is essentially impossible to compare the comprehensive and selective systems without risking significant systematic distortion. Even if we had comparable data at two points in time, say in the 1950s and the 1980s, we would face problems of comparability. A fully selective state-supported system never existed after the Second World War, because some of the earliest post-war rebuilding of heavily bombed areas involved the establishment of comprehensive schools, especially in London, Coventry and Birmingham. Similarly, there has never been a fully comprehensive system. Selective schools (especially grammar schools) continued to exist long after most schools had become comprehensives. But even if there were a 'fully selective' and a 'fully comprehensive period', and even if we had adequate data from both periods, comparisons between them would be subject to distortions owing to other differences between the periods. There might be differences in the overall economic conditions, the quality of teaching staffs, the contents of the curricula, or numerous other factors that could affect the results of a comparative study. In any event, however, there have never been two 'pure' periods on which to base a comparison.

Thus, although they are far from ideal for the purpose, the data available from the NCDS are about as appropriate as we can get to compare the two systems of secondary education. We are necessarily limited to using the kinds of data available here, but it is important to recognise the nature of these data and to understand the limitations of any analysis conducted with them. They are data from a mixed system in which most comprehensive schools were relatively new, having been largely transformed from selective schools, and most selective schools were well-established. We can only guess at the effects of these historical conditions on our results, but it seems likely that the data provide a more valid picture of the selective school system than of the comprehensive school system.

PREVIOUS COMPARATIVE STUDIES

Given the importance, and the frequently controversial nature, of the move towards comprehensive schooling, it may appear surprising that research on the consequences for children's achievement is relatively rare. In part this may reflect the usual lack of enthusiasm among politicians for assessing the effects of action to which they are committed, but there are also technical explanations for the lack of research in this area.

First, the period of time when such research was possible was relatively short. The earliest comprehensive schools, it could be argued, were likely to be special for a number of reasons – the circumstances of their creation, their atypical locations, or the philosophical commitment of those who established them or taught in them – and therefore could not be taken to be representative of comprehensive schools once they were established on a wider scale. Similarly, in more recent times, as comprehensive schools have approached being the norm, the remaining grammar and, particularly, secondary modern schools could not be assumed to represent a fully selective system. Thus, it was only during the late 1960s and 1970s, when both comprehensive and selective schools existed in reasonably large numbers, that adequate comparative research was possible.

Secondly, there are considerable challenges in assembling data which are appropriate for providing generalisable comparisons. Even in the period referred to above, and as illustrated in many of our case-study authorities, comprehensive and selective schools frequently coexisted in the same geographical area, with the result that the most able children were under-represented in the comprehensive schools. Furthermore, because of the link with the political complexion of the Local Authority, comprehensive schools were more likely to be established in less privileged parts of the country and therefore to be less advantaged in the social characteristics and the initial ability of their intakes. Thus, even to compare Local Education Authorities which were entirely comprehensive or selective, or nearly so, would not be to compare like with like and could lead to misleading findings.

For these reasons, it is essential for such research that *either* care is taken to ensure that samples of schools are used such that it can be demonstrated that the comprehensives and the combination of grammars and secondary moderns are equivalent in their intakes *or* sufficient data must be available on their intakes to enable statistical adjustments to be made when comparing their outcomes. In addition, in the latter case it is important that there is clarity and consistency in the unit of analysis, for example that crude regional or local authority data are not used to adjust for differences in analyses which are otherwise at the school or individual level (for a fuller discussion of these issues, see Goldstein, 1984 and Gray, Jesson and Jones, 1984). There are examples of studies, notably Marks, Cox and Pomian-Srzednicki (1983), which attracted considerable attention from the media but which have been severely criticised for failing to meet these criteria (for example, Lacey, 1984 and Fogelman, 1984). A review of other studies which were largely small-scale and local can be found in Reynolds and Sullivan (1987).

There are three studies which do meet the above requirements and represent the best evidence available to date on this issue. (Of course, all three were wider in their scope and purpose than their comparative analyses of attainment.) The first was in fact relatively small-scale and based on nine schools in South Wales (Reynolds and Sullivan, 1987). Its major characteristic is that it was able to take advantage of a situation where the two types of school coexisted within a relatively homogeneous area and also, because of other ongoing research, the researchers had access to a considerable amount of data on the schools' intakes.

The second study was carried out in Scotland (Gray, McPherson and Raffe, 1983), where the researchers were able to use information on school structures and local catchment areas to identify schools which either did or did not contain the full ability range (the latter including some schools designated as comprehensive but known to be affected by their proximity to selective schools). In addition, data on the socioeconomic characteristics of the pupils supported the equivalence in intakes of the two sets of schools, although no direct measure of ability was available.

The third study was based on earlier analyses of the same dataset as we have used in this book, that is, the National Child Development Study, and was thus able to exploit the substantial information available on the children's characteristics before their transfer to secondary schools (Steedman, 1980 and 1983). In fact this showed considerable inequality between the intakes of comprehensive schools and the combination of selective schools, and multivariate analyses were carried out to adjust for these initial differences.

The three studies are not consistent in their findings. The Welsh study took a reading test score as its achievement measure, and found significantly higher average scores in the selective schools. However, the researchers suggest that this could be a function of the particular local circumstances. The other two studies, which both investigated public examination performance (and, in Steedman's case, scores on mathematics and reading tests), were more alike in their conclusions. Both found little or no difference between the two types of school, although Gray *et al.* report a slight increase in average performance for those attending their comprehensive schools.

Thus, on balance, existing research suggests that it is not possible to identify dramatic differences in average attainment associated with attendance at a comprehensive or selective school. This is consistent with more general findings on the relative lack of influence of the administrative characteristics of schools.

SELECTION WITHIN A MIXED SYSTEM

For the reasons discussed in Chapter 11, it is not appropriate to include in any of our analyses those students who attended comprehensives founded after they had entered secondary school. We must assume that such students began their secondary school careers in the selective system. Therefore, in all of the analysis in this chapter we include only those comprehensive school students who, in 1974, were attending comprehensives founded before 1970. Those students are compared with combined groups of students attending grammar or secondary modern schools in 1974. All of our analyses thus compare NCDS students we can assume entered and remained in selective schools with those we can assume entered and remained in comprehensive schools.

It is clear from the previous chapters that comprehensives established in the 1960s were more likely than those established in the 1970s to have been either purpose-built or to have been based on secondary modern schools and less likely to have been based on grammar schools. There is a strong indication that the early comprehensives were more often attended by students with manual family backgrounds and relatively modest prior academic records. Especially in the early period, there appears to have been a degree of selection between the comprehensive and the selective schools. Our initial analysis is designed to assess the validity of that impression.

We conducted a logistic regression analysis comparing the characteristics of students who, in 1974, were attending selective schools (the combined category of grammar and secondary modern schools) and those attending comprehensive schools founded before 1970. The analysis was designed to identify the characteristics of those attending comprehensives as they differed from those attending selective schools. The results of that analysis are presented in Table 12.1.

Those results clearly confirm the impression gained from the earlier chapters. Students attending comprehensive schools in 1974 were more often from families in which the father had a relatively low level of education, but they differed even more sharply from those attending selective schools in having lower prior academic achievements. Their average scores on both the general ability test and the mathematics test taken at age 11 were significantly lower than the average scores of those attending selective schools.

Some of the previous analysis has also suggested that the characteristics of students who attended comprehensives varied depending on the former status of the comprehensive. To assess the validity of that impression, we conducted a multinomial logistic regression analysis in which the dependent categories are the NCDS students who attended the four kinds of comprehensives (purpose-built, ex-grammar, ex-secondary modern and amalgamated) founded before 1970, and the reference category is those students who attended selective schools in 1974. Each set of coefficients thus represents differences between students attending selective schools and those attending comprehensive schools of a particular type.

The results of that analysis are presented in Table 12.2. They do not lend support to the idea suggested by the previous analyses. There are no very noteworthy differences among the sets of coefficients associated with these four types of comprehensive schools. Students who were attending all four were clearly different from those attending selective schools, especially in having lower general ability test scores, but they do not differ from each other in any systematic way. Thus, although comprehensive school students more often came from manual families and had lower academic records than selective school students, those differences did not vary appreciably by the former statuses of the comprehensives they attended.

In several of our case-study LEAs, leaders argued forcefully that unless all of an LEA's schools were changed to comprehensives it was not a truly comprehensive form of reorganisation. The point was that the remaining selective schools were predominantly grammar schools, and they served to 'cream off' the high-ability students from the comprehensives, thus producing 'comprehensives' that were essentially secondary modern schools. Since the majority of LEAs had both comprehensives *and* selective schools, even in 1974, that suggests that 'creaming off' was a system-wide practice. The analyses in Tables 12.1 and 12.2 are consistent with that claim. Overall, the selective schools were 'creaming off' the higher-achieving students from the comprehensives.

ALTERNATIVE COMPARATIVE STRATEGIES

Even if we limit the comprehensive school students studied to those at schools founded before 1970, selective–comprehensive comparisons can be made in several different ways. Those different kinds of comparisons reflect important features of the varied patterns of change we have reviewed in the earlier chapters, and they justify serious consideration of different forms of analysis.

As we have seen, by 1974 there were three kinds of LEAs, viewed from the perspective of our present interests. There were those that had *completely* changed to comprehensive schools, those that had *partially* changed to comprehensives; and those that had retained *pure selective systems*. Among those LEAs that had either partially or completely changed to comprehensive schools, of course, some of the comprehensives were founded in 1970 or later.

We must thus recognise that there were the following kinds of LEAs:[1]

Type A: all selective schools; no comprehensive schools.

Type B: both comprehensive and selective schools; all comprehensives founded before 1970.

Type C: both comprehensive and selective schools; some comprehensives founded before 1970, some in 1970 or later.

Type D: both comprehensive and selective schools; all comprehensives founded in the 1970s.

Type E: all comprehensive schools; all founded before 1970.

Type F: all comprehensive schools; some founded before 1970, some founded in the 1970s.

Type G: all comprehensive schools; all founded in the 1970s.

The analyses presented in Tables 12.1 and 12.2 use different proportions of the students in these seven kinds of LEAs. They use all students in LEA Types A, B and E; some in Types C, D and F; and none in Type G. In fact, comprehensive school students in LEA Type G were also excluded from all of the major analyses in Chapter 11. And, of course, many students in Types C and F have been removed from those analyses. As we noted earlier, among our case studies, Manchester is a Type B LEA, Northumberland is a Type D LEA, and Stoke-on-Trent is a Type G LEA. Thus, all of the comprehensive school students from Manchester are included in our analyses, but none of those from Northumberland or Stoke-on-Trent are included.

There appear to be at least three approaches to making selective–comprehensive school comparisons, given these complications. First, if we believe that the nature of the LEA in which the school is located makes little difference, we can compare students at all pre-1970 comprehensives with students at all selective schools in 1974. This would involve LEAs of all types except Type G. This approach provides the broadest basis for comparison. It is the one used in Tables 12.1 and 12.2.

If we are concerned about the process of 'creaming off', however, we might prefer comparisons that are limited to students at schools in LEAs that were uniformly selective or comprehensive, and including only comprehensive schools that had been founded before 1970. This approach would include only students at schools in LEAs of Types A and E and parts of F. It would provide the narrowest basis of comparison, involving a very small proportion of the LEAs. In what would essentially be the reverse of this approach, we could conduct an analysis that compared students at the two types of schools in LEAs that had both. This approach would limit the analysis to all of the students at schools in LEAs of Type B and some at schools in LEAs of Type C. It attempts to control for the 'creaming off' process by including only LEAs in which it can be assumed that some 'creaming off' had occurred.

Each of these types of analysis has its merits and its disadvantages. The first, which is the broadest (and we will say includes 'all' LEAs), has the merit of including the maximum number of students from the most diverse possible kinds of settings. But it has the disadvantage of including highly varied LEA settings, and thus it may obscure important contrasts. The second form of analysis (which includes only 'pure' LEAs) may appear to be preferable because it compares only pure selective and pure comprehensive cases. There are so few such cases, however, that the size of the sample involved is very small, and the LEAs may be so atypical as to provide an unreliable basis for judging the results. The third form of analysis (which includes only 'mixed' LEAs) might be preferred because it avoids the apparent limitations of the other two. But in doing so, it may introduce another source of error, the conflict within LEAs over the distribution of students into the two contending systems of secondary education.

We believe that the strengths and weaknesses of the three approaches are such that no one method can be chosen with confidence. We have thus conducted analyses using all three, and much of our discussion will involve comparing the results from the three approaches and suggesting general interpretations based on that comparison.

STUDENT 'QUALITY'

Tables 12.1 and 12.2 have suggested that there was a systematic process of selection involved in distributing students into the comprehensive and selective systems such that selective system students were, on average, more academically talented – the selective schools systematically 'creamed off' the high-ability students from the comprehensives. Age 11 general ability test score data relevant to the idea of 'creaming off' are reported in Table 12.3, using the three definitions of the appropriate schools and students to include in the selective–comprehensive comparison.

The most general pattern in Table 12.3 is for the test scores of students at selective schools to be higher than those at comprehensive schools in every comparison using all three sample definitions. The selective school median scores are higher; there are fewer selective school students with scores below 30 and more selective school students with scores above 60. Within that general pattern, however, the sizes of the differences vary a great deal using the three sample definitions. The smallest selective–comprehensive differences are found for the 'pure' definition, and the largest are found for the 'mixed' definition.

Although the overall pattern is consistent with the idea that the selective schools 'creamed off' the high performing students from the comprehensives, a 'creaming off' interpretation of these differences is not consistently appropriate. It is clearly not an appropriate interpretation in the comparison between students in LEAs with 'pure' selective or comprehensive systems. These are differences across LEAs, so what they indicate, rather than 'creaming off', is that LEAs that retained a pure selective system generally had higher-ability students than LEAs that had shifted completely to a comprehensive system. This is consistent with our earlier observation that LEAs that held out against comprehensives tended to be in middle-class areas that strongly supported their well-established grammar schools.

The fact that the greatest difference is found for 'mixed' LEAs is highly relevant to the idea of 'creaming off', however. In LEAs that had both kinds of secondary schools, the selective system was clearly serving more of the high-ability students, while the comprehensive schools had a much less talented student body. The difference between the medians of the comprehensive and selective school students' ability scores is equivalent to more than half a standard deviation of the ability scores for these students. By any standard, the differences shown in Table 12.3 for the mixed category are huge and provide clear evidence of 'creaming off'. The differences using the full set of LEAs largely reflect the differences in the mixed LEAs, but they also reflect the differences in the pure LEAs.

Given these differences between the student bodies participating in the two kinds of secondary school systems, it can be argued that any attempt to compare the two systems would be suspect. Even in the case of the 'pure' LEAs, the difference between the median scores of the two sets of students is equal to one quarter of a standard deviation. To some extent, then, selective–comprehensive comparisons are bound to have a kind of 'apples and oranges' quality. Yet, it is apparent from all of the evidence we have examined in the earlier chapters that the differences we see in Table 12.3 are a part of the actual process of system reorganisation, and would be likely to be found in any reorganisation that permitted a degree of local control over the process.[2]

Our approach to the comparison is thus a cautious one, but we believe it still provides important information and at least establishes a basis for a reasoned discussion of the issues involved in the debate about the relative merits of the two systems. In order to minimise the problems posed by the differences between the kinds of students attending the schools in the two systems, we consistently include in our comparisons controls for the socioeconomic backgrounds and ability test scores of the groups being compared.

SYSTEM PRODUCTIVITY

Proponents of both systems frequently make the claim that their preferred system is actually better for both high- and low-ability students. Those arguing for a selective system reason that low- and high-ability students require different curricula and teaching methods to maximise their potential. Those promoting comprehensive schooling reason that students help each other and that the same curriculum and methods can help all students maximise their potential without negatively labelling those in the lower segment. Both views lead to the prediction that, on average, students perform at higher levels in the preferred system. The most basic test of possible superiority then would be to compare the academic performances of the students in the two systems.

We have proposed that there are at least three possible approaches to defining the appropriate students to include in such an analysis, and there are advantages and disadvantages to each of them. Although Table 12.3 shows that the difference between the student bodies in the two systems is smallest under the 'pure' definition, it also shows that the numbers of students involved are very small. The combination of that limitation and the unusual nature of the pure LEAs makes that a questionable basis for our analysis. Table 12.3 also shows that the impact of 'creaming off' was greatest in those LEAs that included both selective and comprehensive schools, so using that set of LEAs introduces the maximum amount of difference in the students being compared. The 'all LEA' basis for our analysis has the merit of avoiding these difficulties, but it may obscure important differences by combining LEAs with very different characteristics.

To maximise our ability to observe system differences and to minimise the potential sources of error in each of these bases of comparison, we carried out three parallel analyses using the three sets of students indicated in Table 12.3. To spare the reader an extended set of complex tables, however, we present only the detailed results of our analyses using the largest 'all LEA' student samples. However, we also present some of the critical parallel results using the other two, more restricted, samples, noting potentially meaningful differences.

Our initial approach to the question of the relative merits of the selective–comprehensive systems uses a multiple regression analysis in which the academic achievements of students who attended comprehensive schools are systematically compared with the achievements of students who attended selective schools. The purpose of the analysis is to determine if, on average, students had higher levels of achievement under one system than under the other.

As control variables, we use measures of socioeconomic background, gender, and the scores on the general ability test taken at age 11. The focal element in the analysis is a dummy variable indicating whether the individual was attending a comprehensive. The coefficients for that variable show the average difference between comprehensive school students and comparable students who attended selective schools (the reference category in the analysis). The dependent variables used are the same three achievement measures included in several of the analyses in Chapter 11 – scores on reading and mathematics tests taken at the age of 16 and secondary school examinations passed by the age of 18.

The results of this analysis are presented in Table 12.4. The critical coefficient in each analysis is that for the dummy variable representing the comprehensive school cases. It indicates whether, holding the other measures constant, there is a significant difference between the average achievement of students who attended comprehensive schools compared with comparable students who attended selective schools. None of the coefficients is statistically significant, although those for the age 16 reading and mathematics tests approach that level. However, those two coefficients have opposite signs. On average, comprehensive school students had somewhat higher reading test scores, but they also had somewhat lower mathematics test scores. There were no differences between selective and comprehensive school students in their average levels of secondary school examinations passed. That coefficient is essentially zero.

The results in the analyses using the other two definitions of the appropriate samples (the 'pure' and the 'mixed' LEA samples) produce essentially identical results. The comprehensive school dummy variable coefficients are not significant in any of the analyses, and the non-significant reading and mathematics coefficients have opposite signs.

These results can be interpreted as indicating that there is no basis to choose between the two systems. The comprehensive schools functioned just as well as the selective schools did and thus, although nothing may have been gained through comprehensive reorganisation, nothing was lost either. In terms of the overall productivity of the systems, there is no difference between them using any of these three measures. Claims to the contrary, made on behalf of both systems, appear to be unfounded. Yet, as we see in the following section, overall productivity is not the only criterion one can use in comparing the two systems.

INEQUALITIES WITHIN THE TWO SYSTEMS

Previous analyses of these NCDS data (Kerckhoff, 1993) have shown that selective schooling served to enhance the achievements of those in grammar schools and depress the achievements of those in secondary modern schools, compared with comparable students attending comprehensive schools. Since the coefficients in Table 12.4 represent the average net difference between students in the selective and comprehensive systems, they may obscure varying effects depending on the part of the selective system the individual was in. The coefficients may reflect a balance between the advantages for grammar school students and the disadvantages for secondary modern school students. Or, to look at that possibility from the other side, low-ability students attending comprehensive schools may have performed better than they would have in the selective system, but high-ability students may have done less well. To assess the validity of that hypothesis, we added another term to our analytic equation, the interaction of ability with the comprehensive school dummy variable. That term in the analysis indicates whether the effect of being at a comprehensive school (rather than a selective school) varies by the student's ability level. The results of that analysis are presented in Table 12.5.

The results in Table 12.5 are sharply different from those in Table 12.4. In two of the three analyses, the interactions are significantly negative, and the main effects of being at a comprehensive school are significantly positive. The reading test analysis shows neither a significant main effect of being at a comprehensive school nor a significant interaction with ability,[3] but both of the other achievement measures show both main and interaction effects that are significant.

The statistically significant results are what would be expected if the two school systems had the effects just hypothesised. They indicate that, at least on two of these three measures, students at the lowest ability level had higher achievements if they attended comprehensive schools (thus the positive comprehensive school main effect), but as ability level increased, the comprehensive school advantage decreased (thus the negative interaction effect). This pattern is apparent for both the mathematics test and school examinations. Only the reading test analysis completely fails to show this pattern.

The results of the analysis using only LEAs with both selective and comprehensive schools (the 'mixed' definition) are highly similar to those in Table 12.5. The results using only LEAs with fully selective or fully comprehensive systems (the 'pure' definition) are also highly similar for mathematics and examinations, but even the reading analysis shows parallel main and interaction effects. We will discuss those results in greater detail later in the chapter.

These results suggest that comprehensive reorganisation did not alter the average level of academic achievement but that it did lead to a more restricted *range* of achievements. Fewer students performed at very low levels, but fewer also performed at very high levels. The higher-level performances of low-ability comprehensive school students were evidently balanced by the lower-level performances of high-ability students in the same kinds of schools.

One way to estimate the nature of that balance is through the relationship between the sizes of the main effects and interaction effects coefficients in the analyses reported in Table 12.5. Those effects indicate that a low-ability student was advantaged by being in a comprehensive school, but the advantage decreased as ability levels increased. The main effect coefficient indicates the estimated comprehensive school advantage for a student at the lowest ability level (zero in a test or no examinations passed). The interaction effect coefficient indicates the amount of decrease in the comprehensive school advantage for every unit increase in ability. By dividing the main effect term by the interaction term, we can obtain an estimate of the ability level at which the comprehensive school advantage is reduced to zero. Students with ability levels below that point were evidently advantaged and those above that point were disadvantaged by being in a comprehensive school. It is then possible to determine the proportions of comprehensive school students above and below that ability level.[4]

Based on such computations, and using the data from 'all' LEAs, we can estimate the percentages of comprehensive school students who fell below that break-even point and thus appear to have been helped by attending a comprehensive school so far as each academic achievement measure is concerned. Those percentages are 45.2 per cent for the mathematics test and 52.8 per cent for school examinations (Table 12.5 shows no significant main or interaction effect for the reading test, so it is not meaningful to make such estimates for reading). These two percentages straddle the 50 per cent mark, suggesting a rather even balance between the proportions whose scores are higher and lower in a comprehensive school than they might have been in a selective school.

The comparable percentages in the analysis using only mixed LEAs (those with both selective and comprehensive schools) were 42.3 per cent for mathematics and 57.5 per cent for examinations. Again, the two percentages straddle the 50 per cent mark. Using only the pure LEAs, the comparable percentages were: reading test score 82.4 per cent, mathematics test score 40.7 per cent, and school examinations 45.7 per cent. Given the small frequencies involved, it is difficult to know how reliable these estimates are, and the sharp difference between the reading and mathematics test results casts further doubt. But, again we see percentages on both sides of the 50 per cent point.

Table 12.6 summarises the critical results of these analyses for the three definitions of the appropriate samples.[5] In each case, we report the size and significance level of the original ('total') comprehensive school coefficient (from Table 12.4), the main and interaction effect coefficients (from Table 12.5), the ability level at which the comprehensive school effect is reduced to zero, and the percentage of the comprehensive school students with ability scores below that level. It is apparent that the results using the full and mixed sample definitions are very similar. The results using the pure LEA sample definition deviate from the other two in showing fewer than half of the comprehensive school students had obtained superior results in the mathematics test, but they also deviate from the other two in showing that the great majority of the comprehensive school students had superior results in the reading test. The interaction effect for that reading test analysis is not statistically significant,[6] however, so it is not clear how that result should be interpreted.

These analyses provide little evidence that comprehensive schools serve either to increase or to reduce the average academic performances of secondary school students. At the same time, they do indicate that the distribution of academic performances is narrower in comprehensive schools,[7] and that this results from both higher levels of performance of low-ability students and lower levels of performance by high-ability students at comprehensive schools.[8]

These results suggest a trade-off between the advantages and disadvantages of comprehensive versus selective secondary schooling, and it is the kind of trade-off that can lead some to see a half-full glass and others to see a half-empty glass. One can laud either the superior performances of high-ability students in the selective system or the superior performances of low-ability students in the comprehensive system. One can decry either the lower proportion of very high achievement scores in the comprehensive system or the higher proportion of very low achievement scores in the selective system.

Before becoming over-impressed by these results, however, it may be as well to take into account the sizes of the differences they indicate. For instance, Table 12.5 indicates that, in the all-LEA analysis, students with the lowest ability obtained, on average, 0.852 higher level examination passes in comprehensive schools than they would have obtained had they attended a selective (presumably a secondary modern) school. Since the standard deviation of the examinations measure is 2.10 for the comprehensive school students, that is a large increment. Yet, it needs to be remembered that there were very few students at the lowest level. In fact, there were very few students at either the highest or the lowest level (as Table 12.3 shows).

If we accept the estimate of a linear change in the effect of attending a comprehensive school as ability increases, this means that only 6.9 per cent of the comprehensive school students gained as much as half a point on the 8-point examinations measure by going to a comprehensive school. And, making the same assumption about a linear effect across ability levels, only 4.2 per cent of the students can be said to have gained half a point on the examinations measure by attending a selective (presumably a grammar) school. For the same all-LEA sample, using the same linear assumption, only 5.6 per cent gained as much as one point in the 31-point mathematics test by attending a comprehensive school, and only 11.3 per cent gained that much by attending a selective school. Thus, although these results are highly significant statistically, their substantive significance is not so impressive.

A CHOICE OF THE LESSER OF TWO EVILS?

Whether or not the differences we have observed are considered to be 'large', the more basic question is whether these kinds of trade-offs are a necessary part of evaluating the two systems. Do we have to choose between them and accept the bitter with the sweet whichever way we decide to go? We cannot answer that question with any confidence, of course, but we would like to suggest a possible alternative to such a difficult choice.

A major difference between the two systems is in their approach to the education of high- and low-ability students. The selective system tends to focus most of its attention and resources on high-ability students, while the comprehensive system discriminates less sharply among students according to ability level. If we postulate that student achievement is heavily influenced by the resources provided by the school system, the pattern of student achievements reported here can be at least partially explained in terms of the differences in educational resource allocation in the two systems.

The much wider distribution of achievements in the selective system may be due to the heavy allocation of resources to upper-ability students (in the grammar schools) with an associated low level of resources being available to low-ability students (in secondary modern schools). The two kinds of schools undoubtedly do receive different shares of educational resources – teacher talent and effort, facilities (such as libraries and laboratories), and so on.[9] If those same resources are divided more evenly across all secondary school students (in comprehensive schools), it tends to reduce the resources available to high-ability students and increase the resources available to low-ability students. Our analysis suggests that when that is done it lowers the academic achievements of high-ability students and raises the achievements of low-ability students.

Unfortunately, we are unable to test this idea convincingly. Our data do not contain wholly adequate measures of school resources. Two available measures are at least suggestive, however. One is the school's pupil–teacher ratio in 1973; the other is the proportion of teachers who left the school in 1973. The first of these is at least a crude indicator of the school's ability to provide adequate instruction. The second measure gives some indication of programmatic continuity and the stability of the students' academic experience. On average, the lower the pupil–teacher ratio and the lower the teacher turnover, the potentially better the learning environment the school provides.

The great majority of the NCDS students who attended comprehensive secondary schools were in the 'mixed' LEAs, those that had all three types of schools. It is in those LEAs that we can best see the differential allocation of resources under the two systems, since LEAs with wholly selective or wholly comprehensive schools may well have had different overall levels of resources. In this analysis we thus use the mixed LEA definition of the appropriate sample. Our analysis essentially poses the following question: in LEAs that provide schooling in comprehensive, grammar and secondary modern schools, do the resources and stability experienced by students vary depending on the *type* of school they attend?

Table 12.7 reports the averages of the pupil–teacher ratio and attrition measures for the three types of schools in LEAs having all three types. Comparisons are made between all pairs of the three types as well as between the comprehensives and the combined selective school types. The averages of pupil–teacher ratios for the types of schools are consistent with the view of resource allocation just suggested. Secondary modern schools had the highest average pupil–teacher ratio, and grammar schools had the lowest, with comprehensives in between. All of the differences are statistically significant. Although the average pupil–teacher ratio of the combined category of selective schools was larger than the ratio for comprehensives, the difference is not statistically significant at the 0.01 level. The difference *is* significant at the 0.05 level, however.

This pattern of differences undoubtedly reflects two important features of the two systems. First, grammar schools, almost by definition, have lower pupil–teacher ratios than secondary modern schools because of the intensive sixth-form curriculum. Since comprehensives combine pupils who would have attended grammar and secondary modern schools under the selective system, we would also expect the pupil–teacher ratios in comprehensives to fall between the other two. Second, the somewhat smaller pupil–teacher ratio in the comprehensives than in the combined selective school category suggests that the more recently established comprehensives received additional LEA support.[10]

Teacher attrition rates in both secondary modern and comprehensive schools were also significantly higher than in grammar schools. The attrition rate in the comprehensives was actually higher than in both the grammar and secondary modern schools, although the comprehensive–secondary modern difference is not statistically significant at the 0.01 level (although it is at the 0.05 level). The attrition level for the combined category of selective schools was also significantly lower than that for the comprehensives. The high attrition rate in comprehensive schools may reflect teachers' dissatisfaction with the comprehensive school concept. On the other hand, it is at least equally possible that the relatively higher level of teacher turnover reflects the expansion taking place in the comprehensive sector. As new comprehensive schools were created, teachers who were already experienced in such schools were well placed to apply for more senior posts or to schools in more attractive locations, which would lead to higher levels of mobility. Whatever the reason, this would result in less continuity and a possible negative effect on the education of students at comprehensive schools. And grammar school students experienced the highest level of teacher continuity.

The data on both pupil–teacher ratios and teacher attrition rates may have direct relevance to our analyses of the achievement patterns in selective and comprehensive schools. Clearly, students at grammar schools had the most supportive educational conditions – the lowest pupil–teacher ratio and the lowest level of teacher attrition. Both of those conditions should facilitate high achievement levels by the high-ability students who attended grammar schools. By comparison, students at both secondary modern and comprehensive schools had less supportive educational conditions. Those at secondary modern schools had the highest pupil–teacher ratios, and those at comprehensive schools had the highest rates of teacher attrition. These different conditions could be expected to have affected the achievements of students at the three kinds of schools in ways that are consistent with the analyses reported in Tables 12.5 and 12.6. High-ability students at selective schools achieve at higher levels and low-ability students at selective schools achieve at lower levels than comparable students at comprehensives. If there is some validity to a resource allocation explanation of our results, it would appear that an increase in the overall level of resources for comprehensive schools could serve to raise average student performances while maintaining a relatively narrow range of academic achievements. Our results are at least consistent with that expected outcome. Students at selective and comprehensive schools had similar average levels of achievement, given their social status and ability. That is consistent with the assumption that the total resources in the two systems were roughly the same. But students who received greater resources in the comprehensive system (low-ability students) performed better in that system and students who received greater resources in the selective system (high-ability students) performed better in that system. That is consistent with the postulate of a resource–achievement association. In addition, the between-system differences in teacher attrition, a possibly temporary effect of the reorganisation of the schools, may have worked to the disadvantage of comprehensive school students of all ability levels.

It may be true, therefore, that so long as we limit the resources invested in education to the current levels, we may need to choose between higher proportions of very high performances (in a selective system) and lower proportions of very low performances (in a comprehensive system). But it may also be true that an overall increase in the resources invested in comprehensive schooling could produce both of those outcomes. Also, if the teacher attrition rates shown in Table 12.7 were temporary disruptions owing to the recency of the reorganisation, even the differences we have observed may not be indicative of intrinsic differences between the systems.

OVERVIEW

Once we controlled for their ability and family background, there were no differences between the average academic achievements of students in comprehensive and selective schools, irrespective of the specific definition of the appropriate samples to be compared. Yet, there was a general tendency for high-ability students to perform at somewhat lower levels and low-ability students to perform at somewhat higher levels in the comprehensive schools. This suggests that both educational systems have advantages and disadvantages. The selective system seems to help the high-ability students at the expense of the low-ability students, and the comprehensive system seems to help the low-ability students at the expense of the high-ability students.

We have noted, however, that even the statistically significant results reported in this chapter are only limited bases for evaluation of the relative merits of the two systems. We have necessarily used an analysis that assumes a linear interaction effect between the students' ability levels and the system within which they were schooled. Even making that assumption, only small proportions of the samples studied had experienced even modest effects as a result of their locations in the two systems.

Yet, the differences are real, and they are not so small as to be wholly ignored. We thus appear to be faced with the difficult task of deciding on the lesser of two evils. Do we choose a system that sacrifices some of the highest performances in order to facilitate greater achievement by low-ability students, or do we sacrifice achievements by low-ability students in order to offer an enriched academic diet to 'the brightest and best'? Is that the choice we face?

We have offered an alternative view, based on a resource allocation interpretation, that questions the mutually exclusive nature of those two possibilities. This view interprets the distributions of academic achievements under the two systems as a function of postulated distributions of academic resources. The selective system apparently allocates resources disproportionally to high-ability students, thus increasing their achievements while depressing the achievements of low-ability students. Assuming the comprehensive system distributes resources more evenly, it thereby reduces the resources allocated to high-ability students while increasing those allocated to low-ability students, thus altering the achievement levels of both groups.

Although we acknowledge the speculative nature of this reasoning, we are able to offer some limited evidence that is at least consistent with it. An important derivative of this reasoning is that it may not be necessary to choose between the two evils just described if it is possible to increase the resources available to a comprehensive educational system. If the more academically demanding programmes had been weakened under comprehensive reorganisation in order to provide more adequate programmes for all students, additional resources might be used to strengthen those programmes and make them more widely available. If, as the resource allocation perspective would predict, this led to an increase in the proportion of students with high achievements, it would effectively increase the average student achievement. Careful studies of more limited student populations in naturally varying resource allocation situations could serve as an initial test of this perspective, but such studies are beyond the limits of the current research.

Finally, we should return to a matter discussed at several points in this and the two previous chapters. When interpreting the results of the analyses presented here we need to keep two features of the available data in mind. First, all the data we have analysed come from the early part of the transition from the selective to the comprehensive secondary school system. We have seen that most of the comprehensive schools established by 1974 came into existence after 1969, but our analysis is necessarily limited to those NCDS students who entered comprehensives established by 1969 because only they can be assumed to have been in comprehensive schools throughout their secondary school years. It is possible that comprehensives founded later were different from those founded early, and that their students had different experiences and different kinds of achievements from those we have studied. Second, few of the comprehensives founded by 1969 had been in existence very long. The results we have observed may thus be influenced by the recency of the change. They may reflect a period of disruption and adjustment. That may be why we find greater teacher attrition in the comprehensive schools, as reported in Table 12.7. Observations in those same schools a decade later might have provided a different picture.

It is equally important to recognise, however, that these acknowledged limitations also constitute a major strength of the analyses. This is a study of a process of change while it was under way. It is not a study of a stable, well-established comprehensive school system. The kinds of analyses we have conducted could only be based on data collected during this early period, a period in which different kinds of schools with different histories could be compared. Analyses based on a later time period could not include some of the comparisons we have been able to make. But, it is also apparent that further investigation, based on later periods with schools that had a longer stable existence, would help put these findings in clearer perspective.

TABLE 12.1

LOGISTIC REGRESSION ANALYSIS DIFFERENTIATING STUDENTS
ATTENDING SELECTIVE SCHOOLS AND COMPREHENSIVE SCHOOLS
FOUNDED BEFORE 1970

Independent Variables

Father's occupation	–0.010
Father's education	–0.072*
Mother's education	0.001
Number of siblings	–0.003
Gender (female)	–0.035
General Ability Test	–0.018**
Reading Test	0.004
Mathematics Test	–0.014*
Intercept	0.762

† $p<0.05$, * $p<0.01$, ** $p<0.001$.

TABLE 12.2

MULTINOMIAL LOGISTIC REGRESSION ANALYSIS DIFFERENTIATING
STUDENTS ATTENDING SELECTIVE SCHOOLS AND COMPREHENSIVE
SCHOOLS FOUNDED BEFORE 1970, BY THE FORMER STATUS OF
THE COMPREHENSIVE SCHOOLS

Independent Variables	*Former Status of Comprehensive School*			
	Purpose-built	*Amalgamated*	*Grammar*	*Secondary Modern*
Father's occupation	–0.036	0.042	0.091	–0.092†
Father's education	–0.075	–0.091†	–0.023	–0.089
Mother's education	–0.047	–0.015	–0.059	0.130†
Number of siblings	0.012	–0.000	–0.048	0.017
Gender (female)	–0.013	0.018	–0.185	–0.037
General Ability Test	–0.013†	–0.023**	–0.022	–0.017†
Reading Test	0.012	0.052	–0.007	0.010
Mathematics Test	–0.028*	–0.005	–0.006	–0.018
Intercept	–0.543	–0.145	–0.088	–1.871**

† $p<0.05$, * $p<0.01$, ** $p<0.001$.

TABLE 12.3

ABILITY TEST SCORES OF STUDENTS AT SELECTIVE SCHOOLS
AND COMPREHENSIVE SCHOOLS FOUNDED BEFORE 1970

| LEAs Included | Ability Test Scores | | | |
	Median	%<30	%>60	N
All LEAs (Types A, B and E; Parts of C, D and F)				
Selective school students	47.8	16.6	21.4	2,826
Comprehensive school students	40.1	26.0	11.3	1,721
Mixed LEAs (Type B, Parts of C)				
Selective school students	49.3	15.2	23.7	1,564
Comprehensive school students	40.8	25.4	10.8	1,199
Pure LEAs (Types A and E, Part of F)				
Selective school students	43.8	20.5	16.2	327
Comprehensive school students	37.8	25.0	11.3	120

TABLE 12.4

COMPARISONS OF ACADEMIC PERFORMANCES OF STUDENTS
AT SELECTIVE AND COMPREHENSIVE SCHOOLS

| Independent Variables | Achievement Measures | | |
	Age 16 Reading	Age 16 Maths	Age 18 Exams
Father's occupation	0.330**	0.335**	0.169**
Father's education	0.092	0.439**	0.200**
Mother's education	0.230**	0.316**	0.180**
Number of siblings	− 0.468**	−0.167**	−0.103**
Ability	0.269**	0.269**	0.073**
Gender (female)	− 0.873**	−1.960**	−0.013
Comprehensive school	0.228	−0.241	−0.027
Intercept	16.355**	2.903**	−1.069**
Adjusted R^2	0.530	0.503	0.431

† $p<0.05$, * $p<0.01$, ** $p<0.001$.

TABLE 12.5

COMPARISONS OF ACADEMIC PERFORMANCES OF STUDENTS
AT SELECTIVE AND COMPREHENSIVE SCHOOLS, CONTROLLING
FOR VARIATION BY ABILITY

	Achievement Measures		
Independent Variables	*Age 16 Reading*	*Age 16 Maths*	*Age 18 Exams*
Father's occupation	0.331**	0.327**	0.165**
Father's education	0.092	0.437**	0.199**
Mother's education	0.230**	0.309**	0.177**
Number of siblings	−0.467**	−0.169**	−0.104**
Ability	0.267**	0.286**	0.081**
Gender (female)	−0.872**	−1.972**	−0.020
Comprehensive school	0.031	1.787**	0.852**
Comp. school X ability	0.005	−0.047**	−0.021**
Intercept	16.429**	2.144**	−1.403**
Adjusted R^2	0.530	0.505	0.435

† p<0.05, * p<0.01, ** p<0.001.

TABLE 12.6

SUMMARY OF COMPARISONS OF ACADEMIC PERFORMANCES OF
STUDENTS AT SELECTIVE AND COMPREHENSIVE SCHOOLS,
USING DIFFERENT SAMPLES

	Sample Definitions		
Dependent Variable and Effect Measure	*All LEAs*	*Mixed LEAs*	*Pure LEAs*
Reading Test Score			
Total comprehensive effect	0.228	0.324	0.744
Comprehensive main effect	0.031	0.084	3.316†
Interaction effect	0.005	0.005	−0.063
Zero effect point	—	—	52.3
% with comprehensive advantage	—	—	82.4
Mathematics Test Score			
Total comprehensive effect	−0.241	−0.248	−0.676
Comprehensive main effect	1.787**	1.345†	3.700†
Interaction effect	−0.047**	−0.036	−0.108
Zero effect point	37.7	37.0	34.4
% with comprehensive advantage	45.2	42.3	40.7
Secondary School Examinations			
Total comprehensive effect	−0.027	0.011	−0.146
Comprehensive main effect	0.852**	0.835**	1.470*
Interaction effect	−0.021**	−0.019**	−0.040**
Zero effect point	41.2	44.2	36.7
% with comprehensive advantage	52.8	57.5	45.7

† p<0.05, * p<0.01, ** p<0.001.

TABLE 12.7
PUPIL–TEACHER RATIOS AND TEACHER ATTRITION AT COMPREHENSIVE SCHOOLS IN LEAs WITH BOTH TYPES OF SCHOOLS

	School Type			
	Comprehensive	*Selective*	*Grammar*	*Secondary Modern*
Pupil–teacher ratio	17.9	18.7**	17.5##	19.3@@
Teacher attrition	0.166††	0.151*	0.139#	0.157

Comprehensive sig. diff. from grammar:	† <0.01, †† <0.001
Selective sig. diff. from comprehensive:	* <0.01, ** <0.001
Grammar sig. diff. from secondary modern:	# <0.01, ## <0.001
Secondary modern sig. diff. from comprehensive:	@ <0.01, @@ <0.001

NOTES

1. If the distribution of independent schools is taken into account, this classification would become even more complex. The LEAs varied widely in this respect, from having no independent schools to having half of their schools private. Understandably, the smaller LEAs were somewhat more likely to have a high proportion of independent schools. At the same time, the larger LEAs had the largest number of independent schools and the largest numbers of independent school students. Undoubtedly, the distribution of independent schools affected the distribution of kinds of students at selective and comprehensive schools, but it is not feasible to take such factors into account here.

2. The reorganisation of the Scottish secondary schools was centrally controlled to a much greater degree than in England and Wales, which is one of the reasons we have not included Scotland in our investigation. See Gray, *et al.* (1983) and McPherson and Willms (1987).

3. The age 16 reading test was a less than wholly adequate measure of academic achievement because it was the same test administered at age 11. It thus did not sufficiently discriminate among the best readers, producing a ceiling effect on the distributions of scores (see Kerckhoff, 1986).

4. Such a computation necessarily assumes that there is a linear relationship between ability level and the net advantage or disadvantage for comprehensive school students, and that may not be the case. But, short of conducting a set of point-to-point estimates, whose underlying assumptions would be equally questionable, this is the most reasonable assumption we can make.

5. Comparisons across the three sample definitions should be made with caution since different numbers and kinds of cases are involved. It is particularly important to remember that the ability test score distributions of the comprehensive school cases are such that the same test score can be at rather different percentile levels in the three samples.

6. The coefficient is significant at the 0.063 level.

7. The variances of the selective school students' scores on the age 16 mathematics test and the level of school examinations passed were significantly larger than the comparable variances for the comprehensive school students' scores, but the reading test variances for the two groups were very similar.

8. We also considered the possibility that the comparison based on LEAs with mixed types of schools might be biased against the comprehensives since some of them did not provide opportunities for sixth-form courses. To determine if that did bias the results, we conducted the same kinds of analysis as discussed here for the 'mixed' sample definition, restricting the comprehensive school students included to those at comprehensives with sixth forms. The results did differ somewhat from those shown in Table 12.6, but the overall effect was generally the same. In the analyses comparable with those in Table 12.4, comprehensive school students scored significantly higher on the reading test, but there were no significant differences for either mathematics or examinations. Neither the main effect nor the interaction effect was significant for reading in the analyses paralleling those in Table 12.5. However, in both the mathematics test and examinations analyses, the main effects coefficient was significantly positive and the interaction term was significantly negative. The break-even point for the mathematics test showed that 43.3 per cent did better in comprehensive schools, and the break-even point for examinations showed that 61 per cent did better in comprehensive schools. So, removing students at comprehensives without sixth forms produced very similar results to those shown in Table 12.6 for the mixed LEA sample.

9. One 'resource' that is necessarily correlated with the type of school structure is the academic 'quality' of one's peers. If all high-ability students are put together in the same school, they tend both to stimulate and to provide models for each other. But, of course, those high-ability students are then not available to provide the same stimulation and models for low-ability students. To the extent that there is grouping of students within schools, however, even in individual subjects, such peer effects might not differ greatly in comprehensive and selective schools. See Willms (1986) for a discussion of possible contextual effects of this kind.

10. The greater investment in comprehensive than selective schools is also suggested by LEA data 6n per-pupil expenditures. There is a positive association between 1973 per-pupil expenditures and the proportion of the LEA's pupils in comprehensive schools in 1974. This association persists even after controlling for the socioeconomic composition of the student bodies, the number of secondary schools in the LEA, and the nature of the political control in the LEA. Unfortunately, the per-pupil expenditure data are at the LEA level and the allocation of those resources by school type within the LEAs is not known.

13

Variations on a Theme

It is historically accurate to say that the 1960s and 1970s saw a sweeping transformation of the British secondary education system from one that was highly stratified to one that was almost wholly comprehensive. The proportion of state-sector secondary school students attending comprehensive schools increased dramatically from less than ten per cent in the early 1960s to more than 80 per cent in the late 1970s, with a compensating reduction in the proportion of students attending selective schools. There is no question that this was a remarkable period of change, a period in which there was a confluence of several forces that had been building since the end of the Second World War.

The liberal thrust of the Labour Party had consistently sought to reduce the class-bound limitations of the pre-war school system. This initially led to strong support for a tripartite organisation of secondary education, introducing the technical school as a means of recognising and facilitating the increasing involvement of young people in highly skilled technical jobs. The technical school was to serve both the needs of industry and the desire to offer working-class students a set of highly regarded qualifications and work skills. Establishing technical schools required major investments of scarce resources, however, as well as a reconsideration of some of the underlying philosophy of the bipartite system. Very few of these new schools ever appeared, and eventually the impetus that lay behind their establishment was shifted in other directions, a major one being comprehensive reorganisation.

At the same time, the popular demand for secondary schooling was rapidly increasing, and the restrictive limitations of the selective system were being felt in middle-class segments of the population more often than they had before the war. The selective system was organised so as to identify only a small proportion of students for the grammar schools. Both the selective process itself and the physical limitations of grammar and secondary modern school buildings dictated a continued restriction on the proportion of eleven-year-olds who were chosen to attend grammar schools. But the demand continued to increase, and growing numbers of middle-class parents expressed fear and anger about their children's prospects for the future. The all-important 11+ examination became the focus of increasing dissatisfaction.

The demand for secondary education was more general than the middle-class pressure for access to grammar schools, however. There was a more general recognition that schooling, and the credentials it provided, were important and needed to be provided more widely than through a grammar-school education. One indication of that was the increasing pressure to make some form of credential available to secondary modern students. Several LEAs made it possible for secondary modern students to prepare for the O-Level examinations, and later the CSE was introduced.

Comprehensive secondary schooling appeared to be a solution to all of these problems. It was a clearly 'democratic' approach that offered access to the best education the country could offer without restricting that access in some arbitrary way. As Prime Minister Wilson suggested, it made it possible to have 'grammar schools for all'. The much-feared 11+ examination could be set aside. Anxious middle-class parents could be reassured, and ambitious working-class parents could believe in a fair opportunity for their children. As Margaret Thatcher said, '... this great rollercoaster of an idea was moving, and I found it difficult, if not impossible, to stop [it]' (interview with the *Daily Mail*, quoted in Chitty, 1989, pp. 54–55).

Yet, during the rollercoaster ride, a number of things happened to make the outcome less than a uniform transformation from one kind of secondary school system to another. During the early period of change, there was little deviation from the traditional definition that a child entered secondary school at the age of 11. The all-through comprehensive school, offering schooling from ages 11 to 18, was the only type seriously considered in most places. The combination of the discontinuance of the 11+ examination, building size limitations, legislation in 1964 and the Plowden Report (calling for an age 12 entry into secondary school) opened the door to other alternatives. In addition, the general emphasis on increasing the academic quality of those entering the labour force led to an active move to raise the school-leaving age to 16 (which had already been allowed for in the 1944 Education Act). These changes produced a shifting set of conditions and challenges for the LEAs to cope with as they considered comprehensive reorganisation.

The most important change of all came with the publication of Circular 10/65. This not only legitimised the early actions taken by some LEAs to move towards comprehensive schooling, it exerted pressure on the other LEAs to do the same. But, the way in which that pressure was applied was equally important in explaining the resulting transformation described in this book. Circular 10/65 *requested*, it did not require, plans for comprehensive reorganisation, and it explicitly offered a number of alternative forms of organisation that could be subsumed under the comprehensive-school umbrella. That flexibility, together with the general forces of change already under way, when added to the special conditions faced in each LEA, provided the basis for the highly varied results we have observed.

WHAT IS A COMPREHENSIVE SCHOOL?

The early definition of a comprehensive school (which we have observed most clearly in London) was an all-through school with a full intake of students at the age of 11 and providing continuing opportunities through to the sixth form. In concept, the all-through comprehensive was intended to replace the grammar and secondary modern schools completely, and to merge their student bodies into a single entity. The general estimate was that such a school would require the equivalent of a six-form (or class) intake to provide an adequate number of students for the sixth-form classes at ages 16 to 18. This meant that these schools needed to be quite large, enrolling between 1,000 and 1,500 students.

Two kinds of local limitations made it impossible for many LEAs to establish that kind of comprehensive. The most obvious was the need for a large building to house so many students. Without additional building funds, most LEAs could not consider such a school. In the more sparsely populated areas, however, another kind of problem was faced. In order to assemble so many students in a single school, it would be necessary to bring them in from widely scattered and distant locations. There were simply too few students readily available to such a school, even if it could be built.

Three kinds of alternatives to the all-through comprehensive school were suggested in Circular 10/65,[1] and we have seen all three of them in our case-study LEAs. As we have shown, the earliest to be proposed was the *Leicestershire plan* calling for two-tier comprehensives, a high school entered at the age of 11 and an upper school entered at the age of 14. Secondly, there was the *middle-school* form of organisation. This generally called for students to leave primary school at eight or nine years old and enter a middle school from which they would transfer to a comprehensive secondary school at the age of 12 or 13. This form was originally introduced in the West Riding, one of our case-study LEAs. Thirdly, it was possible to limit comprehensive schools to students from the ages of 11 to 16 with transfer at the age of 16 to a *sixth-form college*. Among our case-study LEAs, Stoke-on-Trent provided an example of this form.

Given these varied definitions of what constituted a comprehensive school, simply recording the number of comprehensive schools and the number of students in them does not provide an adequate indication of the reorganisation process or outcome. The youngest pupils in comprehensive schools ranged in age from 11 to 14, and the oldest from 16 to 18. In some of the comprehensives, a very large proportion of the students were preparing for the O-Level or A-Level examinations, while in others no students were preparing for A-Levels and only a small minority were preparing for O-Levels. Whatever their other features, that difference alone meant that they provided different learning environments. Two other factors complicated the picture even further. First, very few of the LEAs had adopted a reorganisation plan that was uniformly applied throughout the authority. Most LEAs considering reorganisation had to cope with limited financial resources, limited numbers of suitable buildings and opposition from loyal supporters of the well-established grammar schools. In most LEAs, therefore, comprehensive schools operated in a system that also included selective schools. And, since the opposition came largely from supporters of grammar schools, the remaining selective schools were predominantly grammar schools. Thus, the selective schools in these mixed system LEAs tended to 'cream off' the more talented students from the comprehensives.

Second, it was very common for LEAs to establish comprehensives both with and without sixth forms. Thus, within many LEAs, some comprehensive school students could prepare for A-Level examinations by continuing their studies in the sixth form of the same secondary school they had entered, while others had to transfer to either a sixth-form college or another secondary school with a sixth form if they were to continue. Again, these two kinds of comprehensive schools provided very different kinds of learning environments.

What may seem to have been a single general process of transformation of a secondary school system from a predominantly selective one to a predominantly comprehensive one was thus actually much more complex and varied than it at first appeared to be.[2] The challenge we have faced was not only to explain why some LEAs reorganised sooner and more completely than others. We have also been faced with the need to try to explain why some LEAs adopted one form of comprehensive school and others adopted another.

THE RATE OF REORGANISATION

Our in-depth analysis of the case of the Inner London Education Authority makes it clear that very soon after the Second World War there were active efforts to establish comprehensive schools instead of the orthodox tripartite system. Our other large city case studies (Manchester, Bristol and Leeds) show some of the same tendencies, although the case of London is especially important because of its national prominence and because it had exceptional rebuilding needs owing to the extensive bomb damage during the war. Yet, early moves towards some kind of comprehensive reorganisation were hardly restricted to the big cities. Even before 1960, Leicestershire had devised the tiered system that made it a focus of intense interest and debate throughout the period we have surveyed. Similarly, the West Riding county LEA was the first to introduce middle schools, so that their secondary schools, even if comprehensive in form, could fit into the existing buildings.

Just as urban–rural differences did not easily explain the early adoption of comprehensive reorganisation, there was no simple association between comprehensive reorganisation and the political control of the LEA. Though London was a bastion of Labour control after the war, Leicestershire was controlled by the Conservatives throughout the period of interest here, as was West Sussex, known for its pioneering comprehensive innovation in Crawley New Town. The Labour Party promoted comprehensive reorganisation *more actively* than the Conservatives, but reorganisation occurred under both parties.

Early moves towards comprehensivisation seemed to depend heavily on local conditions facing LEA leaders. They also depended on the personal efforts and creativity of a number of those leaders, especially the CEOs and the Education Chairmen. Individuals like Patrick Crotty in Leeds, Sir Alec Clegg in the West Riding, Stewart Mason in Leicestershire, and Bob Cant in Stoke-on-Trent made crucial contributions to the comprehensivisation processes in those LEAs. It is difficult to imagine that the timing and the nature of the changes that were introduced would have been the same if these leaders had not been there at the critical times.

It is not wholly surprising, therefore, that we were not very success-ful, using the NCDS data, in identifying characteristics of the LEAs that were significantly associated with their degree of comprehensi-visation by 1974. The socioeconomic characteristics of the LEA were essentially unrelated to the degree of reorganisation. The one clear correlate of early and extensive reorganisation was political control. Even though we used the LEA as the unit of analysis (thus giving small, largely rural, LEAs greater weight than their sizes would justify), control by Labour was clearly associated with greater degrees of comprehensivisation. However, that association was much clearer during the pre-1970 years. Political control explained very little of the reorganisation process in the 1970s.

The 'rollercoaster' of reorganisation referred to by Margaret Thatcher was well on its way by 1970 when she assumed responsibility for education, and we have found no very effective general explana-tion for its rate of progress in the later years. Its early thrust, however, seems to have depended heavily on factors operating most frequently in Labour-controlled areas. Some of those political factors appear in our case studies, largely in the urban LEAs. We do find early moves towards comprehensive schools in our county case studies, but they tend to have been moves involving the alternative forms of compre-hensive schooling, rather than the all-through 11–18 schools favoured in the cities. The early preference for the all-through form in the cities and for alternative forms in the counties provides some basis for further understanding of the overall reorganisation process.

CORRELATES OF THE TYPE OF COMPREHENSIVE SCHOOLS INTRODUCED

At several points in our review of the history of comprehensive reorganisation and of the processes involved in the ten case-study LEAs we have noted that some of the alternative forms of compre-hensive schools appeared to be more favourably viewed by the Conservatives than the all-through form. The alternative forms seemed to be less threatening to those who favoured the tripartite (or, more commonly, the bipartite) selective system. Somehow, the alternative forms seemed more likely to offer a 'grammar school for all' than the huge 11–18 comprehensives.

The two features of the alternative forms that we have been able to study in detail were the later (than 11) age of intake and the lack of a sixth form. These two organisational features were actually associated with each other. Practically all late-intake schools (especially those with intake at ages 13 or 14) had a sixth form, but one-third of those with age 11 intake did not.

The earlier impressions of a link between the Conservative Party and the adoption of the alternative forms were confirmed by our analysis using the NCDS data. But the link was clearer with respect to the locations of comprehensives without sixth forms than it was with respect to the locations of comprehensives with late entry. Most specifically, schools with age 11 intake but without sixth forms were much more likely to be established in LEAs controlled by the Conservatives than those controlled by Labour. In addition, the populations in those LEAs had high proportions of non-agricultural manual workers.[3] Those associations were found throughout the 1960s and early 1970s.

The former status of the comprehensive schools was also associated with the organisational forms they had after becoming comprehensives. Former grammar schools were much more likely to have late intake ages than former secondary modern schools, and former secondary modern schools were much more likely than former grammar schools to have no sixth form. These links between the form of organisation of the comprehensives and their former status in the selective system show a degree of continuity during the reorganisation process. If being without a sixth form weakened a school's claim to being a 'true' comprehensive school, the continuity between being a secondary modern school and being a comprehensive without a sixth form raises important questions. And, since such comprehensives were most likely to be found in LEAs controlled by the Conservatives, the usual source of defence of the traditional grammar schools, it is reasonable to suggest that perhaps some degree of selection was being maintained, even in LEAs that had undergone comprehensive reorganisation.

INCOMPLETE COMPREHENSIVISATION

Showing that the usual defenders of grammar schools were more likely to establish comprehensives without sixth forms is a long way from showing that these no-sixth comprehensives served to perpetuate some of the features of the selective system. This is especially true when we remember that the Conservative-controlled LEAs that were more likely to establish no-sixth comprehensives also had heavily working-class populations. The further question that needs to be faced is whether these comprehensives functioned in ways that paralleled schools in the selective system.

To deal with that question, it is necessary to compare comprehensives with sixth forms and those without sixth forms.[4] If the two kinds of schools actually represent different degrees of continuity with the selective system, they ought to differ in particular ways. Specifically, the no-sixth schools should have students with lower prior academic achievements, and the students should more often be from lower socioeconomic backgrounds. In addition, the no-sixth schools should offer a less challenging academic programme, and their students should have lower levels of academic achievements by the time they leave secondary school.

In order to test these ideas, we had to limit our analyses in some rather rigorous ways. First, we had to restrict the sample used to students who, we had good reason to believe, had spent their full secondary school years at a comprehensive school. That meant that only students in comprehensives that were established before 1970 could be included. We also needed to recognise that, although most LEAs with some no-sixth comprehensives also had comprehensives with sixth forms, not all did. To clarify the purpose and meaning of the analysis, therefore, we included only students at pre-1970 comprehensives in LEAs that had comprehensives both with and without sixth forms.

There is clear evidence of continuity from the selective system to the comprehensive system. Students attending comprehensives without sixth forms more often came from manual family backgrounds, and they had significantly lower scores in ability and achievement tests at age 11. More importantly, their academic achievements by the end of secondary school were significantly lower than those in the same LEAs who had attended comprehensives with sixth forms. The most significant loss experienced by those attending the no-sixth comprehensives was their lower level of secondary school examinations passed. Their level of examination achievement was significantly lower by age 18, even when controls are applied for their socioeconomic background, their ability at the age of 11 and their achievement test scores at the age of 16.

It is clear that, at least in those LEAs maintaining comprehensives both with and without sixth forms, there continued to be a dual system of secondary schools, even though both types of schools were called comprehensive schools. As in the selective system, two kinds of schools were maintained. Students from lower socioeconomic backgrounds and with lower pre-secondary school academic achievements attended the less adequate (also the less 'comprehensive') of the two types, and those students gained less in the most crucial type of academic achievement (examinations passed) while attending that type of comprehensive school. The proportion of secondary school students disadvantaged by attending the no-sixth comprehensives was much smaller than the proportion disadvantaged by attending a secondary modern school under the selective system, and the achievement difference attributable to the type of school attended was smaller than under the selective system. But a dual system continued to function, even among comprehensive schools, and the same kinds of students continued to be disadvantaged by it as under the selective system.

That this kind of dual system was found more often in LEAs with a high proportion of working-class families probably reflects the fact that such LEAs had a sufficiently large working-class population to make it possible to separate students by social class. Under the selective system, working-class neighbourhoods were the most common locations for secondary modern schools. Since the no-sixth form comprehensives tended to be former secondary modern schools, the linkage we have observed between the working-class backgrounds of students and attending a no-sixth form comprehensive undoubtedly reflects the tendency to retain the same catchment areas for these schools, even after they had changed status from a secondary modern to a comprehensive school. Whatever the reason, however, it is clear that working-class students were more likely than middle-class students to attend a comprehensive school without a sixth form, and that put them at an academic disadvantage.

BUT THERE WAS A DIFFERENCE

The continued operation of some of the basic features of the selective system even among schools that were classified as comprehensives, raises the further question of whether comprehensivisation really changed secondary schooling in England and Wales in ways that matter. Our view of this question led us to focus on comparisons between the academic achievements of students under the two systems. We sought to learn whether either system facilitated higher student achievements than were obtained under the other system.

We had to recognise, however, that any attempt to make such an

268

assessment is faced with serious difficulties. At no time has there been a *fully selective* or a *fully comprehensive* system in England and Wales. During the entire period of the 1960s and 1970s there was a mix of selective and comprehensive schools. The proportions changed rapidly from heavily selective to heavily comprehensive, but there was always a mix. In addition, the nature of the mix changed during those two decades. Not only did the proportion of comprehensives steadily increase, but the ratio of grammar to secondary modern schools and students within the selective sector also increased during the same period. These two changes meant that the academic 'quality' of the selective system became progressively 'richer' in relation to that of the comprehensive system.

We can only acknowledge those patterns of change and also acknowledge that the analyses we can conduct are based on data taken from one brief period during those two decades. The achievement measures we have are those made in 1974 and 1976 when the NCDS cohort members were 16 and 18 years old, but they are limited to measures for those in comprehensives founded before 1970. Thus, our comprehensive school sample is taken from schools that were established early in the overall reorganisation movement, and most of them were schools that had not been comprehensives very long. In contrast, the selective schools in our analysis were very largely well-established, and more of them were grammar schools than was the case in the early 1960s. In an effort to avoid errors of analysis or interpretation, we conducted several different analyses restricting the samples involved in different ways. All of our analyses led to the same general conclusion, however. There were essentially no differences in the average achievements of students at selective and comprehensive schools, once we control for their socioeconomic backgrounds and earlier academic achievements. However, there was clear evidence of differences in achievements for students of different ability levels. High-ability students performed at somewhat higher levels in the selective system and low-ability students performed at somewhat higher levels in comprehensive schools. Although the differences were not substantively very large, they were clearly and consistently observed, irrespective of the sample limitations used. It is possible to conclude from these results that it is necessary to choose between two evils: we can adopt a system that operates to the disadvantage of high-ability students or one that operates to the disadvantage of low-ability students. We have proposed an alternative interpretation, however, one based on a resource allocation interpretation of the results of our analyses. If a selective system disproportionately allocates its resources to high-ability students (in grammar schools), it does so by allocating fewer resources to low-ability students (in secondary modern schools). By the same reasoning, if comprehensive schools have the same level of resources available, and if they adopt a more equitable allocation of resources to all students, they must lower the resources available to high-ability students and increase the resources available to low-ability students. If the allocation of resources does affect student achievement, these two patterns of allocation would produce the achievement levels we have observed.

We have only very limited measures of resource allocation, but the data we have are at least consistent with this interpretation. In addition, we have seen that teacher attrition was significantly greater in comprehensive schools in 1973 than in the combined selective school types, suggesting that the newly reorganised comprehensive schools may have experienced greater disruption to their programmes, a factor that could also lead to lower student achievement. These results suggest that an increase in resources allocated to comprehensive schools could both raise the average achievement level and bring the level of achievement of high-ability comprehensive school students closer to that of high-ability selective school students.

We cannot say with confidence that our resource allocation interpretation is valid, but at least it provides a basis for further comparative analyses of the selective and comprehensive systems. However, any further study of this matter should at least attempt to take into account two important and potentially contaminating conditions whose effects we have been unable to assess. One of these is the contrast between the recency of the comprehensive schools' founding and the well-established status of the selective schools. The other is the impressive degree to which the selective schools in these LEAs served to 'cream off' a large proportion of the high-ability students from the comprehensives. We have been able to document these differences between the two kinds of schools being compared, and we have done what we can to control for the effect of the second of them, but we are not confident that they have not seriously affected our results.

SUMMING UP

A sweeping institutional change in the British system of secondary education during the 1960s and 1970s transformed what had been a highly stratified structure into a largely 'levelled' comprehensive one. Although the reorganisation movement seemed to gain momentum during those years, some of the forces that provided the initial impetus also generated a counter-movement that has reversed much of the change that occurred.

A careful analysis of the period of change shows that the seeds of the counter-movement already existed in the reorganisation process. What may have appeared to be a homogeneous new system was actually a highly diversified one. Using the term *comprehensive* to encompass a variety of structures tended to obscure that diversity, but the diversity was there, and it retained many of the features of the stratified selective system.

Stratification continued in two ways. First, the system was never fully reorganised. Only a minority of LEAs reorganised all of their secondary schools to one of the comprehensive forms. Well-established grammar schools continued to function, and they provided an even more rarefied 'upper layer' in the new system. Second, a majority of the LEAs established two kinds of comprehensives, some with and some without sixth forms. The no-sixth form comprehensives replaced the secondary modern schools as the lowest level in the new system.

By the mid-1970s, as the counter-movement was gaining momentum, there was evidence both within and outside the newly created comprehensive school structures that the 'levelling' process had not been as effective as it had first appeared to be. The middle-class dissatisfaction with the selective system had been due to its over-restrictive limitation on access to a 'good' education in a grammar school. The discontinuation of the 11+ examination in most places and the introduction of varied forms of 'comprehensive' schooling provided other means of access to a 'good' education, and those new means of access were effectively used by the same segments of the population that had effectively used the selective system to its benefit. Additionally, of course, some middle-class parents chose to send their children to independent schools.

The comprehensive structure limited the amount of control the middle classes had over the system, however, and that limitation eventually led to the introduction of alternative mechanisms of control.

Our comparison of student achievements at selective and comprehensive schools has suggested that there is no overall advantage of one system over the other, but that low-ability students perform at higher levels in comprehensive schools and high-ability students perform at higher levels in selective (grammar) schools. We have offered a resource allocation interpretation of those findings, which has led us to suggest that an increase in the overall resources allocated to secondary education might well raise the average level of student performance without lowering the achievements of 'the best and the brightest'.

This book, and the research on which it is based, has been largely about developments in the 1960s and 1970s, but it is interesting briefly to consider the implications of our resource allocation hypothesis for more recent educational events in this country. For the past decade and a half the Conservative government has quite overtly pursued policies in education (and in other public services) to increase the influence of market forces. In the name of 'diversity and choice', we have seen the introduction of city technology colleges and grant-maintained schools (which have opted out of local government control). The former have received some support from industry, but both initiatives have largely been fuelled by public funding, thus reducing what is available to the remaining local authority schools.

At the same time, all schools have been required to publish their examination results and other information, often in the form of controversial 'league tables'. While it is laudable that parents should be well-informed, thére is no doubt that underlying such policies is the expectation that some schools will become more popular and attract more students and more funding, while others will wither (or, more realistically, attract only those in their immediate catchment area who cannot afford 'choice').

During the period to which this book mainly relates, the allocation of resources to schools was largely based on tradition and history, tempered by the policies of local authorities, which might have chosen to support particular initiatives, geographical areas or individual schools. Frequently, such policies would have been particularly targeted on schools which served more disadvantaged areas or which had greater proportions of lower-attaining children – in other words, they were exactly designed to *offset* the effects of market forces alone. If our resource allocation hypothesis is correct, then it would lead to the prediction that the effect of recent changes will be to increase inequalities, without, in themselves, bringing about any improvements in overall levels of achievement (although, of course, it remains an open question as to whether other initiatives, such as the introduction of a national curriculum, will have such an effect).

One further recent change has been the Local Management of Schools, devolving financial management and control from Local

Authorities to individual schools. Not only does this reduce the ability of Local Authorities to dilute the effects of market forces, but it also increases the ability of schools to determine resource allocation internally. Thus for now, and for the foreseeable future, it may be at least as powerful and appropriate to study the implications of our hypothesis for the influence on inequalities of such allocation *within* schools as much as among schools and across the educational system.

In the context of such recent changes, our suggestion that an increase in overall resources might raise average achievement levels without detrimental effects on the most able may well be over-naïve, particularly given the ability of the middle class to use whatever educational system is in place to its own advantage. There is mounting evidence that educational reform is seldom effective in reducing the educational advantages of middle-class children (Shavit and Blossfeld, 1993). While we are not able to demonstrate with the data available to us that the same could be said about comprehensive reorganisation in England and Wales, all of the available evidence suggests that the effect was, at best, muted. We have acknowledged the limitations in our comparison of the academic achievements of students under the two systems. Yet, it may be that the analysis we have conducted is fairer and more informative than could be conducted with any more recent data. Given the rather loose definition of what constitutes a comprehensive school, it is likely that, even with large-scale 'opting out', parental choice, and elements of selection being introduced into city technology colleges and grant-maintained schools, the secondary school system of England and Wales will still be referred to as 'predominantly comprehensive'. Yet, there can be little doubt that it will provide middle-class children with *even more* educational advantages than they had in 1974.

NOTES

1. Circular 10/65 actually recognised two additional organisational options besides those discussed here, but they were deemed appropriate only as transitional forms, not as ongoing comprehensive school alternatives.
2. We have necessarily focused our attention on the variation in the forms taken by the newly established comprehensives. It is safe to say, however, that there was also a great deal of variation among the LEAs in the kinds of selective systems that they had before reorganisation became a general movement. We know, for instance, that only some of the LEAs actually had the kind of tripartite system called for by the 1944 Education Act. It is also clear that there was a great deal of variation among the LEAs in the proportions of their selective school pupils who attended grammar schools (ranging from about ten per cent to about 40 per cent). However,

our information about the varied characteristics of the earlier selective system is not sufficient to include them in our systematic analysis.

3. The same LEA socioeconomic characteristics were associated with establishing comprehensives with age 12 intake but without sixth forms, but there was no tendency for Conservatives to establish that kind of school.

4. Although we carried out analyses of entry age that paralleled those of the presence or absence of a sixth form, none of them indicated either that age at entry was used as a selective device or that the schools with normal and late entry had different effects on their students' achievements.

Bibliography

Archer, M.S. (1979) *The Social Origins of Educational Systems* (Beverly Hills and London: Sage).

Banks, O. (1955) *Parity and Prestige in English Secondary Educaton: A Study in Educational Sociology* (London: Routledge & Kegan Paul).

Barker, R. (1972) *Education and Politics 1900–1952: A Study of the Labour Party*, (Oxford: Clarendon Press).

Benn, T. (1987) *Out of the Wilderness: Diaries 1963–67* (London: Hutchinson).

Benn, T. (1988) *Office Without Power: Diaries 1968–72* (London: Hutchinson).

Benn, C. and Simon, B. (1972) *Halfway There: Report on the British Comprehensive School Reform*, 2nd edition (Harmondsworth: Penguin).

Berg, L. (1968) *Risinghill: Death of a Comprehensive School* (London: Penguin).

Bernbaum, G. (ed.) (1979) *Schooling in Decline* (London: Macmillan).

Board of Education (1926) *Report of the Consultative Committee on the Education of the Adolescent* (The Hadow Report) (London: HMSO).

Board of Education (1938) *Report of the Consultative Committee on Secondary Education* (The Spens Report) (London: HMSO).

Board of Education (1941) 'Education After the War' (the Green Book), reprinted in Middleton, N. and Weitzman, S. (1976) *A Place for Everyone: a History of State Education from the End of the 18th Century to the 1970s* (London: Gollancz), pp. 387–462.

Board of Education (1943) *Curriculum and Examinations in Secondary Schools* (The Norwood Report) (London: HMSO).

Boucher, J. (1972) *Tradition and Change in Swedish Education* (London: Pergamon).

Boyle, E. (1972) 'The Politics of Secondary School Reorganisaton: Some Reflections', *Journal of Education Administration and History*, Vol. 4, No. 2, pp. 28–38.

Boyson, R. (1974) *Oversubscribed: The Story of Highbury Grove School* (London: Ward Lock).

Brace, K. (1971) *Portrait of Bristol* (London: Robert Hale).

Bright, J. (1972) 'Stoke-on-Trent's A-Level Academy', *Comprehensive Education*, Vol. 21, pp. 22–3.

Chitty, C. (1989) *Towards a New Education System: The Victory of the New Right?* (London: Falmer).

Clegg, A. (1965) 'West Riding', in Maclure, J.S. (ed.), *Comprehensive Planning* (London: Councils and Education Press), pp. 75–9.

Cole, M. (n.d.) *What Is a Comprehensive School?: The London Plan in Practice* (London: Labour Party).

Connell, J. (1953) 'The London School Plan', *Time and Tide: The Independent Weekly*, 7 March 1953, pp. 294–95.

Cooke, R.L. (1968) 'An analysis of the age structure of emigrants to new and expanding towns', *Journal of the Town Planning Institute*, Vol. 54, No. 9, pp. 430–6.

Cox, C.B. and Boyson, R. (eds) (1975) *Black Paper 1975: The Fight for Education* (London: Dent).

Cox, C.B. and Boyson, R. (eds) (1977) *Black Paper 1977* (London: Maurice Temple Smith).

Cox, C.B. and Dyson, A. (eds) (1969) *Fight for Education: A Black Paper* (London: Critical Quarterly Society).

Crook, D.R. (1992) 'The disputed origins of the Leicestershire two-tier comprehensive schools plan', *History of Education Society Bulletin*, Vol. 50, pp. 55–9.

Crook, D.R. (1993) 'Edward Boyle: Conservative champion of comprehensives?', *History of Education*, Vol. 22, No. 1, pp. 49–62.

Crosland, S. (1982) *Tony Crosland* (London: Jonathan Cape).

Davie, R., Butler, N. and Goldstein, H. (1972) *From Birth to Seven* (London: Longman).

Department for Education (1992) *Choice and Diversity: A New Framework for Schools* (White Paper) (London: HMSO).

Department of Education and Science (1965) *The Organisation of Secondary Education* (Circular 10/65) (London: HMSO).

Department of Education and Science (1967) *Children and Their Primary Schools* (The Plowden Report) (London: HMSO).

Department of Education and Science (1970) *The Organisation of Secondary Education* (Circular 10/70) (London: HMSO).

Department of Education and Science (1978) *Comprehensive Education: Report of a DES Conference* (London: HMSO).

Dibden, H.C. (1965) 'Stoke-on-Trent' in Maclure, J.S., op. cit. (1965), pp. 67–74.

Dodge, J.S. (1980) 'Lutterworth Grammar School and Community College', in Fairbairn, A.N., op. cit., pp. 85–101.

Donnison, D.V. and Chapman, V., *et al.* (eds) (1965) *Social Policy and Administration: studies in the development of social services at the local level* (London: Allen & Unwin).

Fabian Society Research Series (1949) *Next Steps in Education* (London: Fabian Society).

Fairbairn, A.N. (ed.) (1980) *The Leicestershire Plan* (London: Heinemann).

Fearn, E. (1980) 'The local politics of comprehensive secondary reorganisation', in Fearn, E. and Simon, B. (eds), *Education in the 1960s* (Leicester: History of Education Society).

Fearn, E. (1983) 'Comprehensive reorganisation: some priorities in research', *History of Education Society Bulletin* 32, pp. 43–50.

Fearn, E. (1989) 'The Politics of Local Reorganisation', in Lowe, R.A., op. cit., pp. 36–51.

Fenwick, I.G.K. and Woodthorpe, A.J. (1980) 'The Reorganisation of Secondary Education in Leeds: The Role of Committee Chairmen and Political Parties', *Aspects of Education*, Vol. 22, pp. 18–28.

Fenwick, I.G.K. (1976) *The Comprehensive School 1944–70: The Politics of Secondary School Reorganisation* (London: Methuen).

Fiske, D. (1982) *Reorganisation of Secondary Education in Manchester*, Bedford Way Papers 9 (London: University Institute of Education).

Fogelman, K. (ed.) (1976) *Britain's Sixteen-Year-Olds: preliminary findings from the third follow-up of the National Child Development Study (1958 Cohort)* (London: National Children's Bureau).

Fogelman, K. (ed.) (1983) *Growing Up in Great Britain: Collected Papers from the National Child Development Study* (London: Macmillan).

Bibliography

Fogelman, K. (1984) 'Problems in comparing examination attainment in selective and comprehensive secondary schools', *Oxford Review of Education*, 10, 1, pp. 33–43.

Gaziell, H. (1989) 'The Emergence of the Comprehensive Middle School in France: educational policy-making in a centralised system', *Comparative Education*, Vol. 25, No. 1, pp. 29–40.

Goldstein, H. (1984) 'The methodology of school comparisons', *Oxford Review of Education*, 10, 1, pp. 69–74.

Gosden, P.H.J.H. (1976) *Education in the Second World War* (London: Methuen).

Gosden, P.H.J.H. and Sharp, P.R. (1978) *The Development of an Education Service in the West Riding, 1889–1974* (Oxford: Martin Robertson).

Gray, J., Jesson, D. and Jones, B. (1984) 'Predicting differences in examination results between Local Education Authorities: does school organisation matter?', *Oxford Review of Education*, 10, 1, pp. 45–68.

Gray, J., McPherson, A.F. and Raffe, D. (1983) *Reconstructions of Secondary Education: Theory, Myth and Practice since the War* (London: Routledge & Kegan Paul).

Halsall, E. (ed.) (1970) *Becoming Comprehensive: Case Histories* (Oxford: Pergamon).

Harnqvist, K. (1989) 'Comprehensiveness and Social Equality' in Ball, S.J. and Larsson, S. (eds) *The Struggle for Democratic Education: Equality and Participation in Sweden* (Lewes: The Falmer Press).

Hoyles, E.M. (1970) 'The London Plan and Vauxhall Manor School' in Halsall, E. (ed.), op. cit., pp. 39–52.

Hughes, B. (1979) 'In Defence of Ellen Wilkinson', *History Workshop*, Vol. 7, pp. 157–60.

ILEA (1967) *London Comprehensive Schools, 1966* (London: ILEA).

ILEA (1972) *Planning for 1980: A Review of Secondary School Provision in North-East London* (London: ILEA).

ILEA (1973a) *Planning for 1980: A Review of Secondary School Provision in North and North-West London* (London: ILEA).

ILEA (1973b) *Planning for 1980: A Review of Secondary School Provision in South and South-West London* (London: ILEA).

James, P.H. (1980) *The Reorganisation of Secondary Education* (Windsor: NFER).

Jones, D. (1988) *Stewart Mason: The Art of Education* (London: Lawrence & Wishart).

Jones, D.K. (1989) 'The Reorganisation of Secondary Education in Leicestershire, 1947–1984' in Lowe, R.A. (ed.), *The Changing Secondary School* (Lewes: Falmer Press).

Jonnson, I. and Arnman, G. (1989) 'Social Segregation in Swedish Comprehensive Schools' in Ball, S.J. and Larsson, S. (eds), *The Struggle for Democratic Education: Equality and Participation in Sweden* (Lewes: Falmer Press).

Keen, R., (1965) 'Comprehensive Reorganisation in Bristol', *Forum*, Vol. 8, No. 1, pp. 22–6.

Kerckhoff, A.C. (1986) 'Effects of ability grouping in British secondary schools', *American Sociological Review*, 51, pp. 842–58.

Kerckhoff, A.C. (1990) *Getting Started: Transition to Adulthood in Great Britain* (Boulder, CO: Westview Press).

Kerckhoff, A.C. (1993) *Diverging Pathways: Social Structure and Career Deflections* (New York: Cambridge University Press).

Kerckhoff, A.C. and Trott, J.M. (1993) 'Educational attainment in a changing educational system: the case of England and Wales', in Shavit, Y. and Blossfeld, H. (1993), pp. 133–53.

King, H.R. (1958) 'The London School Plan: the present stage', *Forum*, Vol. 1, No. 1, pp. 6–9.

Knight, C. (1990) *The Making of Tory Education Policy in Post-War Britain, 1950–1986* (London: Falmer).

Kogan, M. (1975) *Educational Policy-Making* (London: George Allen & Unwin).

Korner, A. (1981) 'Comprehensive schooling, an evaluation – West Germany', *Comparative Education*, Vol. 17, No. 1, pp. 15–22.

Lacey, C. (1984) 'Selective and non-selective schooling: real or mythical comparisons?', *Oxford Review of Education*, 10, 1, pp. 75–84.

LCC (1947) *London School Plan: A Development Plan for Primary and Secondary Education* (London: LCC).

LCC (1961) *London Comprehensive Schools* (London: LCC).

Litt, E. and Parkinson, M. (1979) *US and UK Educational Policy: A Decade of Reform* (New York: Praeger).

Lowe, R.A. (ed.) (1989) *The Changing Secondary School* (London: Routledge & Kegan Paul).

Maclure, J.S. (ed.) (1965) *Comprehensive Planning* (London: Councils and Education Press).

Maclure, J.S. (1990) *A History of Education in London, 1870–1990* (London: Allen Lane).

Maddock, J. (1983) 'The Comparative Study of Secondary Education Systems. Lessons to be Learned', *Comparative Education*, Vol. 19, No. 3, pp. 245–54.

Mallae, J.R. (1970) 'The Implementation of Swedish Educational Policy and Planning', *Comparative Education*, Vol. 16, No. 2, pp. 99–114.

Marks, J., Cox, C. and Pomian-Srzednicki, M. (1983) *Standards in English Schools* (London: National Council for Educational Standards).

Mason, S.C. (1965) 'Leicestershire' in Maclure, J.S. (1965) op. cit., pp. 51–8.

McCarthy, E.F. (1968) 'The Comprehensive Myth', *Comprehensive Education*, Vol. 10, pp. 25–7.

McCulloch, G. (1993) '"Spens v Norwood": Contesting the Educational State', *History of Education*, 22, 2, pp.163–80.

McCulloch, G. (1989) *The Secondary Technical School: A Usable Past?* (London: Falmer Press).

McPherson, A. and Raab, C.D. (1988) *Governing Education: A Sociology of Policy since 1945* (Edinburgh: Edinburgh University Press).

McPherson, A. and Willms, J.D. (1987) 'Equalisation and Improvement: Some effects of comprehensive reorganisation in Scotland', *Sociology*, Vol. 21, No. 4, pp. 509–39.

Ministry of Education (1945) *The Nation's Schools, Their Plans and Purposes*, (Pamphlet 1) (London: HMSO).

Ministry of Education (1947) *The New Secondary Education* (Pamphlet 9) (London: HMSO).

Ministry of Education (1958) *Secondary Education for All: A New Drive* (London: HMSO).

Morris, M. and Griggs, C. (eds) (1988) *Education: The Wasted Years, 1973–86* (Lewes: Falmer Press).

Müller, D.K., Ringer, F. and Simon, B. (1987) *The Rise of the Modern Educational System, Structural Change and Social Reproduction 1870–1920* (Cambridge: Cambridge University Press).

Bibliography

Neave, G. (1975) *How They Fared: the impact of the comprehensive school upon the university* (London: Routledge & Kegan Paul).

Neave, G. (1975) 'The Reform of Secondary Education in France', *Forum*, Vol. 17, No. 2, pp. 58–61.

Newsam, P. (n.d.) *Inner London Education Authority, 1970–1980: 10 years of change* (London: ILEA).

Newsam, P. (1983) 'Revolution by consent', unpublished IBM Lecture, 4 Nov. 1983.

Northumberland County Council (1952) *County Development Plan* (in Morpeth Records Office).

Northumberland Education Committee (1963) *Education in Northumberland, 1959–62* (Northumberland County Council).

O'Connell, P.J. (1970) 'Administering a comprehensive school on two sites: principles, problems and some solutions', in Halsall, E., op. cit., pp. 53–70.

O'Rourke, J.E. (1978) 'The National Union of Teachers and Education in Stoke-on-Trent, 1878–1978', unpublished manuscript, Hanley Reference Library, Stoke-on-Trent.

Parkinson, M. (1970) *The Labour Party and the Organisation of Secondary Education 1918–1965* (London: Routledge & Kegan Paul).

Paulston, R.G. (1968) *Educational Change in Sweden. Planning and Accepting the Comprehensive School Reforms* (New York: Teachers College Press).

Pedley, R. (1962) 'The Comprehensive School: England', *Forum*, Vol. 4, No. 2, pp. 4–8.

Pedley, R. (1980) review of Fairbairn, A.N., op.cit., *Education* (30 May 1980), p. 458.

Ranson, S. (1990) *The Politics of Reorganising Schools* (London: Unwin Hyman).

Redcliffe-Maud, J. (1981) *Experiences of an Optimist* (London: Hamish Hamilton).

Reeder, D.A. (1987) 'The reconstruction of secondary education in England, 1869–1920', in Müller, D.K., Ringer, F.K. and Simon, B., op. cit., pp. 135–50.

Reeder, D.A. (1993) 'Municipal Activity: Education, Health and Housing', in Nash, D. and Reeder, D.A., *Leicester in the Twentieth Century* (Stroud: Alan Sutton Publishing).

Regional Statistics, Vol. 3 (1967) (Central Statistics Office: HMSO).

Regional Statistics, Vol. 10 (1974) (Central Statistics Office: HMSO).

Reynolds, D. and Sullivan, M. (1987) *The Comprehensive Experiment* (London: Falmer Press).

Ribbins, P.M. and Brown, R.J. (1979) 'Policy making in English local government: the case of secondary school reorganisation', *Public Administration*, Vol. 57, No. 2, pp. 187–202.

Rigby, B. (1975) 'The Planning and Provision of Education in the Foundation and Development of a Post-War New Town: Crawley, West Sussex, 1947–1966', unpublished PhD thesis, University of Southampton.

Ringer, F. (1979) *Education and Society in Modern Europe* (Bloomington and London: Cambridge University Press)

Rubinstein, D. (1979) 'Ellen Wilkinson Re-considered', *History Workshop*, Vol. 7, pp. 161–69.

Rust, V.D. (1990) 'The Policy Formation Process and Educational Reform in Norway', *Comparative Education*, Vol. 26, No. 1, pp. 13–26.

Shavit, Y. and Blossfeld, H. (1993) *Persistent Inequality: Changing Educational Attainment in Thirteen Countries* (Boulder, CO: Westview Press).

Short, E. (1989) *Whip to Wilson* (London: Macdonald).

Simon, B. (1985) 'The Tory government and education, 1951–60: Background to breakout', *History of Education*, Vol. 15, No. 1, pp. 31–43.

Simon, B. (1991) *Education and the Social Order, 1940–1990* (London: Lawrence & Wishart).

Simon, B. (1992) 'The Politics of Comprehensive Reorganisation: a retrospective analysis', *History of Education*, Vol. 21, No. 4, pp. 355–62.

Simon, J. (1986) *Shena Simon: Feminist and Educationalist* (privately printed).

Simon, Lady S. (1962) 'London Comprehensive Schools', *Forum*, Vol. 4, No. 2, pp. 72–3.

Steedman, J. (1980) *Progress in Secondary Schools* (London: National Children's Bureau).

Steedman, J. (1983) *Examination Results in Selective and Non-Selective Schools* (London: National Children's Bureau).

Stenhouse, L. (1965) 'Comprehensive Education in Norway: a developing system, *Comparative Education*, Vol. 2, No. 1, pp. 37–41.

Stewart, M. (1980) *Life and Labour: An Autobiography* (London: Sidgwick & Jackson).

Stoke-on-Trent City Council (1963) *American Journey: a report on the visit to the United States of America, April–June 1963, by the Chairman of the Education Committee and the Chief Education Officer, Stoke-on-Trent, with comments and recommendations* (Stoke-on-Trent).

Stoke-on-Trent Education Committee (1964) *Education 1963* (Stoke-on-Trent).

Stoke-on-Trent Education Committee (1965) *Education 1964* (Stoke-on-Trent).

Stoke-on-Trent Education Committee (1974) *Education 1964–73* (Stoke-on-Trent).

Sutherland, G. (1984) *Ability, Merit and Measurement: Mental Testing and English Education, 1880–1940* (Oxford: Clarendon Press).

Sylvester, G.H. (1965) 'Bristol' in Maclure, J.S., op. cit., pp. 12–19.

Tawney, R.H. (1922) *Secondary Education for All: A Policy for Labour* (London: Allen & Unwin).

Thane, P. (1982) *The Foundations of the Welfare State* (London: Longman).

Thompson, J. (1975) 'Comprehensive schools in Sweden', *Forum*, Vol. 18, No. 1, pp. 28–31.

Weeks, A. (1986) *Comprehensive Schools: Past, Present and Future* (London: Methuen).

West Sussex County Council (1964) *Education in West Sussex, 1959–64* (Chichester: West Sussex Education Authority).

West Sussex County Council (1969) *Education in West Sussex, 1964–69* (Chichester: West Sussex Education Authority).

Willms, J.D. (1986) 'Social class segregation and its relationship to pupils' examination results in Scotland', *American Sociological Review*, 51, pp. 224–41.

Index

Circular 600 (Scotland), 6
City Technology Colleges, 44, 272, 273 (*see also* magnet schools, 'technology schools')
Clapham County Grammar School, London, 76
Clarke, K., 43
Clegg, Sir A., 17, 24, 118, 120, 123–24, 127–29, 131, 134, 145, 168–69, 264
Clifton College, Bristol, 49, 100, 106
Clout, Dr I., 138–39, 142
Cole, M., 59
Collyer's Boys' Grammar School, Horsham, 146–47
comprehensive schools: curriculum, 64–65, 115, 129, 140, 209, 210–11, 216–19, 243, 266; decline of, 37–42; demands for legislation, 32–34; early development of, 1–8, 22–24; foundation dates of, 177–78, 182, 196, 211–13, 222; future of, 42–44; prior status of, 174, 182, 183–86, 188–89, 193, 197, 208–20, 223–25, 234, 238–39, 266; regional distribution of, 176–77; students/pupils, 68, 92, 98, 149, 174, 176, 177, 199, 208–32, 238–39, 244–48; types of, 114, 174, 176, 183–207, 224–25, 233, 238–39, 261–64, 265–66; versus selective schools, 10, 210–11, 233–59, 269 (*see also* Circular 10/65, Circular 10/70, Conservative Party, Labour Party, Local Education Authorities, multilateral schools, National Child Development Study)
Comprehensive Schools Committee (CSC), 29
Connell, J., 63
Conservative government (1951), 18, 20, 62, 124, 138
Conservative government (1970), 34–37, 73–74, 155
Conservative government (1979), 40, 41, 272
Conservative government (1992), 43
Conservative Party (national), 23, 26, 29–31, 34–37, 43, 51, 74, 137 (*see also* Local Education Authorities and political control)
Cooke, R.L., 138
Cornwall, 41
Coventry, 19, 58, 86, 108, 235
Cowbridge Girls' High School, Glamorgan, 150
Cowbridge Grammar School, Glamorgan, 150
Cox, C., 10, 236
Cox, C.B., 38, 69, 73
Crawley New Town, 53, 136, 137, 138–40,

141, 142, 146, 148, 157, 162, 165, 264
Crawley Grammar School, 142
Crook, D.R., 23, 102, 112, 116, 120, 166
Crosland, A., 6, 27–28, 29–30, 31, 36, 39, 69, 73, 88, 95, 97, 101, 114, 129, 146, 148
Crosland, S., 27, 31
Crotty, P., 101–3, 105, 165, 264
Croydon, 25, 110, 111, 113, 116, 143
Cumbria, 41

Daily Telegraph, 28, 67
Davie, R., 205
Davies, E., 158
Davies, E.T., 139
Department of Education and Science (DES) 27–28, 29, 31, 32, 37, 39, 40, 41, 43, 54, 71, 73, 76, 92–93, 95, 97, 101, 112, 113–14, 129, 133, 141, 147, 149, 151, 153–56, 179, 189, 196 (*see also* Board of Education, Ministry of Education)
Dibden, H., 107–112, 116
Digby, S. Wingfield, 46
Diocesan boards, 146, 172
direct-grant schools, 13, 49, 74, 87, 89, 90, 92, 93, 95, 96, 98, 99, 100, 103, 132, 153, 171
Dodge, J.S., 129
Doncaster, 25, 29
Donnison, D.V., 110
Dyson, A., 73

Eastbourne, 183
Eccles, Sir D., 20, 21, 86–87, 120, 140
Eden, A., 20
Education, 28
Education Act (1902), 13
Education Act (1944), 5, 10, 17, 24, 36, 53, 58, 75, 87, 132, 136, 137, 146, 150, 161, 261
Education Act (1964), 24, 25, 128, 141, 261
Education Bill (1969–70), 34, 73, 115, 166
Education Act (1976), 40
Education Act (1979), 41
Education Reform Act (1988), 42
elementary schools, 12, 13, 14, 15
eleven-plus examination, 6, 21, 22–23, 25, 31, 38, 45, 66, 71, 88, 89, 90, 91, 92, 94, 108, 109, 118, 120, 121, 134, 139, 143, 148, 156, 157, 171, 183, 261, 271
Elliott, J., 86, 89–90, 94–95, 104, 133
Elliott, John, 64
Eltham Hill Girls' School, London, 20, 62–63
'enablers', 55, 85, 91, 102, 104, 105, 121, 125, 128, 134, 136, 137, 140, 156–57
Ensham Girls' School, London, 73
examinations, 14, 16, 17, 21, 23, 24, 83, 102,